FROM SINAI TO CALVARY

ONE STORY - TWO COVENANTS - ONE REDEEMER

ROBERT GRIFFITH

GRACE AND TRUTH PUBLISHING
PO Box 338, Gunnedah NSW 2380 Australia
www.graceandtruthpublishing.com.au

ISBN 978-1-7642635-0-4

TABLE OF CONTENTS

PREFACE

I can remember it like it was yesterday, even though it was well over twenty-five years ago. I was the Senior Pastor of a medium sized Baptist church in regional Australia. It was a Friday night, our Girl's Brigade were meeting in the back hall, and they always started with a brief devotion.

On this particular night, we had the leader of our Kids' Church sharing, which should have been fine. I was standing at the back of the hall watching and listening. Like little sponges, thirty girls, aged 7 - 14 years, sat crossed-legged on the floor – each one ready to absorb everything they were about to be told.

The brief devotions commenced with the reading of Psalm 66:18, *"If I have sin in my heart, the Lord will not hear."* These young hearts were then filled with fear as they were told that if they sin, God won't even hear their prayers! My heart sank. I could not believe what I heard, and from someone who had sat under my teaching for the previous two years. Clearly, he had not been listening!

What happened on that night, happens hundreds of times every day across the church and around the world. Someone lifts an Old Covenant verse out of its context and tries to dress it in New Covenant clothes and then preach it as 'truth for today.' Those ten minutes of false teaching took me years to undo for so many of those girls and, I think that experience so long ago was most probably the original catalyst for this book and so much of my teaching over the past twenty-five years.

It's tragic that so many Christians have never been taught to read and interpret the Old Testament (and all the references to the Old Covenant) through the reality of the New Covenant. We live this side of the cross of Jesus Christ – and that changes everything! It is only from that reality that we should ever read, understand and teach the Old Testament. That is why this book was written.

A word of warning before you proceed. This is not a book you can skim read. If you want a genuine understanding of this very important issue, this journey will need some work on your part.

You will need to pause often and reflect – perhaps even re-read some chapters as you go. Whilst the material is not too difficult to grasp, there is a lot to take in and understand. So, pace yourself and give this study the time it deserves.

For some people, explaining the Old and New Covenants and suggesting how we should live today in light of that explanation, would seem relatively simple. Well, if that was true, then this book would contain a lot less than 250 pages! Learning how to read, apply and teach the Old Testament and the Old Covenant in a New Testament / New Covenant era, is a lot like studying a large diamond. It may be stunning and beautiful in its simplicity from a distance, but when you get closer, you discover just how many individual facets make up the whole and how each facet must be studied to appreciate the entire gem.

Continuing with the diamond analogy, it would have been so good if I could just number all the facets of this subject and then just go through them one by one until the end. Unfortunately, it can't be done that way because covenant theology is not linear. You cannot just start at point 1, then move to points 2, 3, 4 etc. Covenant theology is interwoven in a myriad of ways. For this reason, I will address some issues multiple times throughout this book as the context of each chapter changes.

So, when you read statements more than once and notice key Bible passages have also been repeated across chapters, please don't assume there has been an editing failure (or that I may have poor recall). This repetition is deliberate and necessary as I drive home the key truths in our study of the Old and New Covenants and place those statements and some Bible passages in different contexts. I would also remind you that spaced repetition is the best way to learn anything and so it will do you no hard harm to recap and embrace those key points and verses more than once.

I invite you now to come with me on this journey from Sinai to Calvary, as we wrestle with what I truly believe to be one of the greatest challenges facing us today.

- 1 -
WHY THIS MATTERS

Introduction

It was a Sunday morning, much like any other. The congregation was warm, the music uplifting, the preacher sincere. At one point he quoted Deuteronomy 28:12 with great conviction: *"The Lord will open the heavens, the storehouse of his bounty, to send rain on your land in season and to bless all the work of your hands."*

He told his people that if they were faithful, then God promised prosperity, health, and overflowing abundance. Heads nodded, *"Amens"* filled the air, and the people left with great reassurance stamped across their faces.

But for this one woman in the congregation, life did not follow the detailed script she had just been handed. She was faithful in attendance, generous in giving, and very earnest in prayer. Yet she was facing redundancy at work, a chronic illness that would not relent, and deep family tensions that seemed immovable.

As weeks became months, this dear sister began to wonder, *'Has God forgotten me? Am I doing something wrong?'* Doubt sprouted where trust had been sown - not because her God had failed her, but because she had been promised something God had never promised in the era we now inhabit: the New Covenant.

As mentioned in the Preface to this book, stories like this are repeated in churches across the world every single day. Sincere Christians cling to verses from the Old Testament, convinced they apply directly to us now, without realising that those verses were given under a covenant to which we no longer belong.

The result is usually serious confusion, disappointment, and at times, disillusionment with God. Our problem here is not that we value Scripture too highly; our problem is that we often read it without the covenant lens that Scripture itself provides.

Clearly understanding the Old and New Covenants - and how they relate to the Old and New Testaments - is not a scholarly luxury. It is pastoral medicine for bruised consciences, a compass for storm-tossed disciples, and a guardrail for churches that love the Bible but stumble over how to use it. This book was written to offer that medicine, that compass and that guardrail.

The problem beneath many problems

If you trace many theological disputes, pastoral struggles, and personal crises of faith back to their source, you will usually find covenant confusion lurking beneath the surface. Some believers sincerely blend the two Testaments into one flat field, plucking verses from any page as if everything God ever said to anyone at any time applies to us in the same way today.

Others, reacting against that error, swing the pendulum and treat the Old Testament as if it has little relevance - a pre-Christian museum of stories that we visit out of obligation rather than joy.

Both errors inflict deep wounds upon the church. The first error binds consciences with commands and promises that do not belong to them; the second cuts the church off from the rich roots that nourish the gospel's beauty.

Why does this matter so much? It matters because covenants are the very spine of God's self-revelation. Without a spine, the body collapses. Without this covenant framework, our Bible reading collapses into either lawless licence or law-ridden legalism. Jesus Himself taught about this covenant lens.

After His resurrection He told the disciples, *"Everything must be fulfilled that is written about me in the Law of Moses, the Prophets and the Psalms." Then he opened their minds so they could understand the Scriptures."* (Luke 24:44–45)

The verb matters here: He *opened* their minds. Eyes need lenses; minds need to be opened. The lens Jesus provided was Himself - the fulfilment to which the whole story points.

Two Testaments, one story - but not one covenant

The terms 'Old Testament' and 'New Testament' are more than convenient dividers in our bound Bibles. They signal two great movements in God's wonderful redemptive symphony. Yet the Old Testament is not simply 'the Old Covenant book,' and the New Testament is not merely 'the New Covenant book.'

The Old Testament contains a number of covenants (Noahic, Abrahamic, Mosaic, Davidic) and promises of the New Covenant still to come. The New Testament describes and also applies the New Covenant, while constantly reaching back to the Old to show us how Jesus fulfils it. That is why we must hold both Testaments firmly together while distinguishing the covenants properly. If we fail to distinguish, we flatten the story. If we fail to hold them together, we fracture the story.

The Old Covenant - centred on the Law which was given at Sinai - was a real covenant with real blessings and curses for the nation of Israel (Deuteronomy 28). It was holy and good, yet provisional and preparatory. It revealed God's holiness, exposed human sin, and taught the need for a sacrifice that takes away sin. The New Covenant, which was inaugurated in Jesus' blood, is eternal and unbreakable. It brings forgiveness of sins, a new heart, and the indwelling Holy Spirit. The Old Covenant was just a shadow; the New Covenant is the substance. The Old was a tutor; the New is graduation into life with the risen Lord. Both belong to one story; but only one rules the Christian's life today.

How covenant confusion shows up on Sundays

Consider the following common examples where well-meaning Christians misapply the Old Testament because they miss the covenant frame.

1. National promises treated as church guarantees.

2 Chronicles 7:14 says, *"If my people, who are called by my name, will humble themselves and pray ... I will heal their land."* These words were given to Israel whilst under the Old Covenant at a specific moment tied to temple worship and Mosaic obedience.

The principle is precious - God honours humility and repentance - but the form of the promise (national healing tied to covenant faithfulness) is not a New Covenant guarantee for any modern nation or church. As New Covenant people, our hope for the 'healing of the land' is ultimately the new creation secured by Christ's resurrection and promised at His return.

2. Tithing preached as law rather than generosity taught as grace.

Under Moses, tithes supported a Levitical system which was tied to the temple. In the New Covenant there is still joyful, sacrificial giving, but it is always grounded in grace. 2 Corinthians 9:6–8 tells us: *"Whoever sows sparingly will also reap sparingly ... God loves a cheerful giver."* Setting a fixed percentage of giving as a moral law for every Christian today results in us re-importing the structures of a covenant God has fulfilled and set aside.

3. Sabbath kept as a test of righteousness rather than Christ received as our rest.

The Sabbath was a sign between God and Israel (Exodus 31). Paul tells believers, *"Do not let anyone judge you ... with regard to ... a Sabbath day. These are a shadow of the things that were to come; the reality, however, is found in Christ."* (Colossians 2:16–17). The New Covenant does not abolish rest; it deepens it. Jesus is Lord of the Sabbath and the giver of true rest for weary souls.

We could add others that often circulate: Malachi 3:10 treated as a guaranteed financial investment if one "tests God" by tithing; Isaiah 54:17 used as a personal shield against every difficulty; Leviticus 26 cited to promise bumper crops or modern business success. The problem is not the truthfulness of these texts; the problem is our failure to recognise their covenant context.

Jesus the fulfilment - not the destructor - of the Law

When Jesus says, *"Do not think that I have come to abolish the Law or the Prophets; I have not come to abolish them but to fulfil them"* (Matthew 5:17–18), He locates Himself as the goal toward which the entire Old Testament moves.

Fulfilment is stronger than cancellation. Abolishing would erase; fulfilling brings to completion. Jesus obeyed the Law perfectly, bore its curse for law-breakers at the cross, and rose to launch a new era. When He died, *"the curtain of the temple was torn in two from top to bottom."* (Matthew 27:50–51).

Access to God is now through His Son, Jesus Christ, not through the priesthood of Aaron. The sacrifices, feasts, and purity codes served their blessed purpose; today, their meaning is found in Jesus Christ.

Hebrews speaks with luminous clarity: the old system was, *"only a shadow of the good things that are coming – not the realities themselves."* (Hebrews 10:1). The sacrifice of Christ was *"once for all."* (Hebrews 10:10), perfecting for all time those who are now being made holy. The shift from shadow to substance is not a downgrade but an upgrade - the very upgrade the Old Covenant itself taught Israel to expect.

The first-century struggle - and why it never really ended

The earliest Christians were Jewish men and women who loved the Law. Their struggle was not whether the Old Covenant was good; it was how to follow the Messiah Who fulfilled it. Acts 15 records the Jerusalem Council dealing with exactly this: must Gentile believers be circumcised and keep the Law of Moses? The apostles answer: *'No, salvation is by grace through faith in Jesus, and the Spirit falls on the Gentiles as on Jews without circumcision.'*

Paul had to fight this battle repeatedly. To the Galatians he writes with holy fire, *"After beginning by means of the Spirit, are you now trying to finish by means of the flesh?"* (Galatians 3:3). He warns that returning to the Law as covenant is not spiritual maturity but a massive step back into slavery (Galatians 5:1).

Why do you think covenant mixing still happens today? Because our hearts crave visible handles. Rules feel safer than reliance on the Spirit. Checklists feel clearer than just walking by faith. And preachers, so eager to motivate obedience or to inspire hope, sometimes reach for a verse that sounds strong without asking the essential covenant question first.

The result can be impressive in the moment and damaging over time. Faith that begins in the Spirit quietly shifts back toward the flesh. It is subtle most times, but the consequences are severe.

What 'covenant' meant back then

In the ancient world, covenants were not just sentimental words. They were very solemn, binding, relational arrangements - often confirmed by sacrifice, public ceremony, and signs. Kings made covenants with their vassals, spelling out obligations, blessings for loyalty, and curses for rebellion. When God covenants, He stoops to use relational forms we can understand, but He fills them with His faithfulness.

Consider the drama of Genesis 15: God alone passes between the pieces, pledging Himself to Abraham's future. Consider the gravity of Sinai: thunder, cloud, and commandment, a nation constituted by God's voice. Consider David's promise: an eternal throne that finds its *'yes'* in Jesus the Son of David. Consider Jeremiah's promise: *"I will put my law in their minds and write it on their hearts ... For I will forgive their wickedness and will remember their sins no more."* (Jeremiah 31:33–34)

Covenants are not mere legal scaffolding; they are the spine of a true love story. They show that God is not unreliable. He binds Himself by His promise; He advances His purposes through structured mercy; He is inviting human response within His gracious initiative. Understanding this gives you a map for the whole Bible.

What changes from old to new - and what does not

Some of us fear that New Covenant teaching erases holiness. The opposite is true. What changes are the covenant structures that governed Israel's national life - priesthood, sacrificial system, food laws, calendar observances, boundary-marking signs like circumcision. What does *not* change is God's character or His moral will. The New Testament does not shrink holiness; it intensifies and internalises it: *"Walk by the Spirit, and you will not gratify the desires of the flesh."* (Galatians 5:16)

The law of Christ (Galatians 6:2) is not a lighter ethic but a deeper one - love from a renewed heart producing the fruit of the Spirit: love, joy, peace, forbearance, kindness, goodness, faithfulness, gentleness, self-control (Galatians 5:22–23). Therefore, the New Covenant does not teach antinomianism (lawlessness). Rather, it teaches Christ-centred obedience empowered by the Spirit. The difference is not whether we obey, but how and why we obey.

Under the Old Covenant, Israel's obedience was firmly bound to a national charter with curses and blessings tied to land, temple, and political life. Under the New Covenant, obedience flows from our union with Christ and it is shaped by His teaching and the apostolic witness.

Jesus fulfils the moral law and lifts it to its true height: love of God and neighbour from the heart (Matthew 22:37–40), carried into every sphere of life.

The pastoral cost of covenant confusion

Let's make this as practical as possible. When covenant lines are blurred, spiritual damage will definitely follow:

Guilt without grace: A believer hears a sermon that ties God's acceptance to keeping rules that belonged to Israel's civic or ceremonial system. They leave either proud (if they think they kept them) or crushed (if they know they didn't). In either case, the cross shrinks at that point.

Promises without a cross: Another believer will grasp at a verse promising material abundance which is actually tied to Israel's land blessings. When the promotion doesn't come or the illness continues, they feel betrayed by God, not realising that God never pledged New Covenant people a pain-free life. He pledged His presence, His forgiveness, and future glory.

Division without necessity: churches split hairs over food, drink, festival days, or calendar observances that the apostles explicitly refused to bind on the church (Romans 14; Colossians 2:16–17). Fellowship fractures where Christ intends freedom.

Shallow discipleship: Without the covenant lens, we skim the Old Testament as a book of moral examples ('be like David, don't be like Saul') and miss the pulsing heartbeat: **it all points to Jesus.** The Old Testament becomes either a burden or a blunted set of stories rather than a field of gold that leads us to the Messiah.

Clarity about covenants does not make every debate disappear, but it does give us better instincts. It teaches us to ask the right questions, to handle Scripture with reverence and courage, to avoid both legalism and licence, and to cherish the gospel as the very centre of God's plan.

How to read the Old Testament as New Covenant people

Reading the Old Testament rightly does not mean ignoring laws and promises that no longer bind us in the same way. It means understanding *why* they were given and *how* they are fulfilled.

Always start by asking questions: *Who was the original audience? Under which covenant was this word given? How does this text point to Christ? What is the timeless moral principle, and how is it refracted through the New Covenant?* Take the dietary laws (Leviticus 11). Jesus declared all foods clean (Mark 7:18–19). Peter received the vision in Acts 10 to drive the point home. The food laws served a beautiful purpose back then - marking Israel as holy - and they pointed forward to a deeper holiness now written on the heart. The principle of distinctiveness remains; the form has changed.

Or consider the temple. The Old Covenant made temple worship the absolute centre of Israel's whole life. In the New, *we* are the temple, individually and corporately, because the Spirit dwells within us (1 Corinthians 3:16; 6:19). Thus, we read the Psalms of ascent with joy, not by booking a flight to a specific city, but by drawing near to God through Jesus Christ, engaging in gathered worship, and living as His holy house in the world.

Promises to Abraham of blessing for the nations (Genesis 12:3) explode into vibrant colour in Christ in Galatians 3:8: *"Scripture ... announced the gospel in advance to Abraham: 'All nations will be blessed through you.'"*

The seed is Christ (Galatians 3:16). The land promise becomes a down payment of the world renewed. The story expands, not contracts.

Case studies in misuse - and healthier readings

Jeremiah 29:11 is beloved: *"For I know the plans I have for you ... plans to prosper you and not to harm you."* Applied as a universal, immediate guarantee of smooth circumstances, it sets people up for disappointment. In context, this is a letter to exiles in Babylon, promising eventual return after seventy years.

The timeless truth is glorious: God's purposes for His people are good, and He keeps His promises. But the form of fulfilment is not always quick relief; it may be patient hope in trials. The New Testament frames our hope as ultimate: *"Our light and momentary troubles are achieving for us an eternal glory that far outweighs them all."* (2 Corinthians 4:17)

2 Chronicles 7:14 we have already mentioned, and it's a great verse when applied *in principle.* A healthier reading honours the original setting — Solomon's temple dedication — while drawing a proper and important New Covenant line: God loves humility and repentance; the church is called to prayer and holiness; yet the healing we all most deeply need is delivered in Christ and finally completed when He makes all things new.

Malachi 3:10 challenges Israel to bring the whole tithe. Preached as a mechanical formula — *"give 10%, receive guaranteed wealth"* — it completely distorts grace. Preached as an invitation to trust God's generous character and to support the vital gospel work joyfully, it harmonises with the New Covenant ethic of cheerful, Spirit-led generosity.

Grace is not soft - it is strong

Some worry that if we say, *"We are not under law but under grace."* (Romans 6:14), people will just sin more. Paul anticipated the objection: *"Shall we sin because we are not under the law but under grace? By no means!"* (Romans 6:15).

Grace is not the permission slip to do as we please; it is the power to become what Christ calls us to be. The Spirit writes God's law on our hearts (Jeremiah 31:33), producing the obedience of faith. Grace trains us, says Titus 2:12, *"to say 'No' to ungodliness and worldly passions, and to live self-controlled, upright and godly lives in this present age."*

The New Covenant does not lower the bar; it changes the engine. Instead of pushing a boulder uphill in our own strength, we walk by the Spirit Who indwells us.

This is why covenant clarity produces joy. Law without Christ crushes. Christ without holiness is counterfeit. Christ fulfilling the law and giving the Spirit liberates us to love as we have been loved. That is New Covenant Christianity at its best!

The gospel at the centre

At the molten core of covenant clarity stands the gospel: Christ died for our sins according to the Scriptures, He was buried, and He was raised on the third day (1 Corinthians 15:3-4). The Old Covenant mapped the problem — God's holiness and our sin — and sketched for us the silhouette of a coming Saviour. The New Covenant fills the silhouette with the face of Jesus.

Everything I write in this book will turn on that centre of gravity. I am not advocating a niche hermeneutical hobby. I am calling the church back to the clear grammar of grace that Scripture itself teaches: promise and fulfilment, shadow and substance, tutor and maturity, law and Christ.

This is why Jesus Christ, walking with confused disciples on the Emmaus road that day, does not scold them for reading the Old Testament. He scolds them for reading it <u>without Him</u>: *"How foolish you are, and how slow to believe all that the prophets have spoken! … And beginning with Moses and all the Prophets, he explained to them what was said in all the Scriptures concerning himself."* (Luke 24:25, 27) The problem was not their Bible; it was their lens. He gave them the lens, and their hearts burned.

How this book will help

My aim across the chapters to come is simple: to give you a clean, sturdy, Christ-centred lens for reading every page of Scripture. Together, we will trace God's whole covenant story from Noah to Abraham to Moses to David to Jesus; we will look at why the Law was given and how the Law functions; we will focus on Jesus' fulfilment and the New Covenant's promises - a new heart, forgiven sin, indwelling Spirit; we will ask how New Covenant believers should use the Old Testament today; I will challenge common misreadings with pastoral gentleness and biblical firmness; and I will hopefully put tools in your hands so that private devotions, small groups, and pulpit ministry all sing the same grace-filled melody.

You can certainly expect each chapter to mix careful exegesis with concrete examples. When I say, *"This promise was for Israel under Moses,"* I will also say, *"Here is how its principle lives on in Christ."* When I say, *"This command's ceremonial form has been fulfilled,"* I will also say, *"Here is the moral beauty that still binds our hearts."* I will not leave you with theory; but give you a way of reading that strengthens faith and steady's ministry.

A Pastor's word to the weary and the zealous

If you have felt disappointed because you were taught to expect from God what He did not promise in this age, take heart. He has not failed you. He has given you what no covenant before the cross could give: full forgiveness, a new heart, the Holy Spirit, adoption into His family, union with Christ, and future glory that cannot be taken away.

"Since we have been justified through faith, we have peace with God through our Lord Jesus Christ." (Romans 5:1). The peace you seek is not found in re-creating Israel's calendar; it is found in resting in Christ's finished work.

If you are zealous for holiness and worry that grace will weaken the church, take courage. Grace is the only power strong enough to produce holiness from the inside out.

The New Covenant does not turn soldiers into spectators; it turns slaves into much-loved sons and daughters who gladly bear the family resemblance. Your zeal is not wasted; just let the Holy Spirit aim it correctly for you.

If you are a preacher or teacher, the covenant lens will help you handle texts you love but have hesitated to preach. It will help you warn without crushing, comfort without deceiving, exhort without lapsing into legalism, and inspire without peddling fantasies. It will help you preach Christ from the whole Bible with a clear conscience and a full heart.

A symphony, not a medley

Think of Scripture as a symphony in two major movements. The first movement (Old Testament) introduces themes - holiness, covenant, sacrifice, king, temple, land, blessing, curse - building tension and longing. The second movement (New Testament) brings those themes to fulfilment in Christ - He is the true temple, the perfect sacrifice, the Son of David Who reigns forever, the Lamb Who takes away sin, the seed of Abraham in Whom the nations are blessed.

If you try to play both movements in the same way at the same time, you produce dissonance. But when you let the first movement lead you to the second, your ears catch the resolution your heart craves.

This is not an argument for sidelining the first movement. It is an argument for really hearing it properly, so that when the second begins, you recognise the music. The Old Testament is not *replaced* by the New; it is *realised* in the New. The promises are not erased; they are kept - but kept in Christ, sometimes in ways more spiritual and global than the original hearers imagined, always in ways more glorious than we expected.

What you should expect to feel

Good theology should make you think, but it should also make you sing. As covenant clarity settles into your bones, expect to feel three things:

First, **relief.** You are not a second-class Christian because you don't keep a calendar of feasts or diet restrictions. You are not under a system of curses and blessings tied to a piece of earth. You are actually in Christ. He is your righteousness, holiness, and redemption. You can exhale now.

Second, **reverence.** The Old Testament will soon feel much taller, not shorter. You will see the deep wisdom of God in structuring Israel's life, the seriousness of sin that demanded blood, and the patience of God weaving centuries of promise into the tapestry that frames the manger, the cross, and the empty tomb.

Third, **resolve.** Grace will not make you lazy. It will make you loving - and love will make you brave. You will want to obey, not to earn God's smile, but because you already have it in Christ. You will want to read Scripture more, not less, because the story is now coherent and the Saviour now shines.

A final pastoral picture

Imagine reading a map from the wrong century. The roads exist, but many of them have been rerouted; the borders have shifted; landmarks have new names. If you insist on applying the old map literally to the new terrain, you will get lost, frustrated, and perhaps angry with your guide.

The Old Covenant is a true map of where God's people were and how God led them to Christ. The New Covenant is the map of where we now live today. When you overlay them properly - honouring both - you will see the wisdom of God's whole plan, and you will find your way home.

The aim of this book is to put that proper overlay in your hands and in your heart. We will not rush. We will walk through the covenants with Scripture open, eyes on Jesus, and feet planted in real church life. We will wrestle with hard questions and find plain answers. We will keep the gospel at the centre and your joy in view. And we will pray, as Jesus did for His disciples, that God would open our minds to understand the Scriptures.

As we now come to the end of this introductory chapter, allow me to offer a summary and then issue an invitation:

> The confusion about covenants is not academic; it is pastoral and personal.

> The Old Covenant was holy, good, and provisional, designed to lead us to Christ.

> The New Covenant brings forgiveness, a new heart, and the Spirit; it governs Christian life today.

> Misusing the Old Testament by ignoring covenant context creates legalism, disappointment, and division.

> Reading the Old Testament through Christ does not diminish it; it dignifies it and shows its fulfilment.

> Our journey will trace God's covenant story and put practical tools in your hands for faithful, joyful Bible reading.

So, come and walk the path from promise to fulfilment. Feel the first movement rise, let the second resolve, and listen as the whole symphony draws you into worship.

The next chapter will set out the covenants themselves - Noahic, Abrahamic, Mosaic, Davidic, and the promised New Covenant - so you can see the contours of the story that leads straight to Jesus and the freedom of life we are meant to experience in Him.

- 2 -

GOD'S COVENANT STORY

If the first chapter pleaded with us to put on the right 'lenses' for reading Scripture, this chapter walks us through the panorama those lenses reveal. The Bible is not a loose anthology of moral tales. It is one unified story of a faithful God binding Himself to people by solemn promises - covenants - and then keeping those promises in ways that are both tender and terrifyingly holy.

Each of the covenants is like a great arch that bears the weight of salvation history. Remove even one and the structure sways; but see them together and the whole cathedral of Scripture stands in luminous symmetry.

We will move deliberately: first asking what a covenant is and why God chose to speak in that form, then tracing the five great covenants that shape the biblical storyline: Noahic, Abrahamic, Mosaic, Davidic, and New, before stepping back to see how they interlock in Jesus Christ.

Along this journey we will note common misreadings that arise when we flatten these covenants into a single plane or when we rip verses free from their proper home. The goal is not academic neatness; it is pastoral health. Covenant clarity will restore our confidence in God; it will also steady the church's preaching, and free consciences to live in the joy of the New Covenant.

What a covenant is - and why God uses them

In the world of the Bible, a covenant was the weightiest bond two parties could enter into. Kings used covenants to seal alliances; families used them to settle land and marriage; nations used them to end wars.

To 'cut a covenant' often meant blood was shed, not as a macabre decoration but as a sober pledge: *'May I be like this sacrificed animal if I fail to keep my word.'*

Two basic forms were common. *Parity* covenants bound equals to mutual fidelity. *Suzerainty* covenants bound a powerful king (the suzerain) to a vassal people: the king recited his past mercies (a historical prologue), set out stipulations (how loyalty would look), promised blessings for allegiance, warned of curses for rebellion, and provided a sign to memorialise the oath. When Scripture uses covenant form, God stoops to speak in a language His people understood, then fills that form with His own grace and holiness.

Notice how this dignifies history. God does not relate by whim. He binds Himself by oath, not because He must, but because He loves. He chooses to be known and trusted, not merely feared. He sets promises on public record - sometimes unconditional (He will do it), sometimes conditional (Israel must walk in His ways) - and then He moves history to keep them, even at the cost of His own Son. As I have already said, covenants are not cold contracts; they are the spine of a love story.

The Noahic Covenant - mercy that stabilises a shaken world

The flood narrative is a sobering one. *"The Lord saw how great the wickedness of the human race had become on the earth, and that every inclination of the thoughts of the human heart was only evil all the time."* (Genesis 6:5) Judgment fell like a tidal wall; then silence. When the waters receded and the ark settled, God spoke mercy into the quiet: *"I now establish my covenant with you and with your descendants after you and with every living creature that was with you... Never again will all life be destroyed by the waters of a flood; never again will there be a flood to destroy the earth."* (Genesis 9:9, 11)

This covenant is breathtaking for its scope: not only Noah's family but every living creature is included here. Its sign is the rainbow: *"Whenever I bring clouds over the earth and the rainbow appears in the clouds, I will remember my covenant... Never again will the waters become a flood to destroy all life."* (Genesis 9:14–15)

What does this achieve? First, it stabilises history. *"As long as the earth endures, seedtime and harvest, cold and heat, summer and winter, day and night will never cease."* (Genesis 8:22)

Redemption requires a stage; Noah's covenant secures it. It also reveals God's patience. Judgment has fallen, yet mercy will now frame the ages so the promise can now ripen. Third, it dignifies creation. God's care extends to animals and ecosystems; His covenant memory embraces sparrows and seasons.

Pastorally, this means we are neither naïve optimists nor are we panicked fatalists. We steward creation seriously while resting in God's pledge that history will not spin out of His hands. The rainbow is more than meteorology; it is a mercy banner stretched across the sky.

The Abrahamic Covenant - A people, a land, a blessing to the nations

Where Noah's covenant preserves the theatre, Abraham's brings the cast on stage and states the plot. Into a pagan world, God speaks to one man: *"Go from your country, your people and your father's household to the land I will show you. I will make you into a great nation, and I will bless you; I will make your name great, and you will be a blessing. I will bless those who bless you, and whoever curses you I will curse; and all peoples on earth will be blessed through you."* (Genesis 12:1–3)

The promise has three cords: seed (offspring), land, and blessing to the nations. In Genesis 15, God seals it in a ritual that still startles. Animals are halved, the path between their pieces is then marked, and Abram falls into deep sleep as *"a smoking fire pot with a blazing torch"* passes between the pieces (Genesis 15:17).

In the ancient world, both parties walked the blood-path. Here, only God does. He shoulders the curse-oath: *'If this covenant fails, let the penalty fall on Me.'*

Then we hear the foundational words: Abraham believes, and *"it was credited to him as righteousness."* (Genesis 15:6) Later, in Genesis 17, God gives circumcision as a sign and expands Abram's name to Abraham, *"father of many."* The New Testament turns the diamond to show deeper facets.

Paul writes: *"The promises were spoken to Abraham and to his seed. Scripture does not say 'and to seeds,' meaning many people, but 'and to your seed,' meaning one person, who is Christ."* (Galatians 3:16). Those who belong to Christ - Jew or Gentile - *"are Abraham's seed, and heirs according to the promise."* (Galatians 3:29).

The missionary thrust of the church is not a late innovation; it is built into God's call of Abraham. So, we preach the gospel not merely because people need it, but because God promised the nations to Abraham in the Messiah. The Abrahamic covenant is oxygen for weary hearts: righteousness is credited by faith, not earned by works; God bears the covenant's ultimate cost.

The Mosaic (Old) Covenant - A holy nation under Law

Four centuries after Abraham, his descendants groaned under Egypt's whip. God redeemed them with a mighty hand and brought them to Sinai. Redemption first, then law:

"You yourselves have seen what I did to Egypt, and how I carried you on eagles' wings and brought you to myself. Now if you obey me fully and keep my covenant, then out of all nations you will be my treasured possession. Although the whole earth is mine, you will be for me a kingdom of priests and a holy nation." (Exodus 19:4–6)

This covenant is conditional. The Ten Commandments declare God's moral will (Exodus 20). Civil laws will now order justice and compassion. Ceremonial laws govern worship: a priesthood mediates; sacrifices atone; feasts remember. God dwells among His people in the tabernacle - a portable Eden if you like - then in the temple.

Deuteronomy chapter 28 lays out the covenant's blessings and curses with gritty detail. Obedience means flourishing in land, womb, and field; disobedience means famine, defeat, exile. This is a national charter. It binds Israel as a people in a particular land under God's direct rule. But the law is more than statute; it is also pedagogy. *"Through the law we become conscious of our sin."* (Romans 3:20)

The sacrificial system is a drama of holiness: *"without the shedding of blood there is no forgiveness."* (Hebrews 9:22) Yet, *"it is impossible for the blood of bulls and goats to take away sins."* (Hebrews 10:4). The law radiates real glory, and yet it is a glory that fades in the presence of the One to come (2 Corinthians 3:7–11).

Why, then, was the law given? Paul answers clearly: *"The law was our guardian until Christ came that we might be justified by faith."* (Galatians 3:24) A guardian restrains and tutors but is never the final destination. The Old Covenant is holy and good, but provisional. It reveals, restrains, anticipates. It cannot give the new heart it demands (Deuteronomy 29:4; 30:6).

The Davidic Covenant – a throne that will not fail

Israel asked for a king and got Saul; God then raised up David. With enemies subdued and the ark in Jerusalem, David longed to build a house for God. God then reversed the proposal and promised to build David a house - a dynasty: *"The Lord declares to you that the Lord himself will establish a house for you… I will raise up your offspring to succeed you, your own flesh and blood, and I will establish his kingdom… I will establish the throne of his kingdom forever… Your house and your kingdom will endure forever before me; your throne will be established forever."* (2 Samuel 7:11–16)

Psalm 89 sings this promise even through the ache of failure. When David's line disobeyed, God disciplined them, but His steadfast love did not depart. The covenant banks Israel's hope on a coming Son of David — a righteous King who embodies obedience and brings justice and peace.

The New Testament turns fanfare into fulfilment. The angel announces to Mary: *"The Lord God will give him the throne of his father David, and he will reign over Jacob's descendants forever; his kingdom will never end."* (Luke 1:32–33)

The cross of Jesus Christ looks like royal defeat; His resurrection is royal enthronement. Ascended and reigning, He pours out the Spirit and summons nations to His banner.

The Davidic hope matures into the confession, *"Jesus is Lord"* - a title not only personal but political, not partisan but cosmic.

Pastorally, the Davidic covenant reorders allegiance. Christians render to Caesar what is Caesar's - taxes, respect, prayers - but we never grant Caesar the worship owed only to David's greater Son. Our hope is not in a cycle of elections but in a throne that cannot be toppled.

The New Covenant - hearts made new and sins remembered no more

Exile exposed Israel's problem: not merely bad behaviour but a bad heart. The prophets announced a future greater than any past: *"The days are coming,"* declares the Lord, *"when I will make a new covenant with the people of Israel and with the people of Judah. It will not be like the covenant I made with their ancestors when I took them by the hand to lead them out of Egypt... This is the covenant I will make... I will put my law in their minds and write it on their hearts. I will be their God, and they will be my people... For I will forgive their wickedness and will remember their sins no more."* (Jeremiah 31:31-34)

Ezekiel adds the surgery: *"I will give you a new heart and put a new spirit in you; I will remove from you your heart of stone and give you a heart of flesh. And I will put my Spirit in you and move you to follow my decrees and be careful to keep my laws."* (Ezekiel 36:26-27)

You will remember that on the night Jesus was betrayed, He lifted the cup and said: *"This cup is the new covenant in my blood, which is poured out for you."* (Luke 22:20)

At the cross this covenant was cut; at the resurrection it was then confirmed; at Pentecost it was applied. Hebrews gathers the threads: Jesus is mediator of a better covenant, founded on better promises (Hebrews 8:6). The old is obsolete (8:13). Animal blood covered sin; Christ's blood cleanses the conscience (9:14). Priests stood daily; the Son *"offered for all time one sacrifice for sins"* and then *"sat down at the right hand of God."* (10:12)

The gifts of the New Covenant are lavish: full forgiveness, new birth, indwelling Spirit, direct access to the Father through the Son, a global people formed by faith not ethnicity, a mission to the nations, and a kingdom that cannot be shaken.

Grace is not lax in any way. Paul anticipates the objection: *"Shall we sin because we are not under the law but under grace? By no means!"* (Romans 6:15) Grace does what law could never do: it gives new desires. The Holy Spirit writes God's law within, so obedience becomes worship, not wages.

How the covenants interlock in Christ

Now we can step back and see the staircase:

> **Noah:** The stage is secured. History will hold steady for redemption's drama.

> **Abraham:** The cast is called and the plot announced: blessing to the nations through a promised seed.

> **Moses:** The script is given to shape a holy people and reveal the need for a perfect Mediator.

> **David:** The king is promised who will embody obedience and reign forever.

> **New Covenant:** The summit arrives: Jesus fulfils and transforms all that came before.

This is one glorious story, not five parallel tracks. The covenants are progressive revelation, not some relay where the baton is dropped and something different then begins. The Old does not contradict the New; it leads to it. The New does not despise the Old; it realises it. As Paul says, *"No matter how many promises God has made, they are 'Yes' in Christ."* (2 Corinthians 1:20)

Typology also helps here. The temple becomes Christ's body and then the church by the Spirit. The sacrifice becomes the cross. The priesthood becomes our Great High Priest and a kingdom of priests offering spiritual sacrifices. The land promise swells into *"the meek… will inherit the earth."*

The king in Zion becomes Lord of the nations. The law written on stone is now written on human hearts. The exodus out of Egypt becomes our exodus from sin and death. Nothing is wasted; everything is fulfilled. It is all the same story.

Reading the whole Bible with covenant clarity

Here are four simple questions to help you keep your footing:

(a) *Who was this written to, and under which covenant?*
Honour the original audience. Don't hand Old Covenant, land-tied, temple-tethered guarantees to New Covenant believers or modern nations. Do receive the character of God and the principles of wisdom that shine through.

(b) *How does this text point to or find fulfilment in Christ?*
Laws, sacrifices, feasts, kings - follow the arrows to Jesus. He is not an illustration; He is the fulfilment.

(c) *What timeless moral beauty is here, and how does the New Covenant carry it forward?* The forms change; the holiness does not. Love is still the fulfilment of the law (Romans 13:10), now empowered by the Spirit.

(d) *What encouragement or warning does this give the church?* Romans 15:4 says the Old Testament was written *"to teach us… so that through the endurance taught in the Scriptures and the encouragement they provide we might have hope."* The stories train our endurance; the promises lift our eyes.

What this changes - worship, conscience, mission, hope

Worship: Covenant clarity turns duty into doxology. The Old Testament becomes a vast hymnbook for Christ. The sacrifices preach the cross; the festivals anticipate resurrection; the psalms give language for lament and praise in Jesus' name.

Conscience: Legalism loses all its leverage. You are not under a curse-and-blessing regime which is tied to a strip of land. You are in Christ - justified, adopted, sealed by the Spirit. The fear that God will drop you for failing a ceremonial code evaporates in the light of a better covenant.

Mission: Evangelism is not a church growth tactic; it is covenant fulfilment. The gospel to the nations is the Abrahamic promise going global through the risen Son. We don't apologise for this scope; we exult in it.

Hope: We can now stop claiming guarantees God has not made (unbroken prosperity, national dominance) and start clinging to the promises He has: His presence in trouble, peace that guards hearts, the Spirit's power, and an inheritance kept in heaven. Suffering no longer feels like covenant breach; it feels like cross-shaped discipleship on the way to glory.

A pastoral reminder for preachers and people

Let me say again, if you preach, then covenant clarity will change your pulpit. You will warn without crushing, comfort without deceiving, exhort without lapsing into law-keeping as your gospel, and inspire without promising what God has simply not pledged. You will preach Christ from Genesis to Malachi with clean hands and a full heart. If you are bruised by misapplied texts, hear this: God has not failed you. He never promised in the New Covenant what someone told you to expect from the Old.

What He has promised, He keeps without fail: forgiveness, His Spirit, His presence, wisdom when you ask, grace sufficient in weakness, and a future that is not fragile. *"He who calls you is faithful, and he will do it."* (1 Thessalonians 5:24). If you are zealous for holiness and worry that grace will soften the church, take courage. Grace is the only engine strong enough to produce holiness from the inside out. The New Covenant will never produce lax disciples; it produces Spirit-filled ones.

The panorama from Genesis to Jesus

Stand on a high ridge and look back:

- After the storm, a rainbow bends like a bow unstrung: the world will hold.
- Under a night sky, an old man counts stars he cannot count and believes.

- At a smoking mountain, a redeemed people receive a law that glows and a tabernacle where God draws near.
- On a throne in Jerusalem, a shepherd-king hears a promise no empire can cancel.
- In an upper room, a Rabbi lifts a cup and says that His blood seals the covenant all the others foreshadowed.
- On a hill outside the city, the Lamb of God bears the curse so the blessing may flood the nations.
- In an empty tomb, the new creation dawns.
- At Pentecost, the Spirit writes the law on hearts of flesh.
- And at the end, a voice says, *"Look! God's dwelling place is now among the people... He will wipe every tear from their eyes."* (Revelation 21:3–4)

That is the covenant story. Promise and fulfilment. Shadow and substance. Tutor and Son. Law and Christ. The arches hold. The cathedral stands. And it truly is magnificent. The whole Bible then comes alive!

Summary

We have traced the staircase of the covenants and watched it rise to Christ. The Noahic covenant secures history's stage. Then the Abrahamic covenant announces a people and a promise for the nations. The Mosaic covenant shapes a holy nation and exposes our need for a new heart. The Davidic covenant fixes hope on a righteous King. Then the New Covenant delivers all this in Jesus Christ: forgiveness, the Spirit, access, mission, and a kingdom that will not fail.

In the next chapter, we will step inside the Old Covenant itself to understand its purpose, structure, beauty, and limits. We will linger at Sinai, walk through the Law, watch the sacrifices smoke, and listen to the prophets' ache for a heart made new - so that when we turn again to the New Covenant, its surpassing glory will stun us afresh.

3

THE OLD COVENANT IN GOD'S PLAN

From the opening pages of the Bible, we see a God Who speaks, initiates and covenants with humanity. His self-disclosure is not abstract but deeply relational. As we begin to examine the Old Covenant in its richness and historical context, we must avoid two common extremes: one that dismisses the Old Covenant as obsolete and irrelevant, and the other that seeks to reinstate it as a binding framework for Christian living today. Both distortions hinder our understanding of the gospel. To grasp the wonder of the New Covenant, we must first understand the divine purpose of the Old Covenant.

The term 'Old Covenant' refers primarily to the covenant God made with Israel through Moses at Mount Sinai. This covenant, often called the Mosaic Covenant, was not the first covenant God made, but it certainly became the dominant framework for Israel's national identity, worship, and moral life. It was a covenant of law, promises, blessings, and curses; a covenant that revealed God's holiness, Israel's sinfulness, and the need for a better mediator.

A Covenant with a nation

The Old Covenant was born in the fires of redemption. God had delivered His people from slavery in Egypt *"with a mighty hand and an outstretched arm."* (Deuteronomy 5:15). Redemption came before the law. This order is critical: the Israelites were not saved because they kept the law; they were given the law because they had already been saved. God said, *"I am the Lord your God, who brought you out of Egypt, out of the land of slavery."* (Exodus 20:2). Only after this declaration of grace did He proceed to give the Ten Commandments and then the rest of the Mosaic Law. This covenant was made with a specific people — the descendants of Abraham, Isaac, and Jacob — and it formed them into a nation. Unlike the Abrahamic Covenant, which was unilateral and based solely on God's promise, the Mosaic Covenant was now bilateral, conditioned on Israel's obedience.

God said, *"Now if you obey me fully and keep my covenant, then out of all nations you will be my treasured possession."* (Exodus 19:5). The blessings of the covenant were always contingent upon Israel's faithfulness.

The purpose of the Law

The heart of the Old Covenant was the Law, called the Torah, which included moral laws (such as the Ten Commandments), civil laws governing Israelite society, and ceremonial laws related to worship and sacrifice.

The Law was comprehensive, touching every aspect of life. Its purpose was not simply to control behaviour but to reveal the character of God and to set Israel apart as *"a kingdom of priests and a holy nation."* (Exodus 19:6).

The Apostle Paul explains the Law's purpose further in the New Testament. He writes, *"It was added because of transgressions until the Seed to whom the promise referred had come."* (Galatians 3:19). The Law acted like a guardian or a tutor, highlighting sin and pointing forward to the need for a Saviour. *"Through the law,"* Paul says, *"we become conscious of our sin."* (Romans 3:20). The Law was never intended to justify anyone before God; rather, it exposed human inability to attain righteousness apart from divine grace.

The tabernacle and the sacrificial system

Integral to the Old Covenant was the tabernacle — the tent of meeting where God's presence dwelled among His people. The detailed instructions for the tabernacle, its furnishings, and its rituals underscore God's holiness and the barrier that sin created between humanity and Him. Entry into God's presence required the shedding of blood, the intercession of priests, and meticulous observance of purification laws.

The sacrificial system was a constant reminder of seriousness of sin. Day after day, animals were slaughtered, their blood sprinkled, their bodies burned. Leviticus 17:11 declares, *"It is the blood that makes atonement for one's life."*

Yet these sacrifices were never sufficient in themselves. The writer of Hebrews affirms that, *"It is impossible for the blood of bulls and goats to take away sins."* (Hebrews 10:4) They pointed beyond themselves to a greater sacrifice — one that would truly cleanse the conscience and bring final atonement.

The conditional nature of the Old Covenant

The Old Covenant is unique because of its conditional structure. Blessings for obedience, curses for disobedience — this was the framework of the Law. Deuteronomy 28 outlines this vividly. If Israel obeyed, they would experience prosperity, peace, and God's favour. If they disobeyed, they would face famine, disease, exile, and devastation. Tragically, the latter became Israel's story.

The prophets were the covenant prosecutors. Time and again, they would call Israel to account for their failure to uphold the covenant. Idolatry, injustice, and spiritual adultery plagued the nation. The exile to Assyria and to Babylon was not simply a political catastrophe — it was a covenantal consequence.

Yet even in that judgment, God's mercy prevailed. He promised restoration and hinted at a new and better covenant to come — one not written on tablets of stone but on hearts of flesh.

A temporary covenant with eternal lessons

It is vital to recognize that the Old Covenant was never meant to be permanent. It had a beginning, a purpose, and an end. Paul writes in Galatians 3:24, *"The law was our guardian until Christ came that we might be justified by faith."* The Law restrained sin, preserved Israel as a distinct people, and prepared the world for the coming of the Messiah.

But now that Christ has come, we are no longer under that guardian. Hebrews 8:13 says, *"By calling this covenant 'new,' he has made the first one obsolete; and what is obsolete and outdated will soon disappear."* Obsolete does not mean useless — it means fulfilled. The Old Covenant served its purpose magnificently.

It displayed God's holiness, humanity's sinfulness, and the deep chasm that separated the two. It revealed the need for a mediator who could bridge that gap forever.

Yet while the Old Covenant has been fulfilled in Christ and is no longer binding upon believers, it remains inspired Scripture — profitable for teaching, rebuking, correcting, and training in righteousness (2 Timothy 3:16). We do not discard it; we read it through the lens of the cross. We see in its shadows the shape of our Saviour.

The continuity and discontinuity between the covenants

One of the great challenges in understanding the Old Covenant is discerning what continues and what has now ceased under the New Covenant. This requires wisdom, biblical literacy, and theological care. Jesus said He did not come to abolish the Law or the Prophets, but to fulfil them (Matthew 5:17). That fulfilment changes how we relate to the law, but it does not render the Old Testament irrelevant.

The moral principles reflected in the Ten Commandments, for example, remain valid not because they were part of the Mosaic Covenant but because they reflect the eternal character of God. We do not murder, commit adultery, or steal — not because of Sinai, but because our love for God and neighbour compels us (Romans 13:8–10). These commands are reaffirmed in the New Testament as consistent with life in the Spirit.

However, the ceremonial and civil aspects of the law — the sacrifices, dietary laws, temple rituals — have been fulfilled and set aside. Hebrews 9 explains that Christ entered the Most Holy Place once for all by His own blood, securing eternal redemption. The temple veil was torn in two. The shadow gave way to the substance. The confusion often arises when believers attempt to extract Old Covenant principles without any reference to the fulfilment found in Christ. For example, invoking Old Testament curses or promises tied to obedience under the Mosaic Law — such as those found in Deuteronomy — can lead to legalism or false expectations.

The covenant context matters. Israel's blessings and curses were bound to a specific theocratic nation under a specific covenantal arrangement. Applying those conditions wholesale to Christians today disregards the finished work of Jesus Christ and the new realities of the Spirit-led life.

This does not mean we cannot glean much wisdom from the Old Testament - quite the opposite. The stories of Israel's journey, the wisdom of the Proverbs, the passion of the Psalms, and the warnings of the prophets are all rich with spiritual nourishment. But we must read them as Christians, not as Israelites under the Law. As Paul writes in Romans 15:4, *"Everything that was written in the past was written to teach us, so that through the endurance taught in the Scriptures and the encouragement they provide we might have hope."*

Israel's failure and God's faithfulness

The Old Covenant reveals more than just Israel's shortcomings; it also reveals God's unrelenting faithfulness. Despite repeated rebellion, idolatry, and injustice, God never abandoned His people. He may have disciplined them, yes — but always with the intention of restoration. Through the prophets, He promised a new day, a new heart, and a new covenant.

Consider the words of the prophet Hosea. God tells him to marry an unfaithful woman as a picture of Israel's spiritual adultery. Yet in Hosea 2:19–20, God declares, *"I will betroth you to me forever... in righteousness and justice, in love and compassion. I will betroth you in faithfulness, and you will acknowledge the Lord."* This is covenant language — but it anticipates a covenant far greater than Sinai.

Jeremiah, too, speaks of this coming transformation: *"The days are coming... when I will make a new covenant with the people of Israel and with the people of Judah."* (Jeremiah 31:31). God Himself promises to write His Law on their hearts and forgive their sins. The New Covenant, as we shall see more fully in later chapters, is inaugurated by Jesus Christ and sealed with His blood.

The Old Covenant thus functions as both a mirror and a map — revealing our need and pointing us toward the only One Who can meet it. Israel's story becomes our warning and our hope. *"These things happened to them as examples,"* Paul writes, *"and were written down as warnings for us, on whom the culmination of the ages has come."* (1 Corinthians 10:11).

Jesus and the Old Covenant

When Jesus arrived, He came not as a rebel against the Law but as its perfect fulfiller. In every way, He met the demands of the Old Covenant. He obeyed perfectly, loved fully, and submitted to the will of His Father, even unto death. His entire ministry was shaped by faithfulness to the Law — not merely to uphold it, but to bring it to completion. On the Mount of Transfiguration, Jesus appeared with Moses and Elijah — the personifications of the Law and the Prophets. And a voice from heaven declared, *"This is my Son, whom I love; with him I am well pleased. Listen to him!"* (Matthew 17:5). The torch was being passed. The age of the Law was yielding to the age of the gospel.

At the Last Supper, Jesus took the cup and declared, *"This cup is the new covenant in my blood, which is poured out for you."* (Luke 22:20). The Old Covenant had been ratified with the blood of animals (Exodus 24:8); the New Covenant was ratified with the blood of God's own Son. This covenant would not be based on external law but on internal transformation. It would not depend on human obedience but on divine grace. It would not require repeated sacrifices but rest on one perfect sacrifice forever. Jesus did not just patch up the Old Covenant. He did not reform it, renovate it, or repackage it. He fulfilled it — and in doing so, rendered it obsolete as a governing system for God's people. The veil in the temple was torn from top to bottom. Access to God was no longer mediated through priests and rituals but through the risen Christ, our great high priest.

Why the old still matters

If the Old Covenant has been fulfilled and superseded, why does it still matter? Why devote entire books of the Bible — even this chapter — to something which is no longer binding?

Because the Old Covenant reveals God's holiness, humanity's need, and the framework for understanding Jesus' redemptive work. Without the Law, grace has no real context. Without the priesthood, Christ's intercession loses its depth. Without the sacrificial system, the cross becomes a mere tragedy rather than the fulfilment of a divine pattern.

Moreover, the Old Covenant lays the whole foundation for understanding the clear continuity of God's redemptive plan. The gospel did not appear out of thin air. It is the culmination of centuries of covenantal history. As Jesus told the disciples on the road to Emmaus, *"beginning with Moses and all the Prophets, he explained to them what was said in all the Scriptures concerning himself."* (Luke 24:27).

To neglect the Old Testament is to read the climax of a story without its beginning. But to read the Old Testament without Christ is to miss the point entirely. He is the key, the lens, the fulfilment. All Scripture points to Jesus Christ. The Old Covenant prepares the stage; the New Covenant unveils the drama of redemption in full.

Avoiding the two errors

In light of all this, Christians must be careful not to fall into two equal and opposite errors. The first is *legalism* — the attempt to impose Old Covenant laws and practices on New Covenant believers. This might include observing Old Testament feasts as mandatory, enforcing dietary laws, or suggesting that salvation depends on adherence to certain Mosaic regulations. Paul strongly opposed such teachings, especially in his letter to the Galatians 5:4, *"You who are trying to be justified by the law have been alienated from Christ; you have fallen away from grace."* Returning to the Law as a system of righteousness is a rejection of the gospel.

The second error is *lawlessness* — the idea that grace means we can disregard all of God's moral commands. As we saw earlier, Paul counters this in Romans 6:15: *"Shall we sin because we are not under the law but under grace? By no means!"*

The moral standards of God have not been abolished; they have been written on our hearts by the Spirit. Grace does not nullify holiness — it empowers it. The New Covenant does not set us free to sin; it sets us free from sin. The Spirit of God now enables what the Law could never achieve: obedience from the heart. As Paul writes in Romans 8:3-4, *"For what the law was powerless to do... God did by sending his own Son... in order that the righteous requirement of the law might be fully met in us."*

Learning to read the Old Covenant correctly

For Christians today, the Old Covenant is not our covenant, but it is our heritage. We are not under its legal demands, but we are enriched by its truths. We must learn to read it with discernment, always asking:

➤ What does this reveal about God's character?

➤ How does this point forward to Christ?

➤ What principles still apply in the light of the New Covenant?

➤ How does this deepen my understanding of grace?

Take, for example, the book of Leviticus. At first glance, it will appear arcane and irrelevant. But when read through the lens of the gospel, it becomes a treasure. Every sacrifice, every priestly garment, every ritual of cleansing whispers the name of Jesus. He is our sacrifice, our priest, our purity. Leviticus is not about rules — it's about relationship, holiness, and access to God, now fulfilled in Christ. Likewise, the narratives of Israel's journey, their wilderness wanderings, conquests, exiles, and returns, mirror our own spiritual journey. They remind us of our tendency to wander, our need for grace, and the faithful Shepherd Who leads us home.

Embracing the fulfilment

The Old Covenant sets the stage, but the New Covenant tells the story in full. To live as New Covenant believers today means embracing Christ not only as Saviour but as the fulfilment of all that came before.

Jesus is the true temple, the perfect sacrifice, the final priest, the living Law, the faithful Israelite, and the ultimate King. In Him, all the promises of God are *"Yes"* and *"Amen"* (2 Cor. 1:20). This means we no longer approach God through the shadows of the old, but through the substance of the new. The sacrificial system was a shadow — but Christ is the substance. The priesthood was a shadow — but Christ is our high priest. The tabernacle was a shadow — but now we are God's dwelling place by His Spirit. To return to the shadows when we have the substance is to regress, not grow.

The writer to the Hebrews makes this point repeatedly. *"The law is only a shadow of the good things that are coming — not the realities themselves."* (Hebrews 10:1). Again and again, Hebrews contrasts the Old and New: old sacrifices versus Christ's once-for-all offering; earthly priests versus the eternal Son of God; external regulations versus internal transformation.

"For this reason," Hebrews 9:15 declares, *"Christ is the mediator of a new covenant, that those who are called may receive the promised eternal inheritance."* The old was temporary; the new is eternal. The old brought condemnation; the new brings life. The old was written on stone; the new is written on hearts.

Living as New Covenant people

Understanding the Old Covenant's role helps us live more fully under the New. It clarifies our identity, sharpens our mission, and fuels our worship. We are no longer striving to obey a written code to gain God's approval. We have been accepted in Christ and empowered by the Spirit to walk in joyful obedience. This doesn't mean we ignore the commands of Scripture — far from it. But we obey not to earn God's favour, but because we already have it. The law once said, *"Do this and live."* The gospel says, *"Live, and now do this."* The order has changed — and that changes absolutely everything.

As New Covenant believers, we now live from a different foundation. We are not children at Mount Sinai, trembling in fear. We are citizens of Mount Zion, rejoicing in grace.

Hebrews 12 captures this contrast beautifully: *"You have not come to a mountain that can be touched and that is burning with fire… But you have come to Mount Zion, to the city of the living God… to Jesus the mediator of a new covenant."* (Hebrews 12:18, 22, 24).

Our lives are not governed by the tablets of stone but by the Spirit Who is within us. Our righteousness is not self-produced but Spirit-formed. Our confidence is not in our performance but in Christ's perfection.

The old in light of the new

Let's consider a few practical implications of living, in light of this truth.

1. How we use the Old Testament:

We must read the Old Testament through a Christ-centred lens. When we see laws about sacrifices, we reflect on the cross. When we read about the tabernacle, we remember God's presence in us. When we hear prophetic calls to justice, we respond not with external compliance, but with Spirit-led transformation.

We also resist the temptation to claim promises made to Israel under the Old Covenant as though they now apply directly to the church today. While the character of God is unchanging, the covenantal context matters. Promises tied to obedience under the Mosaic law are not guarantees for us under grace. That doesn't diminish their beauty — it deepens our gratitude that in Christ, we receive far better promises.

2. How we understand holiness:

The Old Covenant emphasized external holiness — clean versus unclean, pure versus impure. These categories taught important truths about God's holiness and humanity's sinfulness. But they were temporary pictures. Under the New Covenant, holiness is a matter of the heart. Jesus declared all foods clean, but He also taught that it's what comes out of a person — not what goes in — that defiles them (Mark 7:15). The Spirit now writes God's laws on our hearts, not our menus.

This doesn't lead to moral laxity but to deeper transformation. Holiness is no longer about rules to follow but about reflecting the character of Jesus Christ. We pursue purity, love, justice, and humility — not because we fear condemnation, but because we are new creations.

3. How we worship:

Old Covenant worship centred on a place, a ritual, and priestly mediation. Whereas New Covenant worship is in Spirit and in truth (John 4:24). We are the temple. Jesus is the mediator. Every believer is a priest.

This means worship is not confined to buildings or ceremonies. It's a lifestyle — presenting our bodies as living sacrifices, holy and pleasing to God (Romans 12:1). It's gathering as the church not to re-enact sacrifice, but to celebrate the one perfect offering already made for us. Our songs, prayers, and sacraments are not attempts to reach God — they are responses to His grace already given. The veil is torn. The throne of grace is open. Worship is now a feast of joy, not a burden of duty.

4. How we disciple others:

Understanding the covenants helps us disciple wisely. We don't load new believers with outdated regulations or confuse them with mixed messages. We teach them the whole counsel of God, rightly divided. We show them how the Old Testament leads to Christ and how the New Testament equips them to walk in freedom.

We also help people distinguish between the moral, civil, and ceremonial aspects of the law — recognizing what was fulfilled, what was for Israel's national life, and what reflects timeless moral truth. This is not always easy, but it's necessary if we want to honour both Scripture and the gospel.

5. How we live with confidence:

Perhaps most importantly, having a right understanding of the Old Covenant gives us assurance. We are not on probation with God. We are not one failure away from rejection.

The Old Covenant was conditional — blessings came through obedience. The New Covenant is based on Christ's obedience, not ours. This is why Paul could write with boldness, *"Therefore, there is now no condemnation for those who are in Christ Jesus."* (Romans 8:1). The law condemns. The gospel liberates. Under the Old, the priest had to return again and again. Under the New, Jesus sat down at the right hand of God — His work is done. We can rest now. We can rejoice. We can live with confidence, not in ourselves, but in the covenant sealed by the blood of Christ.

Conclusion: holding the story together

The Old Covenant is not a mistake which had to be discarded — it's a masterpiece to be understood. It reveals God's holiness, humanity's need, and the unfolding plan of redemption.

But it is not the final word. That word is Jesus. In Him, the story finds its climax. In Him, the Law is fulfilled. In Him, the promises are kept. In Him, we find grace upon grace upon grace. To understand the Old Covenant is to marvel at the New. To know the weight of the Law is to cherish the wonder of the gospel.

As we move forward in this book, we will explore more fully what the New Covenant entails — its promises, its implications, and its beauty. But we do so with gratitude for the Old, for it led us here. And we do so with eyes fixed on Jesus, *"the author and perfecter of our faith."* (Hebrews 12:2).

4

THE NEW COVENANT PROMISED

The need for a New Covenant

Let's take a step back for a moment. From the earliest pages of Scripture, we see the unfolding of God's covenantal dealings with humanity. Each covenant God made was a step toward His ultimate redemptive plan. But as we've seen, the Old Covenant — centred on the Law given through Moses — though holy and good, was never intended to be the final or sufficient covenant. It pointed to something far greater, to a new and better way through which God would bring lasting reconciliation and transformation. The prophets of the Old Testament began to stir hope in the hearts of God's people as they spoke of a time when a new covenant would replace the old.

The need for a New Covenant was born out of human inability to live according to the righteousness which was required by the Law. Despite Israel's unique relationship with God, the nation continually fell into cycles of sin, judgment, and then temporary restoration.

The Law could expose sin, but it could not empower obedience. It could reveal the holiness of God, but it could not transform the human heart. The sacrificial system was repetitive and external; it could atone for sin, but it could never cleanse the conscience. All of this created a yearning for something more, something better, something new.

Prophetic promises of a new way

Promises of a New Covenant began to emerge in the prophetic books, especially during periods of national crisis and exile. In those dark times, when Israel and Judah faced the consequences of their covenant unfaithfulness, God offered glimpses of a future in which He would act decisively to heal, redeem, and restore. Perhaps the most well-known prophetic declaration of the New Covenant is found in the book of Jeremiah:

"'The days are coming,' declares the Lord, 'when I will make a new covenant with the people of Israel and with the people of Judah. It will not be like the covenant I made with their ancestors when I took them by the hand to lead them out of Egypt, because they broke my covenant, though I was a husband to them,' declares the Lord.

'This is the covenant I will make with the people of Israel after that time,' declares the Lord. 'I will put my law in their minds and write it on their hearts. I will be their God, and they will be my people. No longer will they teach their neighbour, or say to one another, "Know the Lord," because they will all know me, from the least of them to the greatest,' declares the Lord. 'For I will forgive their wickedness and will remember their sins no more.'" (Jeremiah 31:31–34).

This stunning passage reveals key aspects of the promised covenant. It would be:

➤ **New**: It would not be a renewal of the old, but something entirely different in nature.

➤ **Internal**: God's law would be written on hearts and minds, not tablets of stone.

➤ **Relational**: It would bring a deeper intimacy between God and His people.

➤ **Universal among believers**: All would know God directly.

➤ **Forgiving**: Sin would no longer be merely covered; it would be fully forgiven.

This promise must have seemed revolutionary to the people of Jeremiah's day, living as they were under the heavy weight of exile, judgment, and the memory of a failed covenant. Yet this message was not one of condemnation, but of hope. God was not done with His people. He was preparing something greater.

Ezekiel's vision of inner renewal

The prophet Ezekiel also contributed profound insights into the nature of the coming covenant. Speaking to exiles in Babylon, Ezekiel shared a vision of God's redemptive action that would transform the very core of human identity:

"I will give you a new heart and put a new spirit in you; I will remove from you your heart of stone and give you a heart of flesh. And I will put my Spirit in you and move you to follow my decrees and be careful to keep my laws." (Ezekiel 36:26–27)

The newness of the covenant is shown not only in the forgiveness of sin but in the transformation of human nature. This is not simply external compliance with divine rules, but inner change through the indwelling presence of God's Spirit. The promise of a new heart and a new spirit sets the stage for the Holy Spirit's vital role in the New Covenant. God Himself would empower His people to live in faithfulness.

Isaiah and the Servant of the Lord

Isaiah, too, contributed to the picture of this New Covenant. He foretold the coming of a Servant who would suffer for the sins of the people and establish justice on the earth. In Isaiah 42, God declares: *"I, the Lord, have called you in righteousness; I will take hold of your hand. I will keep you and will make you to be a covenant for the people and a light for the Gentiles."* (Isaiah 42:6)

And again, in Isaiah 49: *"I will also make you a light for the Gentiles, that my salvation may reach to the ends of the earth."* (Isaiah 49:6)

The Servant of the Lord would not merely bring a new covenant; He would be the covenant itself. In Him, the promises of God would find their fulfilment. The covenant would no longer be written merely in words but embodied in a person.

Isaiah 53 then shows the Servant suffering for the sins of many: *"Surely he took up our pain and bore our suffering, yet we considered him punished by God, stricken by him, and afflicted. But he was pierced for our transgressions, he was crushed for our iniquities; the punishment that brought us peace was on him, and by his wounds we are healed."* (Isaiah 53:4–5)

These prophecies not only point to the coming of Jesus Christ but reveal the nature of the New Covenant He would establish: one that is based on sacrificial love, substitutionary atonement, and universal hope.

God's initiative and faithfulness

A critical theme that runs through all these prophetic visions is that the New Covenant would be initiated by God Himself. It would not depend on human obedience or achievement but on God's sovereign grace and faithfulness. This distinguishes it fundamentally from the Old Covenant, which was conditional and repeatedly broken by the people.

In the New Covenant, God takes the first step. He provides the means. He writes the law on the heart. He grants the Spirit. He forgives the sin. He restores the relationship. And He does so through the person and work of His Servant, the Messiah.

When the Old Testament era drew to a close, these promises hung in the air like morning dew waiting for the warmth of the sun. God's people waited — longing, hoping, praying for the day when the New Covenant would come.

The stage is now set ...

The promise of a New Covenant is the promise of a better hope. The prophets did not present this covenant as a vague spiritual idea but as a real and radical intervention in human history. The Old Covenant, though divinely given, was not sufficient to bring about the kind of transformation God desired for His people. The New Covenant would be God's final word on the whole matter of redemption. It would be written on hearts, empowered by the Spirit, secured through the Servant, and offered to all.

The promises of the New Covenant are not isolated or sudden revelations, but the culmination of a redemptive arc that spans the entire biblical narrative. In the prophetic literature of the Old Testament, especially in the exilic and post-exilic periods, we find these promises rising like dawn after a long night of failure and exile. The people of Israel, though chosen, had not fulfilled their covenant obligations. The Law had exposed their sin but could not heal it. The sacrificial system had covered guilt but could not cleanse the conscience. What was needed was a better covenant, founded on better promises.

A covenant of transformation

One of the most profound distinctions of the New Covenant is that it promises internal transformation. The Old Covenant had been written on tablets of stone, but the New Covenant is written on the hearts of God's people.

This inner engraving of the law points not only to an intellectual understanding but to a deep alignment of desire and will with God's purposes. Under the Old Covenant, obedience was often external and driven by duty or fear of punishment. Under the New Covenant, obedience flows from a heart that has been changed by grace. This heart-level transformation is the work of the Holy Spirit, who indwells believers and empowers them to live according to God's ways. This is not a moral improvement program; it is a spiritual rebirth. It is regeneration.

A covenant of intimacy

The New Covenant also promises a deeper intimacy with God. Jeremiah continues in his prophecy: *"No longer will they teach their neighbour, or say to one another, 'Know the Lord,' because they will all know me, from the least of them to the greatest."* (Jeremiah 31:34).

This is revolutionary. In the Old Covenant, knowledge of God was mediated through priests and prophets. Access to God's presence was limited and regulated through temple rituals and sacrifices. But in the New Covenant, there is a democratization of access to God. Every believer is invited into a personal, direct relationship with the Lord. This intimacy is made possible through the mediating work of Jesus Christ.

As the author of Hebrews writes, *"There is one mediator between God and mankind, the man Christ Jesus."* (1 Timothy 2:5). He is the great High Priest who entered the Most Holy Place once for all by his own blood, securing eternal redemption. Through Him, we have access to the Father by one Spirit. The curtain has been torn. The barrier is gone. This intimacy is not merely positional but experiential. The Holy Spirit enables believers to cry out, *"Abba, Father."*

The Spirit bears witness with our spirit that we are children of God. We are no longer servants standing outside the house, but sons and daughters who dwell in the Father's presence.

A covenant of forgiveness

At the heart of the New Covenant is the promise of full and final forgiveness. Jeremiah declares, *"For I will forgive their wickedness and will remember their sins no more."* (Jeremiah 31:34). This is not a temporary covering, as in the sacrificial system, but a definitive cleansing. The sacrifices of bulls and goats could never take away sins. They were but shadows pointing to the substance, which is Christ.

In Jesus, the Lamb of God, the penalty for sin has been paid in full. As Hebrews proclaims, *"By one sacrifice he has made perfect forever those who are being made holy."* (Hebrews 10:14).

The New Covenant does not leave sin partially dealt with, nor does it require repeated offerings. The work is finished. The debt is cancelled. The record is erased. This forgiveness is not earned but received by faith. It is rooted in the grace of God, who delights in mercy. It is secured by the righteousness of Jesus Christ, Who fulfilled the law on our behalf. It is sealed by the Spirit, Who applies this grace to our hearts.

Forgiveness under the New Covenant is also transformative. It does not lead to lawlessness but to love. As Jesus said, *"Whoever has been forgiven little loves little,"* but the one who knows the depth of their forgiveness will respond with deep devotion (Luke 7:47). The grace that pardons also purifies. The blood that cleanses also consecrates.

A covenant of universality

Another vital aspect of the New Covenant is its universality. While the Old Covenant was made specifically with the nation of Israel, the New Covenant extends to all nations. This was always God's intention, even in His covenant with Abraham: *"All peoples on earth will be blessed through you."* (Genesis 12:3).

Isaiah foresaw this when he wrote, "*It is too small a thing for you to be my servant to restore the tribes of Jacob... I will also make you a light for the Gentiles, that my salvation may reach to the ends of the earth.*" (Isaiah 49:6). Jesus completely fulfilled this vision when He commissioned His disciples to make disciples of all nations. Paul, the apostle to the Gentiles, celebrated the mystery that had been hidden for ages but was now revealed: that the Gentiles are fellow heirs, members of the same body, and partakers of the promise in Christ Jesus through the gospel.

The New Covenant tears down the dividing wall between Jew and Gentile. It forms one new humanity in Christ. It brings near those who were far off. It unites people from every tribe and tongue and nation under one Lord, one faith, one baptism. This universality does not erase ethnic identity but transcends it in a higher unity.

This has profound implications for the church. We are not a continuation of Israel as a nation-state, nor are we under the civil and ceremonial laws of the Mosaic covenant. We are a new creation, a holy nation, a royal priesthood, called to proclaim the excellencies of Him who called us out of darkness into His marvellous light. Our identity is not in our lineage but in our union with Christ.

A covenant initiated by God

Perhaps the most humbling aspect of the New Covenant is that it is entirely initiated and enacted by God. It is not a mutual agreement, nor is it dependent on human performance. God says, "*I will make a new covenant... I will put my law in their minds... I will be their God... I will forgive their wickedness... I will remember their sins no more.*" (Jeremiah 31). The repeated "*I will*" statements emphasize the unilateral nature of this covenant.

This reflects the character of a God who is both just and merciful. He does not abandon His people in their failure but steps in to do what they could never do. He upholds both His righteousness and His love. The New Covenant is not 'plan B' but the fulfilment of a plan that was in the heart of God from the beginning.

This divine initiative is seen most clearly at the cross. While we were still sinners, Christ died for us. He did not wait for us to improve or promise better behaviour. He took the initiative. He bore our sin. He offered Himself as the mediator and guarantor of a better covenant. Our response is not to negotiate but to surrender. Not to earn but to receive. Not to strive but to trust. The New Covenant begins and ends with grace. It is a covenant not of demand but of provision. Not of fear but of freedom. Not of exclusion but of embrace.

This divine authorship assures us of the covenant's permanence. If it depended on us, it would surely fail. But because it is grounded in God's unchanging purpose and secured by Christ's finished work, it cannot be broken. It is an everlasting covenant, written not in ink but in blood, not on stone but on hearts, not with the threat of curse but with the promise of life.

The next movement in this covenantal progression reveals how all these promises converge in the person and work of Jesus Christ, who stands as the fulfilment and embodiment of all God's covenantal hopes and declarations. The promise of the New Covenant is not a peripheral doctrine in the Bible.

It is the culmination of God's redemptive plan, the fulfilment of His unchanging purpose to dwell with His people and restore what was broken by sin. The anticipation of this covenant reverberated throughout Israel's history, and its realization in Christ changed the trajectory of the world.

God's heart revealed in the New Covenant

One of the most beautiful aspects of the New Covenant is that it unveils the very heart of God. Unlike a contract rooted merely in law, the New Covenant is born out of love, grace, and divine initiative.

This is not a God of distant judgment but one of intimacy and restoration. The use of relational language (*"I was a husband to them"* and *"I will be their God, and they will be my people"*) underscores the deep covenantal bond God desires.

The New Covenant is not merely about moral adherence or religious ritual. It is about communion. God is not merely handing down a revised list of rules; He is calling a people into a personal, transformative relationship.

The internalisation of the Law

The Old Covenant placed the law on stone tablets. The New Covenant places it within the human heart. This internal shift is monumental. Under the old system, obedience came under the pressure of external demands. In the new, obedience flows from inward transformation.

God promises, *"I will put my law in their minds and write it on their hearts."* This is a shift from compulsion to conviction, from duty to delight. The Spirit of God now indwells believers, enabling them to live in accordance with His will not out of fear of punishment but from love and new desires. Ezekiel 36:26–27 echoes this promise: *"I will give you a new heart and put a new spirit in you; I will remove from you your heart of stone and give you a heart of flesh. And I will put my Spirit in you and move you to follow my decrees and be careful to keep my laws."*

This is not reform but rebirth. It is a change in nature, not merely behaviour. The transformation envisioned in the New Covenant is deep, enduring, and Spirit-wrought. The believer is no longer externally conformed to God's will but internally renewed to reflect His nature.

A forgiven and redeemed people

Another central feature of the New Covenant is its provision of complete and final forgiveness. The Old Covenant had rituals for atonement, but they pointed forward to a greater reality. Hebrews 10:1–4 reminds us that the law was only *"a shadow of the good things that are coming"* and that animal sacrifices *"can never take away sins."* But under the New Covenant, God declares, "For I will forgive their wickedness and will remember their sins no more" (Jeremiah 31:34). This is a radical promise. Forgiveness is no longer temporary, provisional, or conditional upon repeated sacrifice. It is final. It is complete. It is secured in Christ.

Jesus, in instituting the New Covenant at the Last Supper, held up the cup and declared, *"This cup is the new covenant in my blood, which is poured out for you."* (Luke 22:20). His blood did what the blood of bulls and goats never could. It cleansed the conscience, reconciled us to God, and secured eternal redemption. The New Covenant community is a forgiven community. They are not defined by their failures or bound to their past. They live in the freedom of grace, in the assurance of peace, and in the joy of reconciliation. Their identity is no longer *"sinner"* but *"saint,"* not merely *"servant"* but *"son"* and *"daughter."*

A new community formed

With the New Covenant comes the birth of a whole new people. No longer is covenant membership determined by ethnicity, circumcision, or adherence to ceremonial law. The people of the New Covenant are defined by faith in Christ.

As Paul states in Galatians 3:28: *"There is neither Jew nor Gentile, neither slave nor free, nor is there male and female, for you are all one in Christ Jesus."* This new community is not limited by borders or bloodlines. It spans nations, cultures, and generations. It is the church — the body of Christ, united by the Spirit, called to be the visible expression of God's kingdom on earth.

The early church understood this identity shift. The Jerusalem Council in Acts 15 wrestled with the implications of Gentile inclusion without the requirements of the Mosaic law. Their verdict was clear: salvation is by grace through faith, and the burdens of the Old Covenant law were not to be placed on the necks of new believers. This new community is marked by love, unity, and mission. They live not for themselves but for the glory of Christ. Their shared life is a testimony to the reconciling power of the New Covenant.

Life by the Spirit

Perhaps the most distinguishing feature of the New Covenant is the role of the Holy Spirit. The Spirit is not only the seal of our salvation but the very presence of God within us. The Spirit guides, convicts, empowers, and comforts.

Romans 8:2 declares, *"Through Christ Jesus the law of the Spirit who gives life has set you free from the law of sin and death."* This freedom is not the license to sin but the liberty to live in righteousness. The Spirit enables what the law demanded but could not produce.

Whereas the Old Covenant emphasized human effort and our external compliance, the New Covenant emphasizes divine enablement and internal transformation. As the Apostle Paul says in 2 Corinthians 3:6, *"(God) has made us competent as ministers of a new covenant – not of the letter but of the Spirit; for the letter kills, but the Spirit gives life."* This Spirit-filled life is dynamic. It is not a static observance of rules but an ever-deepening walk with God. The believer is continually being conformed to the image of Christ, bearing the fruit of the Spirit, and living out the kingdom ethic in everyday life.

The New Covenant realised

The New Covenant is not just a future hope; it is a present reality. It has been inaugurated by Christ and is being lived out by His people today. It fulfils the deepest longings of the human heart – for intimacy with God, for forgiveness, for transformation, and for belonging.

Yet, while it is a present reality, it also carries future promise. The fullness of the New Covenant will be realized when Christ returns, and the kingdom of God is consummated. Until then, we live as participants in this covenant, stewards of its grace, and ambassadors of its message.

In every generation, the church must return to the foundation of the New Covenant, not as an abstract doctrine, but as the heartbeat of its life and mission. For in this covenant, God has not only made promises – He has made a people, a redeemed, Spirit-filled community called to live for His glory in a broken world.

THE FULFILMENT OF THE OLD COVENANT IN CHRIST

The shadow of what was to come

When we open the Old Testament, we are stepping into the covenantal relationship God established with the nation of Israel—a covenant built upon promises, laws, sacrifices, and a hope that pointed forward to something far greater. The Old Covenant was not an end in itself; it was a shadow, a signpost pointing ahead. Its fulfilment would come not through Israel's performance, but through a Person - Jesus Christ.

The writer to the Hebrews helps us grasp this truth when he declares, *"The law is only a shadow of the good things that are coming—not the realities themselves."* (Hebrews 10:1). Those ceremonies, the tabernacle, the priesthood, and even the moral laws were types and patterns of something deeper, richer, and eternal. They were temporary scaffolding, necessary for a season, but destined to be dismantled once the true structure—the New Covenant—was revealed in Christ.

Yet for centuries, the people of God clung to this shadow with reverence, not always realising it was never meant to be the final word. The Law served its purpose, but it was never intended to be permanent. Jesus Himself confirmed this when He said, *"Do not think that I have come to abolish the Law or the Prophets; I have not come to abolish them but to fulfil them."* (Matthew 5:17).

Fulfilment, not abolishment

The distinction Jesus makes is profound. He did not come to discard or devalue the Old Covenant; He came to <u>fulfil</u> it—to bring it to its intended climax. Every ritual, prophecy, and symbol in the Old Covenant finds its ultimate meaning in Him. The Passover lamb prefigured His sacrificial death. The high priest foreshadowed His intercessory role. The temple pointed to His body, the true meeting place between God and humanity. This fulfilment means that Jesus completed what the Law required and embodied what the prophets foretold.

Where the Law exposed sin, Jesus dealt with it. Where the covenant demanded obedience, Jesus supplied it. He met the conditions we could never meet and He bore the penalties we deserved.

As Paul wrote, *"Christ is the culmination of the law so that there may be righteousness for everyone who believes."* (Romans 10:4). The word *"culmination"* (*"end"* in some translations) does not suggest destruction, but completion. The Law's purpose was to lead people to Christ, and now that He has come, its role is fulfilled.

The end of the sacrificial system

Perhaps the clearest sign that the Old Covenant was fulfilled in Christ is seen in the temple system. All those sacrificial rituals, repeated daily and annually, testified not only to God's holiness but also to the insufficiency of animal blood to permanently remove sin. Hebrews again puts it plainly: *"It is impossible for the blood of bulls and goats to take away sins."* (Hebrews 10:4).

These sacrifices were really placeholders, anticipating the one perfect sacrifice that could truly and finally atone for sin. That sacrifice came through Jesus, who, according to Hebrews 10:12, *"offered for all time one sacrifice for sins"* and then *"sat down at the right hand of God."* The posture of sitting is significant—He sat down because His work was finished.

The tearing of the temple curtain at Jesus' death (Matthew 27:51) was no mere coincidence. It signified the final end of the Old Covenant's sacrificial system and the opening of a radically new and living way into God's presence, made possible by the blood of Jesus (Hebrews 10:19–20). This wasn't a symbolic or partial change; it was a decisive fulfilment. The old was not needed anymore because the new had come.

A better covenant, built on better promises

The Old Covenant was glorious in its time, but it was never designed to last forever. It was, as Paul described, a *"guardian until Christ came"* (Galatians 3:24). It restrained sin, preserved Israel as a people, and pointed to the holiness of God.

But it could not change the human heart. It could not impart life. It could only reveal the standard and the shortfall. That is why God, through the prophet Jeremiah, announced a new covenant in Jeremiah 31:33: *"This is the covenant I will make with the people of Israel after that time,"* declares the Lord. *"I will put my law in their minds and write it on their hearts. I will be their God, and they will be my people."*

The writer of Hebrews quotes this prophecy at length and then says, *"By calling this covenant 'new,' he has made the first one obsolete; and what is obsolete and outdated will soon disappear."* (Hebrews 8:13).

Jesus inaugurated this New Covenant with His own blood. At the Last Supper, He lifted the cup and said, *"This cup is the new covenant in my blood, which is poured out for you."* (Luke 22:20). With those words, He declared that the old had given way to the new — not because it had failed, but because it had succeeded in leading us to Him.

Jesus as the True Israel

Another way Christ fulfilled the Old Covenant is by being the true embodiment of Israel. Where Israel had failed in obedience, Jesus succeeded. Where Israel grumbled in the wilderness, Jesus triumphed in the desert. He recapitulated their story and rewrote it in perfect faithfulness.

Matthew's Gospel, in particular, portrays Jesus as the true and better Israel. Just as Israel passed through the Red Sea, Jesus was baptized in the Jordan. Just as Israel wandered forty years in the wilderness, Jesus fasted forty days in the desert. Just as Moses ascended the mountain to receive the law, Jesus climbed the mountain to deliver the Sermon on the Mount.

In all this, Jesus is not only fulfilling prophecy but also fulfilling identity. He is the Son whom God called *"out of Egypt"* (Matthew 2:15; Hosea 11:1). He is the vine that bears fruit where Israel failed (John 15:1–2). He is the faithful servant who brings justice and salvation to the nations (Isaiah 42:1; Matthew 12:18–21).

To understand Christ's role in fulfilling the Old Covenant, we must see that He didn't merely replace Israel – He embodied and redeemed Israel's calling.

Christ, the final High Priest

One of the most profound ways Jesus fulfilled the Old Covenant is through His role as our eternal High Priest. Under the Mosaic law, the high priest served as an intercessor between God and His people. He entered the Most Holy Place once a year to offer sacrifices for the sins of the nation (Leviticus 16:2-34). Yet even this solemn ritual had limitations. The high priest was a sinful man offering imperfect sacrifices. His role was temporary and needed repetition every year.

But Hebrews declares that Jesus is the great High Priest who has passed through the heavens (Hebrews 4:14), and unlike the Levitical priests, He is *"holy, blameless, pure, set apart from sinners, exalted above the heavens."* (Hebrews 7:26). Jesus did not need to offer sacrifices for His own sins, nor did He need to repeat His work. Instead, *"He sacrificed for their sins once for all when he offered himself."* (Hebrews 7:27). The Old Covenant high priest entered the earthly tabernacle. Whereas Jesus entered the true, heavenly tabernacle *"not made with human hands."* (Hebrews 9:11).

This is more than a doctrinal shift—it is a relational revolution. We no longer approach God through a human priestly system, but through Jesus Himself. The veil that separated humanity from God's presence was torn at the moment of Christ's death (Matthew 27:51), signifying that access to the Father was now available to all who come through Christ. Jesus, the true and final High Priest, has inaugurated a new and living way by His blood.

The perfect and final sacrifice

Sacrifice was the heart of the Old Covenant system. Daily offerings and annual rituals emphasized the cost of sin and the necessity of atonement. But the blood of bulls and goats *"can never take away sins."* (Hebrews 10:4). These sacrifices were temporary coverings, not permanent solutions.

Jesus fulfilled this entire system in one decisive act. *"He has appeared once for all at the culmination of the ages to do away with sin by the sacrifice of himself."* (Hebrews 9:26). He is both priest and sacrifice. As John the Baptist declared, *"Behold, the Lamb of God, who takes away the sin of the world!"* (John 1:29). No further offering is needed. His death was sufficient, complete, and eternal.

This means that any attempt to reintroduce or rely again on Old Covenant sacrificial practices denies the sufficiency of Christ's cross. The cross is not just central — it is final. It is the exclamation point at the end of the long sentence of the Old Covenant, declaring *"It is finished."* (John 19:30).

When we grasp the magnitude of this fulfilment, we are set free from guilt-driven religion. We no longer bring our offerings to appease God but come boldly because Christ has already made peace through His blood (Colossians 1:20). The invitation is no longer, *"Bring your lamb,"* but *"Come to Me, all who are weary and burdened, and I will give you rest."* (Matthew 11:28).

The fulfilment of the moral law

One area of confusion for many Christians is the role of the law after Christ. Some argue that if the ceremonial and civil aspects of the Old Covenant were fulfilled in Christ, perhaps the moral law (especially the Ten Commandments) remains binding.

Jesus clarified this tension in the Sermon on the Mount. *"Do not think that I have come to abolish the Law or the Prophets; I have not come to abolish them but to fulfil them."* (Matthew 5:17). Fulfilment does not mean dismissal — it means bringing something to its intended purpose. Jesus did not lower the moral bar; He raised it. Instead of just avoiding murder, we must reject hate. Instead of abstaining from adultery, we must reject lust. He moved obedience from external actions to internal transformation. Paul affirms this shift when he writes, *"Christ is the culmination of the law so that there may be righteousness for everyone who believes."* (Romans 10:4). We are no longer under the law as a system of righteousness, but we now live by the Spirit, who writes God's law on our hearts (Romans 8:2-4).

This is the difference between law-driven and grace-empowered obedience. Under the Old Covenant, obedience was a condition for blessing. Under the New Covenant, obedience is a response to grace and blessing. The Spirit empowers what the law could only demand. We no longer obey in order to be accepted — we obey because we *are* accepted.

Jesus and the prophetic promises

The Old Covenant was not just a legal code or ritual system — it was a rich story – a prophetic narrative pointing toward a future redemption in Christ. Jesus fulfilled not only the commands and ceremonies but the storyline itself.

From Genesis to Malachi, the Old Testament unfolds a tapestry of promises: a serpent-crusher (Genesis 3:15), a prophet like Moses (Deuteronomy 18:18), a suffering servant (Isaiah 53), a king from David's line (2 Samuel 7:12-13), a new covenant written on hearts (Jeremiah 31:31-34). Jesus is the living fulfilment of all these threads.

He is the seed of Abraham through whom all nations are blessed (Galatians 3:16). He is the righteous Branch who reigns as King (Jeremiah 23:5). He is the true Temple (John 2:19-21), the final Passover Lamb (1 Corinthians 5:7), and the light to the Gentiles (Isaiah 49:6).

To read the Old Testament rightly is to see Christ at the center. He told the disciples on the road to Emmaus, *"Everything must be fulfilled that is written about me in the Law of Moses, the Prophets and the Psalms."* (Luke 24:44). The Old Covenant was never the end goal — it was always just the signpost.

Living in the fulfilment

If the Old Covenant has been fulfilled in Christ, what does that mean for how we live today? It means we live in the reality, not the shadow (Hebrews 10:1). We don't look back to the law for salvation — we look to Christ. We don't rebuild what Christ has torn down (Galatians 2:18). We walk by faith, not by law, and we live by the Spirit, not by rituals.

But this doesn't mean the Old Testament is irrelevant. On the contrary, it becomes richer when we read it through the lens of Christ.

The stories, laws, prophecies, and psalms all find new depth when we understand how they each point to Jesus. The Passover becomes a foreshadowing of the cross. The wilderness becomes a picture of our own spiritual journey. The law reveals the holiness that Christ fulfilled on our behalf.

In 2 Timothy 3:16 Paul told Timothy that *"all Scripture is God-breathed and is useful for teaching, rebuking, correcting and training in righteousness .."* and when he wrote this, *"all Scripture"* referred to what we know as the Old Testament. The Old Covenant is still Scripture—but it no longer defines our covenantal relationship with God.

We do not discard the Old Testament; we read it as fulfilled in Christ. We don't quote it as binding law, but as revelation that leads us to the One who has fulfilled the law on our behalf.

From shadow to substance

Let me stress it again: the transition from Old Covenant to New Covenant is not a rejection—it is a fulfilment. Like a shadow gives way to substance, or a sketch gives way to reality, the Old Covenant finds its purpose in Jesus. He is the true tabernacle, the perfect sacrifice, the eternal priest, and the obedient Son.

To live as New Covenant believers is not to be lawless—it is to live in the freedom of Christ. It is to walk in the Spirit, to trust in grace, and to rest in the finished work of Jesus. We honour the Old by embracing the New. We cherish the past by living fully in the present reality of redemption.

"The law was given through Moses; grace and truth came through Jesus Christ."(John 1:17). The law shows us our need, but Jesus meets that need. The law declares us guilty; Jesus declares us forgiven. The law was a guardian, but Christ has come, and now we are sons and daughters of God through faith.

Standing firm in the fulfilment

Many Christians today still wrestle with how much of the Old Covenant applies. Some try to rebuild the Law's rituals; others cherry-pick verses completely out of context. But to do so is to misunderstand the cross. We are not under the Old Covenant — we are under grace, and that grace cost Jesus everything and accomplished everything.

To return to the Law is to return to slavery. To live in Christ is to live free. *"It is for freedom that Christ has set us free. Stand firm, then, and do not let yourselves be burdened again by a yoke of slavery."* (Galatians 5:1). This is our calling, our joy, and our hope: to live as the people of the New Covenant, fulfilled in Christ, and empowered by His Spirit.

- 6 -
LIVING UNDER THE NEW COVENANT

The transformational reality of the New Covenant

The New Covenant, established by the blood of Jesus Christ, is not merely a revision of the Old Covenant; it is an entirely new framework for relationship with God. It is not an upgrade but a fulfilment and a rebirth - a shift from external laws to internal transformation, from shadows to substance, from striving to resting in God's grace. Living under the New Covenant is not about acknowledging doctrinal truths but walking daily in the power, liberty, and intimacy that this covenant makes possible.

As we begin this chapter, it is vital to root ourselves in the central promise of the New Covenant as declared by God through the prophet Jeremiah. Read these words again, *"This is the covenant I will make with the people of Israel after that time,"* declares the Lord. *"I will put my law in their minds and write it on their hearts. I will be their God, and they will be my people."* (Jeremiah 31:33)

This divine declaration unveils the heart of what it means to live under the New Covenant. It is not just about knowing God's law but becoming people who desire and delight in His will. The law is no longer etched on stone but inscribed on hearts. This transformation is not the result of human effort but the work of the Spirit in those who believe.

A life empowered by the Spirit

One of the most striking distinctions between the Old and New Covenants is the role of the Holy Spirit. Under the Old Covenant, the Spirit would come upon specific individuals at specific times for specific purposes. Under the New Covenant, the Holy Spirit dwells within all believers permanently - guiding, comforting, empowering, and sanctifying them. Paul speaks to this reality in his second letter to the Corinthians: *"He has made us competent as ministers of a new covenant — not of the letter but of the Spirit; for the letter kills, but the Spirit gives life."* (2 Corinthians 3:6)

Living under the New Covenant means living by the Spirit. It is through the Spirit of God that we are led, instructed, and also empowered to live in ways that please God. The Spirit does not merely point out our failures as the Law did, but He produces in us the fruit that reflects the character of God: love, joy, peace, patience, kindness, goodness, faithfulness, gentleness, and self-control. (Galatians 5:22–23).

The Spirit is not an accessory to the Christian life; He is essential. Jesus referred to Him as the Helper, the Advocate, the Spirit of Truth. To live under the New Covenant is to live in dependence upon and communion with the Spirit of God, Who now dwells within each of us.

From law to grace

The Old Covenant was marked by commands, obligations, and a sacrificial system designed to atone for sin only temporarily. It demanded obedience but provided no power to fulfil it.

The New Covenant, however, is grounded in grace – a divine empowerment that both justifies and transforms. Paul's words to the Romans highlight this radical shift: *"For sin shall no longer be your master, because you are not under the law, but under grace."* (Romans 6:14)

Grace is more than unmerited favour, as many have defined it over the years. It is divine enablement. It is the empowering presence of God. Grace teaches us to say no to ungodliness and empowers us to live godly lives in this present age as Paul reminds us in Titus 2:11–12. Under the New Covenant, we are no longer trying to earn God's approval – we already have it in Christ. Our obedience flows not from fear of punishment, but from gratitude and love.

The result is a life marked not by religious duty, but by relational devotion. The motivation shifts from external compulsion to internal desire, from rigid obligation to joyful surrender. We no longer serve in the old way of the written code but in the new way of the Spirit (Romans 7:6).

The role of faith

Living under the New Covenant is living a life of faith. The old way relied heavily on visible signs, tangible sacrifices, rituals. The new way calls us to trust in what is unseen, to walk by faith and not by sight. (2 Corinthians 5:7).

The writer of Hebrews reminds us: *"Now faith is confidence in what we hope for and assurance about what we do not see."* (Hebrews 11:1). Faith is the conduit through which the benefits of the New Covenant flow. We are justified by grace through faith, we are sanctified by grace through faith, and we also persevere by grace through faith. Our relationship with God is not maintained by keeping rules but by trusting in His promises, His power, and His presence.

This faith is not passive – it is active and transformative. It causes us to live differently, to love sacrificially, and to endure trials with hope. Faith becomes the lens through which we interpret life and the anchor that holds us steady in the storms.

From temple to indwelling

Under the Old Covenant, worship was centred in the temple. It was a sacred space where sacrifices were made, and God's presence was symbolically manifested. Access was limited, and only the high priest could enter the Most Holy Place – and even then, only once a year.

Under the New Covenant, the veil has been torn down. Jesus, our great high priest, has entered the heavenly sanctuary on our behalf, offering His own blood as the once-for-all sacrifice for sin (Hebrews 9:11–14). Now, we, His children, are the temple of the Holy Spirit (1 Corinthians 6:19). Worship is no longer confined to a place – it is the posture of a surrendered heart.

You will remember what Jesus said to the woman at the well: *"A time is coming and has now come when the true worshipers will worship the Father in the Spirit and in truth, for they are the kind of worshipers the Father seeks."* (John 4:23).

Living under the New Covenant means living lives of continual worship—not just in song, but in how we live, love, and serve. Every moment becomes sacred when lived in the awareness of God's presence within us.

The assurance of forgiveness

One of the greatest blessings of this wonderful New Covenant is the assurance of complete and eternal forgiveness. Under the Old Covenant, sacrifices had to be repeated year after year, and even then, they could never fully cleanse the conscience of the worshiper. They were merely a shadow pointing forward to the substance which is only found in Christ.

The book of Hebrews declares: *"For by one sacrifice he has made perfect forever those who are being made holy."* (Hebrews 10:14). In Christ, we have full atonement. Our sins—past, present, and future—have been nailed to the cross once and for all time. We are no longer under condemnation. We are not waiting for a final verdict to be handed down. The verdict has already been given: we are righteous in Christ.

This assurance does not lead to complacency but to greater love and devotion. We serve not to earn forgiveness but because we have already been forgiven. We obey not to be accepted but because we are accepted.

Freedom with responsibility

Living under the New Covenant brings freedom, but it is not freedom to sin—it is freedom to serve. Paul cautioned the Galatians: *"You, my brothers and sisters, were called to be free. But do not use your freedom to indulge the flesh; rather, serve one another humbly in love."* (Galatians 5:13)

Freedom in Christ is not autonomy, it is alignment. It is not license but liberty. It frees us from guilt and condemnation, from the tyranny of legalism, and from the bondage of sin. But it also calls us to a higher standard—a life of love, sacrifice, and holiness. We are free from the demands of the law but bound by the law of Christ (1 Corinthians 9:21), which is the law of love.

We are free from ritual but called to relationship. We are free from the shadow but filled with the substance.

The ministry of the Spirit: A new dynamic

One of the most defining characteristics of the New Covenant is the gift and indwelling of the Holy Spirit. In contrast to the Old Covenant, where the Spirit came upon individuals for specific tasks or limited periods, the New Covenant introduces a continuous and personal experience of the Spirit for all believers.

As you have already been reminded, Ezekiel foresaw this when he recorded God's promise: *"I will give you a new heart and put a new spirit in you; I will remove from you your heart of stone and give you a heart of flesh. And I will put my Spirit in you and move you to follow my decrees and be careful to keep my laws."* (Ezekiel 36:26–27).

When Paul said, *"He has made us competent as ministers of a new covenant – not of the letter but of the Spirit; for the letter kills, but the Spirit gives life"* (2 Corinthians 3:6), he was not disparaging the Old Covenant; he was stressing the superior nature of the New.

Under the New Covenant, obedience is no longer externally enforced but internally inspired. Believers are no longer striving to uphold laws written on stone tablets; they are actually being transformed by the Spirit Who writes God's law on their hearts.

This internal transformation is the essence of Christian living under the New Covenant. The Spirit not only empowers us to obey but also sanctifies us, leading us into deeper intimacy with Christ.

The fruits of the Spirit listed in Galatians 5:22-23 — love, joy, peace, patience, kindness, goodness, faithfulness, gentleness, and self-control — are not commands to be followed in our own strength but evidence of the Spirit's active work within us.

This new dynamic invites believers into a daily, Spirit-led life where transformation is not only possible but expected.

The law fulfilled, not abolished

A very common misunderstanding in discussions about the covenants is the relationship between law and grace. Some of us assume that grace under the New Covenant means lawlessness or moral laxity. Jesus addressed this misconception directly in Matthew 5:17: *"Do not think that I have come to abolish the Law or the Prophets; I have not come to abolish them but to fulfil them."* Jesus fulfilled the law in every sense: morally, by living a sinless life; ceremonially, by becoming the ultimate sacrifice; and judicially, by satisfying the penalty for sin. His fulfilment means that believers are no longer under the law in terms of their justification or acceptance before God. As Paul writes, *"Christ is the culmination of the law so that there may be righteousness for everyone who believes."* (Romans 10:4)

Living under the New Covenant does not eliminate our moral responsibility — rather, it reorients it. Our motivation is no longer fear of punishment, but love born from grace. Romans 6:14 clarifies this beautifully: *"For sin shall no longer be your master, because you are not under the law, but under grace."* Grace doesn't lower the bar; it raises it by empowering us to live out the righteousness that the Law demanded but could never produce. This understanding transforms how we read the Old Testament. The laws, rituals, and commands were shadows pointing to the substance found in Christ (Colossians 2:17). We honour the Old Testament by seeing its fulfilment in Jesus and allowing that revelation to deepen our worship and obedience.

A new identity in Christ

One of the most profound realities of the New Covenant is the new identity it grants to those who are in Christ. Under the Old Covenant, our identity was primarily national and external — defined by genealogy, circumcision, and observance of the law. But the New Covenant redefines identity in spiritual terms.

Paul makes this clear in Galatians 3:26-29: *"So in Christ Jesus you are all children of God through faith... There is neither Jew nor Gentile, neither slave nor free, nor is there male and female, for you are all one in Christ Jesus."*

This radical redefinition means that believers are united not by race, class, or gender, but by their faith in Jesus. This new identity brings with it a new status: adopted sons and daughters of God (Romans 8:15), citizens of heaven (Philippians 3:20), and members of Christ's body (1 Corinthians 12:27). These truths are not merely theological abstractions; they form the basis of how we live, relate, and serve. Knowing who we are in Christ shapes how we think, how we treat others, and how we face trials. This identity also comes with new responsibilities. As Paul writes in Ephesians 4:1, "*I urge you to live a life worthy of the calling you have received.*" Our behaviour flows from our identity. We don't act righteously to become God's children; we act righteously because we are God's children.

The church: A covenant community

The New Covenant is not just an individual experience; it creates a new community — the church. Jesus inaugurated the church as the gathering of those who are called out by His grace and united by His Spirit. Under the Old Covenant, God's people were identified as a nation; under the New, they are defined by faith in Christ.

Hebrews 12:22-24 paints a beautiful picture of this new assembly: "*But you have come to Mount Zion, to the city of the living God... to the church of the firstborn, whose names are written in heaven... to Jesus the mediator of a new covenant.*" The church is a spiritual entity, composed of believers from every nation, tribe, and tongue, gathered under the lordship of Christ.

Living under the New Covenant means participating in this covenant community. The church is not an optional add-on to the Christian life; it is the context in which the life of the New Covenant is expressed. Through the church, believers receive teaching, accountability, encouragement, and opportunities to serve.

Acts 2:42-47 provides a vivid snapshot of this dynamic: a community devoted to the apostles' teaching, to fellowship, to the breaking of bread, and to prayer.

The church also embodies the mission of the New Covenant. As ministers of reconciliation (2 Corinthians 5:18), believers are sent into the world to proclaim the gospel of grace and demonstrate the love of Christ. The church, therefore, is both a sanctuary and a sending base—a place of formation and a platform for mission.

Unprecedented freedom

The New Covenant offers unprecedented freedom. Galatians 5:1 declares, "*It is for freedom that Christ has set us free.*" But this freedom is not a license for self-indulgence; it is a call to love and service.

Paul continues in Galatians 5:13, "*Do not use your freedom to indulge the flesh; rather, serve one another humbly in love.*"

Living under the New Covenant involves a paradox: we are free, yet bound by love; we are released from the law, yet called to fulfil it through the Spirit. Let me say again, true freedom is not autonomy but alignment with God's will. It is the ability to do what we ought because we want to, empowered by grace.

This freedom also brings responsibility. As recipients of mercy, we are called to be merciful. As forgiven people, we are called to forgive. As those who have received grace, we are to extend grace. The freedom of the New Covenant is not merely personal; it is communal and missional.

James captures this balance well when he describes the law of liberty. "*But whoever looks intently into the perfect law that gives freedom, and continues in it — not forgetting what they have heard, but doing it — they will be blessed in what they do.*" (James 1:25). This is not a return to legalism but a joyful obedience that flows from a heart transformed by grace.

Living under the New Covenant, then, is a life which is now marked by Spirit-led obedience, grace-fuelled identity, Christ-centred community, and gospel-driven mission. It is not a static state but a dynamic journey—one in which we continually discover the riches of God's grace and respond with faith, love, and surrender.

Transformed by grace: Living from acceptance, not for it

One of the most radical differences between life under the Old Covenant and life under the New is the foundation upon which our relationship with God now rests. Under the Old Covenant, Israel was required to live in obedience to the law in order to maintain their standing within the covenant community and receive God's blessings. The law demanded righteousness, and failure to meet its standards brought consequences — both spiritual and societal.

Under the New Covenant, however, the order is reversed: we are not called to live righteously in order to be accepted by God; rather, we live righteously because we are already accepted through Christ and empowered by His grace. This fundamental shift moves us from striving for God's approval to responding to His love. As Paul declares in Romans 5:1, *"Therefore, since we have been justified through faith, we have peace with God through our Lord Jesus Christ."* Our peace with God is secured, not by our own efforts, but by faith in Jesus and His finished work.

This liberating truth is the foundation of New Covenant living. It totally removes the burden of performance-based religion and replaces it with the joy of relationship-based obedience. Instead of asking, *"What must I do to be loved by God?"* the New Covenant believer proclaims, *"I am loved — now how shall I live in response?"*

Grace not only redeems us, it also reshapes us. As we can see in Titus 2:11–12, *"For the grace of God has appeared that offers salvation to all people. It teaches us to say 'No' to ungodliness and worldly passions, and to live self-controlled, upright and godly lives in this present age."*

A new community: the covenant people of grace

Living under the New Covenant also redefines what it means to be part of the people of God. In the Old Testament, covenant identity was tied to ethnic Israel — a physical nation descended from Abraham, marked by circumcision and adherence to the Mosaic law. But under the New Covenant, God's people are defined not by lineage or law but by faith in Jesus Christ.

Galatians 3:28–29 declares, *"There is neither Jew nor Gentile, neither slave nor free, nor is there male and female, for you are all one in Christ Jesus. If you belong to Christ, then you are Abraham's seed, and heirs according to the promise."* This spiritual community — the church — is made up of believers from every nation, tribe, and tongue. We are now one body, united by the Spirit, and called to live in mutual love, service, and mission.

The implications of this are vast. We are no longer isolated individuals pursuing personal righteousness; we are members of a covenant family. The New Testament is filled with exhortations to "one another" — love one another, bear with one another, forgive one another, encourage one another, to name just a few. These commands reflect the communal nature of New Covenant life. We do not walk this path alone. We are shaped and sustained by the body of Christ as we live out our faith together.

The Law fulfilled in love

Many Christians struggle with how we should relate to the law now that we are under the New Covenant. Should we ignore it? Obey it? Modify it? Jesus Himself gave us the answer. Christ fulfilled the law in every sense — its moral demands, its ceremonial requirements, and its prophetic shadows. He is the true High Priest, the final Sacrifice, and the embodiment of God's righteousness. In Him, the law finds its completion. Yet this does not mean the law has no relevance for us. Rather, it is now interpreted and lived out through the lens of love.

Paul writes in Romans 13:10, *"Love is the fulfilment of the law."* When we love God and love our neighbour, we live in alignment with the very heart of God's commands. The Spirit writes this law of love on our hearts and empowers us to live it out. We are not governed by external rules but guided by an internal compass — the love of Christ compelling us (2 Corinthians 5:14).

Thus, the law no longer condemns us; it inspires us. We no longer serve in the old way of the written code but in the new way of the Spirit (Romans 7:6). Love becomes our ethic, our motivation, and our goal. In this way, the law is not abolished but fulfilled — not by obligation but by transformation.

Hope anchored in a better covenant

Living under the New Covenant also gives us a superior hope — one which is anchored in better promises and secured by a better Mediator. Hebrews 8:6 declares, *"But in fact the ministry Jesus has received is as superior to theirs as the covenant of which he is mediator is superior to the old one, since the new covenant is established on better promises."*

Our hope is no longer tied to the rituals, symbols, or shadowy foretelling of the past. It is rooted in the living Christ, who has entered the true heavenly sanctuary on our behalf and secured eternal redemption. We no longer fear condemnation, for there is now no condemnation for those who are in Christ Jesus.

We no longer approach God trembling at Mount Sinai but with boldness at Mount Zion, the city of the living God. This hope shapes how we live right now. It gives us courage in suffering, perseverance in trials, and joy in the face of uncertainty.

We are no longer under the Law but under grace.

We are no longer in the shadows but in the light.

We are no longer bound by fear but filled with the Spirit.

We are heirs of a kingdom that cannot be shaken — and we live in light of that reality every single day!

USING THE OLD TESTAMENT TODAY

The importance of the Old Testament in Christian life

For many modern Christians, the Old Testament is like a distant relative — revered but rarely invited into everyday conversation. Its stories are ancient, its laws seem foreign, and its customs often feel irrelevant in a post-resurrection world. And yet, this portion of Scripture makes up over two-thirds of the Bible. Jesus, Paul, and the early church were steeped in its teachings, nourished by its promises, and directed by its commands. If we neglect it, we sever the very root system from which our New Covenant faith has grown.

The apostle Paul declared unequivocally, *"All Scripture is God-breathed and is useful for teaching, rebuking, correcting and training in righteousness."* (2 Timothy 3:16). At the time he wrote those words, the only Scriptures available to the church were what we now call the Old Testament. He was not speaking about some outdated religious text, but the living Word of God that pointed directly to Jesus Christ. For Paul, and for Jesus Himself, the Old Testament was not peripheral — it was essential.

One story, one Saviour

At the heart of understanding the Old Testament today is the recognition that the Scriptures tell a unified story. It begins in Genesis with the creation of all things, follows the covenantal journey of God's people Israel, and ultimately culminates in the life, death, and resurrection of Jesus Christ. The Old Testament lays the theological, moral, and redemptive groundwork for the New. Jesus said to the Jewish leaders, *"These are the very Scriptures that testify about me."* (John 5:39).

Later, on the road to Emmaus, He explained to two disciples, *"what was said in all the Scriptures concerning himself."* (Luke 24:27). From the Law to the Prophets to the Psalms, Jesus understood the Old Testament as pointing directly to Him.

Therefore, Christians must read it with gospel lenses—not as disconnected history, but as the inspired preparation for the revelation of the Messiah. This unified storyline changes how we approach the Old Testament. We no longer read it as a flat collection of laws and narratives, but as a progressive unfolding of God's plan of redemption. It is not just background; it is the beginning of the same story to which we now belong.

Fulfilment, not abolishment

Perhaps nowhere is the Christian use of the Old Testament more clearly addressed than in Jesus' words in Matthew 5:17: *"Do not think that I have come to abolish the Law or the Prophets; I have not come to abolish them but to fulfil them."* This clear statement is a theological watershed. Jesus affirms the authority of the Old Testament but redefines its purpose in light of His mission. He is not discarding what came before His incarnation. He is bringing it to its intended goal.

The Law pointed to Christ. The sacrificial system foreshadowed His atoning death. The priesthood anticipated His role as our eternal High Priest. The prophets longed for His coming. Every command, symbol, and institution of the Old Covenant finds its fulfilment in Him. Hebrews 10:1 reminds us that *"the law is only a shadow of the good things that are coming—not the realities themselves."* Those realities are now here in Christ. This means there are certain Old Testament laws—especially ceremonial and sacrificial laws—which are no longer binding. We do not sacrifice animals, burn incense on altars, or keep dietary laws to remain clean before God. These practices were signs and shadows that pointed forward to Jesus, and now that the substance has come, the shadows have served their purpose.

Reading the Law through gospel eyes

The Law of Moses included civil, ceremonial, and also moral components. Civil laws governed the daily life of Israel as a theocratic nation; ceremonial laws regulated worship, purity, and sacrifice; moral laws reflected God's unchanging holiness and righteousness.

The New Testament makes clear that Christ fulfilled the civil and ceremonial aspects of the law in His first coming. The Jerusalem Council in Acts 15 confirmed that Gentile believers were not obligated to keep the Mosaic Law in its entirety. Paul declared in Galatians 3:24-25 that the law was our *"guardian until Christ came,"* but now that faith has come, we are no longer under that guardian. However, the moral law—which is powerfully summarised in what we know as the Ten Commandments and rooted in God's character—remains deeply relevant. Jesus affirmed its enduring value when He said the two greatest commandments are to love God and love one's neighbour (Matthew 22:37-40). These two principles encapsulate the moral heart of the Old Testament.

The difference is that under the New Covenant, we are not justified by keeping the Law. Instead, we are indwelt by the Spirit, Who empowers us to live in obedience from the inside out. You will remember Jeremiah's prophecy, *"I will put my law in their minds and write it on their hearts."* (Jeremiah 31:33). The Old Testament law has not been discarded—it has been internalised and fulfilled in us through Christ.

Prophecy and promise

Another key element of the Old Testament is prophecy. From Genesis to Malachi, God's promises to His people permeate the text. Many of these promises were fulfilled in the first coming of Christ. Others look forward to the consummation of all things in His return. Understanding how to interpret these prophecies is crucial to using the Old Testament wisely today.

Not all Old Testament prophecies apply directly to the church. Many were specific to Israel, tied to the land, the temple, or the monarchy. However, because Jesus is the true Israelite, the ultimate Son of David, and the perfect Temple, these promises find their *"Yes"* in Him (2 Corinthians 1:20). Therefore, while we must be careful not to claim every Old Testament promise as a direct word to us, we can see how they find deeper fulfilment in Christ—and by extension, in His people.

For example, God's promise in Isaiah 7:14 of a virgin giving birth was fulfilled in Mary. The suffering servant in Isaiah 53 points clearly to Jesus' passion. The New Covenant, promised back in Jeremiah 31 is inaugurated at the Last Supper. When we read prophecy through the lens of Christ, we see its deepest meaning come alive.

Wisdom and worship in the Old Testament

The Old Testament is a lot more than just law and prophecy. It also contains profound wisdom literature, like Job, Proverbs, Ecclesiastes—and deeply personal prayers and hymns in the Psalms. These vital writings speak across the centuries with remarkable relevance. They address suffering, joy, injustice, family, work, friendship, and the mystery of God's providence.

The Psalms remain the church's prayer book. They teach us how to worship, how to lament, how to give thanks, and how to trust God when life is hard. Jesus quoted the Psalms more than any other book. On the cross, His cry—*"My God, my God, why have you forsaken me?"*—was a direct quotation of Psalm 22. These ancient poems are saturated with gospel truth and raw human experience.

Proverbs and Ecclesiastes provide wisdom for living in a fallen world. Their principles are timeless, though not always absolute promises. They offer insight into human character, the nature of temptation, and the importance of fearing the Lord. To neglect this wisdom is to impoverish our discipleship.

Avoiding misapplication

While the Old Testament is rich with truth, it must be handled with care. One of the most common errors is to misapply texts by ignoring their covenantal or historical context. Note the example I gave earlier, the promise in 2 Chronicles 7:14—*"If my people, who are called by my name..."* was given to ancient Israel in the context of temple dedication. While the principle of humble prayer still applies, it should not be ripped from its original context and applied wholesale to modern nations or churches.

Another common pitfall is treating narrative as normative. Just because David took multiple wives, or Gideon laid out a fleece, does not mean those actions are prescribed for believers today. We must learn to discern between description and instruction. The antidote to this misapplication is to remain Christ-centred at all times. Every passage must be read in light of the gospel, within its literary and its historical setting, and in the broader flow of redemptive history.

Embracing the whole counsel of God

Using the Old Testament today means embracing the whole counsel of God. It means preaching from Genesis as confidently as from John. It means quoting the prophets with understanding. It means seeing Christ on every page, not forcing Him into the text, but recognising that He was always there.

The Old Testament is not a museum of spiritual artifacts. It is living, active, and sharper than any double-edged sword. It convicts, encourages, instructs, and points to the Saviour. When rightly understood, it deepens our worship, strengthens our theology, and equips us for every good work.

This is our inheritance as New Covenant believers: not to discard the Old, but to delight in it — because in its pages, we meet the God who never changes, whose plan has never failed, and whose promises find their fulfilment in Jesus Christ our Lord.

Christ-Centred interpretation of the Old Testament

Understanding how to interpret the Old Testament under the New Covenant requires a profound shift in focus — from law to grace, from the old to the new, from type to fulfilment. Jesus Himself pointed to this transformation when He said, *"These are the very Scriptures that testify about me."* (John 5:39). He was referring to the Hebrew Scriptures — the Old Testament — which He declared ultimately point to Him. This changes everything about how we engage with the Old Testament today. It is not a disjointed set of historical records and ceremonial instructions, nor merely a moral code or cultural artifact.

Rather, it is a revelation that finds its climax in the person and work of Jesus Christ. This Christ-centred lens is what allows Christians today to wisely, faithfully and fruitfully use the Old Testament.

Jesus didn't simply show up in the New Testament. He is the eternal Son, the Word made flesh, who was present *"in the beginning"* (John 1:1). The shadows, patterns, and promises scattered throughout the Old Testament anticipate His coming and mission. From the sacrificial system to the temple, from the kings to the prophets, from the festivals to the moral law — each element points beyond itself to a greater reality fulfilled in Christ.

Discerning what still applies

One of the most common errors in Christian interpretation of the Old Testament is a failure to distinguish between what was specific to Israel under the Old Covenant and what has carried through to the New Covenant. While the entire Old Testament is inspired and profitable for teaching, not every command is directly applicable.

Theologians have historically categorized Old Testament laws into three broad types: moral, civil, and ceremonial.

➤ **Moral laws** will reflect God's unchanging character and His design for human life and relationships. These are timeless truths — such as commands against murder, theft, adultery, and lying. Jesus reaffirmed these in His teaching and even deepened their meaning by addressing the heart, not just external actions.

➤ **Civil laws** were given to Israel as a theocratic nation. These include laws which dealt with property boundaries, judicial procedures, and punishments for various crimes. Since Israel as a nation under God's direct rule no longer exists, these laws are not binding on Christians today. However, they still reveal principles of justice, fairness, and wisdom that can inform modern ethics and governance.

➤ **Ceremonial laws** related to Israel's worship system: priests, sacrifices, the temple, and ritual cleanliness. These pointed forward to Christ and were fulfilled in Him. The book of Hebrews makes it abundantly clear that the old sacrificial system has been rendered obsolete because of Christ's once-for-all sacrifice (Hebrews 10:1–14). These laws are no longer practiced, but they help us grasp the depth of what Jesus accomplished.

This framework helps us read the Old Testament with both reverence and discernment. We are not under the Mosaic Law (Romans 6:14), but the moral truths it reveals remain as guiding lights for the believer.

The prophets and their contemporary echo

Another major component of the Old Testament is the prophetic literature. Books like Isaiah, Jeremiah, Ezekiel, and the twelve minor prophets were written in specific historical and cultural contexts. Yet their words still resonate because they address universal themes: justice, repentance, idolatry, faithfulness, and hope.

Modern readers must avoid the temptation to cherry-pick verses from the prophets without understanding their original context. Verses like *"For I know the plans I have for you ..."* (Jeremiah 29:11) are often quoted in ways that detach them from their covenantal and historical meaning. Jeremiah addressed the exiles in Babylon and so his words formed part of a broader promise of national restoration. To apply such a verse to ourselves today requires careful theological grounding, recognizing that our hope now lies in Christ, not in the restoration of a physical kingdom.

That said, the prophets continue to call God's people to righteousness, mercy, and humility (Micah 6:8). They remind us of God's heart for the oppressed and His disdain for empty religion. They call us to repentance and renew our vision of God's coming kingdom. Their promises of a Messiah and a renewed covenant find their fulfilment in Jesus and the church, making them essential reading for Christians today.

Wisdom literature and the Spirit-filled life

The Old Testament also includes wisdom literature — books like Proverbs, Ecclesiastes, and Job — which address practical living, the search for meaning, and the complexities of life. These are deeply human books, full of observation, reflection, and insight.

Proverbs offers general principles for wise and righteous living. Its admonitions on diligence, honesty, speech, and relationships remain relevant, though not always guarantees. For example, *"Train a child in the way he should go, and when he is old he will not turn from it,"* (Proverbs 22:6) is a principle - it's not a promise. It encourages faithful parenting but doesn't negate the reality of free will or the complexity of spiritual development.

Ecclesiastes confronts the vanity of life *"under the sun"* and drives the reader to look beyond this world for true significance. Its final message — *"Fear God and keep his commandments, for this is the duty of all mankind."* (Ecclesiastes 12:13) — is a sobering conclusion that harmonizes with New Testament calls to live for with eternity always on our mind.

Job, arguably the most emotionally raw of all biblical books, addresses suffering and the sovereignty of God. Its message is not one of easy answers but of trusting a wise and just God even when life makes no sense. For New Covenant believers, Job's perseverance and God's ultimate vindication point us toward the suffering and exaltation of Jesus Christ. These books provide practical and theological insights for the Spirit-filled life. When read through the lens of Christ and the gospel, they help shape a life of wisdom, humility, and worship.

Psalms: Worshipping in every season

The book of Psalms, the hymnbook of ancient Israel, has always had a central place in Christian devotion. It gives voice to the full range of human emotion: joy, sorrow, fear, anger, repentance, and hope. While written under the Old Covenant, the Psalms transcend their original context because they speak to the heart of human experience and direct that experience toward God.

David and other psalmists cry out to God in both celebration and despair, reminding us that our faith is not limited to the mountaintop moments. The Psalms teach us how to lament, how to wait, how to rejoice, and how to praise. They model honesty before God and trust in His faithfulness.

Psalm 22's vivid description of suffering finds its ultimate fulfilment in the crucifixion of Jesus Christ. Psalm 23's shepherd imagery is echoed in John 10:11, when Jesus said, *"I am the good shepherd."* Psalm 110's royal priest language is directly applied to Jesus Christ in Hebrews. These connections reinforce the Psalms' enduring relevance, inviting us to see Christ in our worship, suffering, and hope.

For the New Covenant believer, the Psalms are not just poetic reflections but Spirit-inspired prayers that align our hearts with the heart of God. They remain a vital tool for personal and corporate worship.

Typology: seeing Christ in the old

Typology is the study of how Old Testament people, events, and institutions prefigure Christ. It's one of the most powerful ways the Old Testament speaks to New Covenant believers. The sacrifices, the temple, the high priest, the exodus, the manna, the serpent on the pole, and even figures like Moses, David, and Joseph — all are types that point forward to Jesus.

Paul makes this clear when he calls Adam *"a pattern of the one to come."* (Romans 5:14). Jesus is the second Adam who undoes the curse of sin. The Exodus becomes a type of salvation, with Jesus as the greater deliverer. The Passover lamb foreshadows the Lamb of God who takes away the sin of the world.

However, typology must be used responsibly because not every Old Testament figure or event is a type of Christ, and forced allegories can distort the text. But when guided by Scripture itself and the illumination of the Holy Spirit, typology opens a rich window into the unity of the Bible and the majesty of Christ.

Caution against proof-texting

One of the greatest dangers in using the Old Testament today is the misuse of isolated verses to support personal opinions or doctrines. This practice—commonly called proof-texting—rips Scripture from its context and too often leads to legalism, false teaching, or confusion.

For example, quoting Malachi 3:10 about tithing without first understanding its covenantal and national context can lead to guilt-based giving rather than Spirit-led generosity. Misapplying promises meant for Israel can foster unrealistic expectations or twisted theology.

Scripture must interpret Scripture. Context is king. We must ask, *"To whom was this written?" "Under what covenant?" "How does this point to Christ?" "How does the New Testament treat this theme?"* Such questions will help us prevent misuse and promote faithful interpretation. The Old Testament is not a bag of motivational quotes. It is a cohesive, divinely inspired testimony that leads us to Jesus. Rightly handled, it strengthens our faith, informs our lives, and glorifies God.

The prophetic lens: Christ in the Old Testament

As already mentioned, one of the most powerful and enduring ways the Old Testament speaks to us under the New Covenant is through its prophetic witness to Christ. The prophets, the psalms, the laws, the stories—all of them ultimately point to the coming of the Messiah. When we learn to read the Old Testament through this lens, a whole new world opens before us, rich with meaning, foreshadowing, and fulfilment.

Take, for example, the suffering servant passages in Isaiah, especially chapter 53. This chapter describes one who would be *"pierced for our transgressions," "crushed for our iniquities,"* and by whose wounds *"we are healed"* (Isaiah 53:5). Although Isaiah lived centuries before Christ, the vivid imagery and theological depth in this prophecy resonates so clearly with the life, death, and resurrection of Jesus that it is almost as if he had seen the cross himself.

The early church saw this clearly. Philip the evangelist, in Acts 8, encountered the Ethiopian eunuch reading this very passage, and *"beginning with that very passage of Scripture, told him the good news about Jesus."* (Acts 8:35).

Understanding the prophetic role of the Old Testament enhances our worship and deepens our faith. The Bible becomes more than a collection of disconnected texts. It becomes a unified story, culminating in the person of Jesus Christ.

The prophecies of old are not just ancient promises — they are the voice of God preparing humanity for final redemption. They build anticipation, reveal God's character, and underscore the seriousness of sin and the extravagance of grace.

Moreover, the sacrificial system in the Old Testament, while no longer practiced today under the New Covenant, serves as a theological precursor to the ultimate sacrifice made by Christ. The blood of bulls and goats, we are told, could never truly take away sins (Hebrews 10:4), but they pointed forward to a perfect and sufficient sacrifice. Jesus is described as *"the Lamb of God, who takes away the sin of the world."* (John 1:29), echoing the Passover lamb and the entire Levitical system.

Thus, when we read the Old Testament today, we must do so with Christ-centred eyes. As Jesus taught the disciples on the road to Emmaus, *"beginning with Moses and all the Prophets, he explained to them what was said in all the Scriptures concerning himself."* (Luke 24:27). See the interpretive key: not allegorizing every detail, but recognizing the trajectory of the story, the shadows that anticipate the substance found in Christ.

Wisdom Literature and the Life of the Believer

The wisdom books of the Old Testament — Job, Psalms, Proverbs, Ecclesiastes, and Song of Songs — continue to hold a vital place in the life of the believer. These books are not tied to the old covenant in the same way the Mosaic Law is. Rather, they offer reflections on life, suffering, joy, love, and the fear of the Lord.

While the context of some proverbs or psalms may be rooted in the ancient Israelite experience, the truths they express will often transcend time and culture.

Proverbs, for instance, is filled with timeless principles. *"A gentle answer turns away wrath, but a harsh word stirs up anger."* Taken from Proverbs 15:1, this verse is as true today as it was when first penned. These are not covenantal commands but observations of how life generally works. They do not guarantee outcomes but reveal patterns aligned with God's wisdom.

Similarly, Ecclesiastes confronts us with the futility of a life lived apart from God. Its cry that *"everything is meaningless"* (1:2) leads us to the ultimate conclusion in 12:13: *"Fear God and keep his commandments."* In the light of Christ, this fear is not terror but awe-filled reverence and joyful obedience.

The Psalms, in particular, remain central to Christian worship and devotion. Jesus quoted the Psalms frequently. On the cross, He cried out words from Psalm 22:1, *"My God, my God, why have you forsaken me?"* He used them to express anguish, joy, and dependence on the Father. For centuries, the church has prayed the Psalms, sung them, meditated on them. They give voice to our innermost thoughts and provide language for every season of life.

Importantly, while the Psalms are embedded in Old Covenant Israel, they are not law — they are prayer. They model for us a relationship with God that is raw, emotional, and honest. In them, we learn how to bring our whole selves before the Lord. They invite us into communion with God, not based on ritual, but on real, heartfelt engagement. Under the New Covenant, they still serve this purpose, drawing us into deeper worship.

Historical Narratives and God's Sovereign Purpose

The historical books of the Old Testament — Joshua through to Esther — also serve a valuable purpose today. These narratives recount the formation of the people of Israel, their struggles, victories, sins, and restoration.

Though we no longer stand under the same covenant as Israel, we see in these stories the hand of a faithful God who keeps His promises and works out His redemptive plan in real time.

These accounts are more than just records; they are theological narratives. In the story of Ruth, we see God's providence in the life of a foreign woman who would become an ancestor of Jesus. In the life of David, we see a man after God's own heart who foreshadows the true and better King. In the rise and fall of Israel, we see the consequences of covenant unfaithfulness, and yet we also see God's persistent grace.

Paul tells us, *"These things happened to them as examples and were written down as warnings for us."* (1 Corinthians 10:11). The lessons of Israel's past are not dusty moral tales—they are spiritual guideposts. They remind us of the seriousness of sin, the perils of idolatry, and the unwavering nature of God's mercy.

When we read the Old Testament stories today, we are not looking for heroes to imitate but for the God who sustains flawed people and fulfils His promises despite them.

These narratives also help us understand the world into which Jesus came. The exile, the return, the prolonged silence of the intertestamental period—set the stage for the Messiah to come. The failures of earthly kings made room for the arrival of the true King. The longing of the prophets and the brokenness of the people find their answer in the Word made flesh.

The Law as a witness, not a burden

The most controversial aspect of using the Old Testament today lies in how we relate to the Mosaic Law. As we've already established, the law was given to Israel as part of the Old Covenant, which Christ has fulfilled. Yet the Law continues to have value—not as a rulebook for Christians, but as a witness to the holiness of God and the gravity of sin. Paul describes the law as our *"guardian until Christ came"* (Galatians 3:24), not as our ongoing master.

Paul affirms that *"the law is holy, and the commandment is holy, righteous and good."* (Romans 7:12), but he also makes clear that believers are *"not under the law, but under grace"* (Romans 6:14). This balance is absolutely essential. We do not discard the law; we understand its place.

The Ten Commandments, for example, are too often treated as universal moral imperatives. While they do reflect God's moral character, they were given in a specific covenant context. That said, many of the principles found in the Law — honesty, sexual purity, justice, worship of the one true God — are reaffirmed in the New Testament many times and are consistent with life in Christ. The key difference is that we now live out those moral principles empowered by the Holy Spirit, not to earn God's favour but as a response to God's amazing grace.

So, when reading the Law today, we should ask: *What does this reveal about God? What does this show me about human nature? How does this point me to Christ?* Rather than seeking to re-enact every command, we examine the Law for wisdom, for theology, for understanding. It can still teach us, guide us, and humble us — but it does not bind us.

Cautions and commitments

While affirming the enduring value of the Old Testament, we must also be cautious in its application. Misuse of Old Testament texts can lead to confusion, legalism, or even spiritual harm. Pulling verses totally out of context, imposing Old Covenant expectations and rules on New Covenant believers, or using Old Testament promises to justify unbiblical behaviour must all be avoided.

For instance, claiming national blessings promised to Israel (like those in Deuteronomy) as if they apply unconditionally to modern nations, distorts both Scripture and theology. Likewise, invoking the imprecatory psalms as personal vengeance tools misrepresents the gospel of grace. Instead, we must approach the Old Testament with reverence, study, and care.

We should seek to understand its original context, its place in redemptive history, and how it ultimately leads us to Christ. This requires both humility and diligence. We must be committed to rightly dividing the word of truth (2 Timothy 2:15), ensuring our interpretations are anchored in sound doctrine and Christ-centred understanding.

Cleaders and teachers bear particular responsibility here. They must guide congregations away from superficial or legalistic readings and toward a mature, Spirit-led engagement with all of Scripture. This involves teaching biblical theology, equipping believers to read the whole Bible well, and modelling how to handle difficult texts with grace and clarity.

Making the most of ALL that God has given us

To live faithfully under the New Covenant does not mean we must discard the Old Testament. It means embracing it for what it is—a foundational, inspired, and Christ-pointing portion of God's Word. It reveals God's character, displays His redemptive plan, and enriches our understanding of the gospel.

The Old Testament is not our lawbook, but it is our storybook. It tells the story of creation, fall, promise, and preparation. It sets the stage for the gospel. It helps us understand Jesus. It gives us language for prayer, models of faith and failure, songs of lament and praise, and insights into the heart of God.

By reading the Old Testament in light of the New, with Christ at the centre and the Spirit as our guide, we can rightly use these sacred writings today. Not as a burden to bear, but as a treasure to cherish.

- 8 -
COMMON MISUNDERSTANDINGS AND MISUSE

Misapplying the Old Testament in the New Covenant era

I have already addressed this issue in part in previous chapters. However, it is important enough to devote a whole chapter now to what was my primary motivation in writing this book: that is, the misuse and misinterpretation which still plagues the church as we try to deal with the whole Bible in a responsible manner.

Many believers today continue to wrestle with questions like: *Are all the Old Testament laws still relevant? Should Christians observe the Sabbath? What about dietary laws, tithing, or Old Testament promises made to Israel?* These are not merely academic queries — they affect how people live, worship, and view God.

The misunderstanding often stems from a failure to grasp the radical nature of the monumental shift which occurred with the death, resurrection, and ascension of Jesus Christ. The New Covenant did not merely update or add to the Old — it fulfilled it and, in many ways, replaced its function.

As Hebrews 8:13 declares, "*By calling this covenant 'new,' he has made the first one obsolete; and what is obsolete and outdated will soon disappear.*" When believers overlook this, they risk dragging Old Covenant obligations into their New Covenant life, all too often binding others with them.

Confusion about the Mosaic Law

Perhaps the most widespread misunderstanding is about the role of the Mosaic Law. The Law was central to the covenant God made with Israel at Mount Sinai. It included moral, ceremonial, and civil regulations meant to govern Israel as a nation set apart for God's purposes. However, Paul is clear in Romans 10:4 that "*Christ is the culmination of the law so that there may be righteousness for everyone who believes.*" This culmination means the Law, as a covenantal structure, has come to its intended end.

Yet too many Christians still attempt to extract moral rules or behavioural standards from the Mosaic Law as though they are binding commands under the New Covenant.

While the Law reveals God's character and righteousness, its primary function was always to lead us to Christ by highlighting our inability to fulfil it. As Paul writes in Galatians 3:24, "*So the law was our guardian until Christ came that we might be justified by faith.*"

To be clear, this does not mean that moral principles found in the Old Testament are now irrelevant. But their authority over the believer now must come through their affirmation in the New Covenant, not because they are written in the Law of Moses.

Jesus and the apostles reiterate many moral truths—such as prohibitions against murder, theft, and adultery—but always in the context of the New Covenant's call to love. You can see this in Matthew 22:37-40 and Romans 13:8-10.

Legalism in disguise

Some Christians, often with sincere hearts, fall into a form of legalism by picking and choosing Old Testament commands to follow and/or impose upon others. For example, insisting on the tithe as a required percentage for giving, treating the Sabbath as a strict Saturday observance, or quoting Old Testament dietary laws as binding commands can all be examples of this tendency.

This kind of selective legalism is often justified by appealing to the unchanging nature of God or by claiming that certain laws are 'moral' while others are 'ceremonial.' While this distinction has some theological value, it was not how the Jews viewed their Law. The Law was a unified covenant package, and to break one part was to break the whole (James 2:10).

Moreover, Paul warned the Galatians that to return to the Law was to fall from grace (Galatians 5:4). The Law, once fulfilled by Christ, cannot be partially retained without distorting the gospel.

Promises taken out of context

A different but related problem is the misuse of Old Testament promises. Scripture is often quoted without considering the covenantal context in which it was given.

The most often quoted verse, which I have mentioned more than once already here, is Jeremiah 29:11. "*'For I know the plans I have for you,' declares the Lord, 'plans to prosper you and not to harm you, plans to give you hope and a future.'*" This is a favourite verse for encouragement. While this is a powerful statement, it was given to exiled Israelites in Babylon as part of a specific promise about their eventual return to the land.

Similarly, many Christians claim Old Testament blessings — such as those in Deuteronomy 28 — without recognizing that these were covenant blessings tied to Israel's obedience under the Mosaic Law. Applying them directly to believers today without adjusting for the New Covenant context can lead to confusion, disillusionment, or even prosperity gospel distortions.

Of course, that is not to say the Old Testament has no relevance for believers today. Of course it does! But every passage must be interpreted through the lens of Jesus Christ. As Paul said to the Corinthians, "*For no matter how many promises God has made, they are 'Yes' in Christ.*" (2 Corinthians 1:20). In other words, the promises find their ultimate fulfilment in Him, not in national Israel or in our selective application of covenantal texts.

Ritual and symbolism misunderstood

Another area of some misuse is the attempt to reintroduce Old Testament rituals or symbols into New Covenant worship. The sacrificial system, temple festivals, and even priestly garments hold deep theological significance — but they are fulfilled types, not practices for modern Christians.

The book of Hebrews devotes a lot of attention to explaining that the entire priestly and sacrificial system pointed to Jesus, our great High Priest and perfect sacrifice (Hebrews 10:1-18).

Attempts to revive these practices— through reenactments of Jewish feasts or integrating temple symbolism into Christian worship—can obscure the finality and sufficiency of Christ's work. The danger is not merely aesthetic or liturgical—it is theological.

When we act as though we must add to Christ's finished work with ancient symbols or rituals, we imply that His once-for-all sacrifice is somehow insufficient.

Paul warned the Colossians against this very error: "*Therefore do not let anyone judge you by what you eat or drink, or with regard to a religious festival, a New Moon celebration or a Sabbath day. These are a shadow of the things that were to come; the reality, however, is found in Christ.*" (Colossians 2:16–17). To return to the shadow is to miss the substance.

Moralism over Gospel transformation

One of the more subtle but widespread misuses of the Old Testament is the moralistic use of biblical stories. Preachers and teachers sometimes present characters like David, Moses, or Joseph primarily as role models to emulate. While their lives can certainly inspire, this approach can reduce the Bible to a book of moral lessons rather than a revelation of God's redemptive work.

The story of David and Goliath, for example, is often taught as a lesson in courage and faith—which it is. But more importantly, it points us to Christ, the true anointed King who defeats the giant of sin and death on our behalf. Similarly, the exodus is not just a tale of liberation—it foreshadows our deliverance from sin through Christ, the true Passover Lamb. (1 Corinthians 5:7)

If we read the Old Testament merely for principles and not for Christ-centred transformation, we miss its purpose. As Jesus told the Pharisees, "*These are the very Scriptures that testify about me, yet you refuse to come to me to have life.*" (John 5:39–40).

The point is not to find ourselves in every story but to find Christ—and then, through Him, understand ourselves better.

The role of the Old Testament today

Despite these and many other misuses and misunderstandings, the Old Testament remains a vital part of Christian Scripture. But how we use it is important. We must interpret every passage through the lens of the gospel, the cross, and the New Covenant. This does not diminish the Old Testament—it fulfils it. When understood rightly, the Law drives us to grace, the stories lead us to the Saviour, and the shadows give way to the reality. The Old Testament is indispensable, but it is not our covenant. It is the foundation on which the house of the gospel stands, but it is Christ who is the cornerstone.

Understanding this difference guards us from error and equips us to rightly divide the Word of truth. It enables us to love the Old Testament without misusing it and to walk in the fullness of the New Covenant, rooted in grace and truth.

The danger of selective obedience

One of the more troubling tendencies I can see in contemporary Christianity is the practice of 'selective obedience.' This is when we pick certain Old Testament laws or practices to uphold while ignoring others. This inconsistency is often unintentional, arising from a genuine desire to honour God's Word. However, this reflects a serious misunderstanding of how the Old and New Covenants relate and it is a failure to see the completed work of Christ as the decisive dividing line in redemptive history.

Many Christians, for example, may insist on Old Testament dietary restrictions, Sabbath observance, or purity laws, while simultaneously ignoring sacrificial commands, temple worship requirements, or ritual washings—all of which are part of the same covenantal framework. James warns us against this kind of compartmentalised obedience: *"For whoever keeps the whole law and yet stumbles at just one point is guilty of breaking all of it."* (2:10).

The Law is a unified whole. To take up one part as binding is to place oneself under the entire Law, with all its demands and penalties.

Paul repeatedly stressed that justification and sanctification do not come through selective obedience to the Law but through faith in Jesus Christ alone. *"I do not set aside the grace of God,"* Paul says, *"for if righteousness could be gained through the law, Christ died for nothing!"* (Galatians 2:21).

The call of the gospel is not to return to the Mosaic Covenant in part or in whole, but to walk in the Spirit and live under the law of Christ—the new way of life shaped by grace, empowered by the Spirit, and focused on love. We see this in Galatians 5:18 and 1 Corinthians 9:21.

The seductive appeal of legalism

Legalism is one of the oldest distortions of the gospel and one of the most persistent. It thrives on the misuse of the Old Covenant and flourishes wherever believers are tempted to earn God's favour through rule-keeping and personal performance against the benchmark of the Law. Legalism will often masquerade as holiness, but it will actually enslave the believer rather than set them free.

This danger was already present in the early church, as Paul's letter to the Galatians makes clear. Some Jewish Christians were insisting that Gentile believers must be circumcised and obey the Law of Moses to be fully accepted into God's people. Paul's response was uncompromising: *"You foolish Galatians! Who has bewitched you?"* (Galatians 3:1). He reminded them that they had received the Spirit by believing, not by observing the Law.

Today, legalism can be seen in rigid religious structures, moral superiority, and harsh judgmentalism. All these are built upon a foundation of misunderstood Scripture. When churches or individuals try to impose Old Covenant laws as binding on Christians—whether in dress codes, food laws, Sabbath rules, or tithe obligations—they are not actually pursuing holiness but resurrecting the very yoke Christ came to remove! *"Stand firm, then,"* Paul urges, *"and do not let yourselves be burdened again by a yoke of slavery"* (Galatians 5:1).

True holiness comes not through externally imposed rules, but through the internal transformation brought about by the Spirit. Legalism offers control and predictability, but it cannot produce the freedom, joy, or power of a life rooted in the grace of Christ.

The confusion of covenantal identity

Another widespread misunderstanding stems from confusion over who the people of God are under the New Covenant. Many Christians still operate with a dual-covenant mindset, treating Israel and the church as two separate entities with two different destinies. This has led to some theological frameworks that reintroduce distinctions that Christ came to dismantle.

The New Testament teaches that in Christ, God has created *"one new humanity out of the two."* (Ephesians 2:15). The dividing wall between Jew and Gentile has been broken down. Believing Gentiles have been grafted into the olive tree of God's covenant people (Romans 11:17) and now share in the promises originally given to Abraham—not by natural descent, but through faith.

Paul writes, *"Understand, then, that those who have faith are children of Abraham."* (Galatians 3:7). He goes on to say that *"If you belong to Christ, then you are Abraham's seed, and heirs according to the promise."* (Galatians 3:29). The church, therefore, is not some parenthesis in God's plan or a second-best people; it is the true 'Israel' of God, composed of all who believe in Jesus—Jew and Gentile alike. Misunderstanding this identity leads to further confusion in interpreting Old Testament prophecies. Many are wrongly applied to ethnic Israel or modern nations, rather than being seen as fulfilled in Christ and His church. This not only distorts our eschatology but weakens our understanding of the gospel's unifying power.

Prosperity theology and the Old Covenant

Perhaps no distortion of Scripture has been more damaging in recent decades than the rise of prosperity theology. This teaching often hinges on Old Covenant promises of wealth, health, and victory, removed from their historical and covenantal context and applied to Christians today as divine guarantees.

Verses from Deuteronomy and Proverbs are frequently quoted to suggest that obedience will automatically result in financial blessing and physical health. Malachi 3:10 is regularly cited to encourage giving with the promise that God will *"throw open the floodgates of heaven."* These messages, though appealing, totally misunderstand the nature of the covenants and the kind of blessings God has promised His people.

Under the New Covenant, the blessings which God bestows are primarily spiritual, not material. Paul teaches in Ephesians 1:3 that believers have been *"blessed... with every spiritual blessing in Christ..."* and that suffering and hardship are not signs of God's displeasure but often the means through which He refines and strengthens us (Romans 5:3–5).

Jesus, our Lord, had no place to lay His head. The apostles faced persecution, hunger, and poverty. Paul wrote from prison, not from a palace. To teach that health and wealth are the expected rewards of faith is to contradict the example of Christ and the teaching of the New Testament. It is to turn the gospel into a means of personal gain (1 Timothy 6:5), and that is a grave misuse of the Old Covenant.

Rebuilding the temple in theology and practice

Among certain Christian groups, especially those with a futurist eschatology, there is a belief that the Old Testament temple will one day be rebuilt in Jerusalem, and that animal sacrifices will resume as part of God's plan for the end times. This belief is based on a literal reading of Old Testament prophetic texts such as Ezekiel 40–48 and Daniel 9, often reinforced by news from modern Israel.

However, this view fails to account for the clear New Testament teaching that the temple has already been fulfilled in Jesus Christ. He is the true temple (John 2:19–21), and in Him the fullness of God dwells bodily (Colossians 2:9). The church, which is His body, is now to be regarded as the temple of the Holy Spirit (1 Corinthians 3:16–17), and there is no need for a return to stone, altars, or sacrifices.

The idea of rebuilding the temple and reintroducing sacrifices is not only unnecessary; it is a denial of Christ's finished work. The book of Hebrews makes this abundantly clear: *"We have been made holy through the sacrifice of the body of Jesus Christ once for all."* (Hebrews 10:10). To suggest that God desires a return to animal sacrifices is to misunderstand the nature of fulfilment and the finality of the cross.

Christians must be cautious not to let political or religious enthusiasm override sound biblical theology. The shadows of the Old Covenant have passed; the substance belongs to Christ.

The misuse of the law in cultural battles

In today's moral and political climate, many Christians have turned to Old Testament laws to support their views on justice, sexuality, crime, punishment, and a lot more. While Scripture certainly speaks to these issues, the direct application of Old Covenant laws to modern society can lead to serious errors.

Quoting Leviticus or Deuteronomy to shape national legislation without regard for the covenantal context is both theologically flawed and politically dangerous. It ignores the theocratic nature of Israel and assumes that the church or the state today has the same mandate. This is particularly common in the so-called 'theonomy' or 'Christian reconstructionist' movements.

The New Testament provides a better framework for Christian ethics. Rather than imposing ancient laws, it calls believers to embody those kingdom values of humility, love, mercy, and justice. Jesus said, *"My kingdom is not of this world."* (John 18:36), and His followers are to live as salt and light, influencing society through transformed lives, not imposed legislation.

The Law's moral truths remain relevant—not because we are under the Law, but because they reflect the character of God, now written on our hearts by the Spirit. Our calling is not to make the world conform to Sinai, but to make disciples who follow Jesus in every sphere of life.

Misunderstanding God's character through the covenants

One of the subtle but pervasive misuses of the Old Testament involves having a distorted perception of God's character. Some Christians read the Old Testament and conclude that God was primarily angry, punitive, and harsh—contrasted with the loving, gracious Jesus we encounter in the New Testament. This false dichotomy leads to confusion, fear, and sometimes rejection of the Old Testament altogether.

Yet this is a failure to read Scripture as one continuous revelation of God's unfolding plan of redemption. The same God who gave the Law also revealed His compassion, mercy, and steadfast love (Exodus 34:6). The God who judged sin at Sinai also promised a new heart and a new Spirit through the prophets (Ezekiel 36:26).

Likewise, Jesus did not come to reveal a different God but to reveal the Father more fully (John 14:9). The cross shows both the justice and the mercy of God in perfect harmony. Paul tell us that, God presented Christ as a sacrifice in order to, " .. *demonstrate His righteousness... so as to be just and the one who justifies those who have faith in Jesus."* (Romans 3:26).

When the Old Testament is misunderstood or misused, it distorts not just doctrine but our very vision of who God is. A Christ-centred, covenant-aware reading of Scripture is essential to rightly understand the God we worship.

The dangers of moralism and typology not anchored in Christ

A subtle but widespread misunderstanding in handling the Old Testament is the tendency toward moralism — extracting isolated moral lessons from Old Testament narratives while bypassing their deeper theological purpose. Stories like David and Goliath, Joseph in Egypt, or Daniel in the lions' den are often reduced to inspiring tales of courage, integrity, or perseverance. While these virtues are present, they are not the central message. When moral principles are emphasized without any reference to God's overall redemptive plan, the Old Testament becomes a collection of ethical fables rather than a unified witness to Jesus Christ.

Take David and Goliath, for example. A moralistic reading might tell Christians to *"face their giants"* with great confidence and determination. While that message may encourage some, it misses the theological richness of the narrative. David is not just a brave shepherd boy — he is a messianic figure, a type of Christ, who represents God's anointed king defeating the enemy on behalf of helpless people. The true giant in Scripture is not merely personal adversity but sin and death, which only Jesus — the greater David — can conquer.

Typology, when properly understood, is a powerful and valid interpretive tool. Paul uses it well in 1 Corinthians 10 when he identifies Israel's wilderness journey as a type for Christian experience, and in Romans 5 when he calls Adam *"a pattern of the one to come."* But typology must be grounded in the narrative of redemption and fulfilled in Christ. When types become moral allegories or speculative theological constructs, we lose sight of the gospel and distort the text's intent.

Misunderstanding the role of the prophets

Another widespread misuse arises in the way Christians handle the prophetic literature. Prophets like Isaiah, Jeremiah, and Ezekiel were not fortune-tellers predicting the future in vague terms for distant generations. They were covenant prosecutors — speaking on behalf of God to Israel and Judah, calling the people to repentance, announcing judgment, and proclaiming hope.

Too much of modern popular Christianity misappropriates the prophets by mining their texts for personal encouragement or political insight, often disconnected from their historical and redemptive contexts. Jeremiah 1:5 — *"Before I formed you in the womb I knew you"* — is too frequently quoted to affirm personal identity or calling. While this verse beautifully affirms God's sovereignty, its original context is God's call to Jeremiah to be a prophet to the nations in a time of national upheaval.

Likewise, Isaiah's oracles of judgment are sometimes applied wholesale to modern governments or societies, as though the prophet was speaking directly to today's headlines.

But Isaiah spoke into a covenantal framework—a relationship between God and His chosen nation, Israel. While his words reveal timeless truths about God's holiness, justice, and mercy, their application must be filtered through the reality that we now live under the New Covenant, not the Old.

Furthermore, the prophets ultimately point forward to Christ. As Peter declared, *"the prophets…spoke of the grace that was to come to you…they were not serving themselves but you, when they spoke of the things that have now been told you by those who have preached the gospel."* (1 Peter 1:10–12). The prophetic voice, when it is rightly understood, will always culminate in the revelation of Jesus as the fulfilment of all God's promises (2 Corinthians 1:20).

Overlooking the corporate and covenant nature of Old Testament texts

A major area of misuse lies in individualizing passages that were meant to be understood corporately or covenantally. Western Christianity, with its strong emphasis on individualism, often reads Scripture as if it were written to *'me'* rather than to *'us.'* This leads to misunderstanding texts like 2 Chronicles 7:14 – *"If my people, who are called by my name, will humble themselves…"* – which, as I stressed in an earlier chapter, was addressed to Israel under the terms of the Mosaic Covenant, not to the church or to modern nations.

Again, I stress that this does not mean such texts are irrelevant. On the contrary, they clearly reveal God's heart for repentance, humility, and restoration. But to apply them rightly, we must acknowledge the shift from a covenant based on national identity and law to one which is based on faith in Christ and the indwelling Spirit. The church is now the people of God—not a geopolitical nation, but a global body united by grace.

The covenantal structure of the Old Testament also means that blessings and curses were often corporate, not merely individual. Psalm 122:6 – *"Pray for the peace of Jerusalem"* – is frequently quoted as a call to support modern political Israel. But the original intent was to seek the welfare of the city where God's presence dwelt.

Today, the presence of God no longer resides in a temple or geographic location, but in His people (us) through the Holy Spirit (1 Corinthians 3:16; Ephesians 2:19–22). We are to pray for peace and justice everywhere, not just in one region, because the kingdom of God transcends borders and is not of this world.

The misinterpretation of Old Testament promises

Old Testament promises are rich with meaning and relevance, but they must be interpreted through the lens of the New Covenant. Many Christians claim promises that were given to specific individuals or to the nation of Israel in that time, without considering the covenantal conditions attached to them. For example, Psalm 91 is often cited as a blanket promise of divine protection: *"No harm will overtake you, no disaster will come near your tent."* Yet this psalm is poetic and conditional, expressing confidence in God's protection for those who dwell in His presence and trust in Him.

Jesus Himself was tempted by Satan using this very psalm (Matthew 4:6), and Jesus responded by refusing to test God's promises out of context. That interaction highlights an essential truth: promises are not to be used presumptuously. Under the New Covenant, God promises His presence, His sustaining grace, and ultimate deliverance—not immunity from suffering or danger. Paul, who suffered immensely for the gospel, still declared, *"The Lord will rescue me from every evil attack and will bring me safely to his heavenly kingdom."* (2 Timothy 4:18), indicating both present trials and ultimate security.

Similarly, the promise in Malachi 3:10—about opening the windows of heaven and pouring out blessings for those who tithe—is often cited in prosperity circles to motivate giving. Yet this promise, as I mentioned earlier, was made to Israel within the covenant of law, and the tithe was part of their national theocratic system.

The New Testament calls believers to generous, cheerful giving (2 Corinthians 9:7), but without a legal requirement or a transactional promise of material blessing.

Theological systems that blur the covenant distinctions

The misuses of the Old Testament are very often reinforced by theological systems that fail to maintain any clear distinctions between the covenants. For example, some forms of covenant theology risk flattening the biblical narrative by treating the Old and New Covenants as essentially the same, thereby continuing to apply Old Covenant regulations or principles without due regard for their fulfilment in Christ. On the other hand, some dispensational approaches may separate the covenants too starkly, creating a rigid division that severs the deep continuity of God's redemptive plan.

A biblical theology of the covenants recognises both continuity and discontinuity. The moral character of God remains the same, and His plan for redemption unfolds progressively, culminating in Christ. Yet the Old Covenant was temporary and preparatory, while the New Covenant is eternal and consummative. Hebrews 8:13 is decisive: *"By calling this covenant 'new,' he has made the first one obsolete; and what is obsolete and outdated will soon disappear."*

Any system that tries to obscure the movement from shadow to substance, from type to reality, from law to grace, will mislead believers and encourage improper use of the Old Testament. Good theology does not diminish the value of the Old Testament but places it within its proper framework—preparing the way for Christ and serving the church through instruction, wisdom, and worship.

Practical consequences of misusing the Old Testament

The misuse of the Old Testament is not only an academic problem—it has tangible consequences in the life of the church. Misinterpretation can lead to guilt-based religion, legalism, confusion about God's character, misplaced nationalism, and even spiritual abuse. Christians who are taught that their suffering must be a result of disobedience (drawing from Old Testament curse passages) will often become disillusioned or feel abandoned by God. Believers who are urged to *"claim"* Old Testament promises may lose faith when outcomes do not match expectations.

On a broader scale, when churches or ministries build their theology or practice on a flawed application of Old Testament texts, they often hinder true discipleship. Rather than equipping believers to follow Jesus in grace and truth, they burden them with outdated rituals, nationalistic ideologies, or prosperity teachings that have no basis in the New Covenant. The result is often a shallow faith built on selective verses, rather than a deep relationship with the living Christ.

Restoring the Old Testament to its proper place

Despite these dangers, the answer is not to sideline the Old Testament but to restore it to its rightful place within the whole counsel of God. Paul told Timothy that *"all Scripture is God-breathed and is useful for teaching, rebuking, correcting and training in righteousness."* (2 Timothy 3:16) — and at the time, the Old Testament was the primary Scripture he had in view.

The Old Testament is absolutely vital to us in our understanding creation, sin, covenant, justice, worship, and redemption. It gives us the Psalms to pray, the Proverbs to guide us, the prophets to awaken us, and the narratives to inspire and instruct. But above all, it gives us a portrait of the coming Christ — one that blossoms fully in the pages of the New Testament.

To read the Old Testament correctly, we must learn to ask the right questions: *How does this passage reveal God's character? What does it teach about humanity's need for redemption? How does it point forward to Christ? How do its principles shape us as members of the New Covenant community?*

These questions transform our reading from mere information gathering to gospel formation. The Old Testament, when read through the eyes of faith in Christ, becomes not a minefield of misused texts but a treasure chest of divine wisdom.

GOD'S UNIFIED PLAN

A story that binds heaven and earth

The Bible is not merely a collection of religious teachings, wise sayings, or moral rules—it is, at its core, a divine story. It is the story of God's covenant relationship with humanity, a narrative that stretches from creation to new creation, binding heaven and earth in a drama of redemption. At the heart of this story is God's unwavering faithfulness, His covenant love, and His steadfast determination to dwell with His people.

From the moment God breathed life into Adam, He initiated a relational dynamic rooted in trust, obedience, and blessing. This relationship was shattered by sin, but it was not destroyed. What follows throughout the pages of Scripture is a long, intricate, and beautiful covenant love story - a bond stronger than contract, deeper than mere promise. The covenant is the vehicle through which God clearly reveals His character, His purposes, and His unrelenting grace.

This chapter explores that unfolding covenant story, tracing how the various covenants of Scripture, each interconnected, and yet distinct, form one unified plan culminating in Jesus Christ. To understand the Bible, to grasp the gospel, and to live as New Covenant believers, we must learn to see this story not as just a patchwork of ancient texts, but as one God-breathed narrative that invites us into the heart of God's redemptive plan.

The covenant with creation: A world of blessing

The first covenantal framework is found in Genesis 1–2. Though the word *"covenant"* is not used explicitly in the creation account, the structure, language, and divine-human relationship clearly reflect a covenantal reality. God creates the world in beauty and order, places humanity at the pinnacle of His creation, and entrusts them with the responsibility of ruling, stewarding, and multiplying (Genesis 1:26–28).

This covenant of creation—or the Edenic covenant—rests on divine generosity and human obedience. God's command is simple: enjoy all that He has made, but do not eat from the tree of the knowledge of good and evil (Genesis 2:16-17). The promise of life and the warning of death are covenantal in nature. Humanity's role is to trust and obey; God's promise is to provide and bless.

This original covenant sets the pattern: God initiates, reveals His will, offers blessing, and calls for obedience. When Adam and Eve sin, the covenant is broken, but God does not abandon His creation. Instead, He introduces a promise that becomes the seed of all future covenants: that the offspring of the woman will one day crush the serpent's head (Genesis 3:15). This proto-gospel— often called the *"first good news"* – is foreshadowing a coming Redeemer and the restoration of all things.

The covenant with Noah: preserving creation

After the fall, sin escalates to such a degree that God judges the earth through the flood, preserving only Noah and his family. In this context, God makes a formal covenant with Noah. This is a covenant not only with humanity but with every living creature (Genesis 9:8-17). This covenant is unconditional. God promises never again to destroy the earth with a flood, and He gives the rainbow as a sign of this perpetual promise.

The Noahic covenant reveals God's commitment to sustain the world despite human sinfulness. It is a covenant of preservation. While it does not resolve the problem of sin, it ensures the stability of the created order so that God's redemptive purposes can unfold in history.

This covenant is significant because it reaffirms the value of life, establishes basic principles of justice (Genesis 9:5-6), and reveals God's faithfulness to all creation. It provides the foundation upon which the redemptive covenants to follow will be built. The world is preserved not because it deserves preservation, but because God is faithful to His purposes.

The covenant with Abraham: the promise of a people and a land

In Genesis 12, God calls a man named Abram and makes a profound promise: *"I will make you into a great nation... and all peoples on earth will be blessed through you."* (Genesis 12:2-3). This is the beginning of the Abrahamic covenant—a defining moment in the covenant story. Then in Genesis 15 and 17, the covenant is formalized. God promises Abraham descendants, land, and a role in blessing the nations. He commands Abraham to walk before Him and be blameless, and He gives circumcision as the sign of the covenant.

The Abrahamic covenant is both unilateral and bilateral. God initiates it, guarantees its fulfilment, and binds Himself to it through a symbolic act—passing between the animal pieces in Genesis 15. Yet God also calls Abraham to a life of obedience and faith. Therefore, this covenant is missional in nature: Abraham's descendants are not chosen for privilege alone, but to be a conduit of blessing to the world.

Crucially, the New Testament reveals that this covenant will ultimately find its fulfilment in Jesus Christ. Paul writes, *"If you belong to Christ, then you are Abraham's seed, and heirs according to the promise."* (Galatians 3:29). The Abrahamic covenant was never simply about a physical nation or a strip of land—it was always about the coming of the Messiah and the gathering of a people from every tribe, language, and nation.

The covenant at Sinai: The Law and the nation

Four hundred years after Abraham, God then delivers his descendants from Egypt and brings them to Mount Sinai. There, He enters into a covenant with them as a nation. This Mosaic Covenant is outlined fully in Exodus 19–24. It includes the Ten Commandments and a host of other laws governing worship, justice, and daily life. This covenant is conditional: blessings for obedience and curses for disobedience (see Deuteronomy 28). It is a covenant of law, designed to set Israel apart as a holy nation and to reveal God's character through their national life.

At its heart, it is relational: *"I will be your God, and you will be my people."* (Exodus 6:7). The law was never intended as a means of salvation, but as a tutor to lead Israel—and ultimately the world—to Christ. Paul writes in Galatians 3:24 that *"the law was our guardian until Christ came that we might be justified by faith."* The law revealed sin, restrained evil, and pointed to the need for a Redeemer. It also provided the structure for Israel's worship, with sacrifices and a priesthood that foreshadowed the work of Christ.

Importantly, the Mosaic covenant was never the final word. It was temporary, preparatory, and eventually made obsolete by the New Covenant in Christ (Hebrews 8:13). Yet it plays a vital role in the covenant story, showing both God's holiness and humanity's inability to live up to His standard.

The covenant with David: A king forever

In 2 Samuel 7, we read where God makes a covenant with King David, promising that his throne will be established forever. *"Your house and your kingdom will endure forever before me; your throne will be established forever."* (v.16). This Davidic covenant adds a royal dimension to the covenant story. It confirms that the Messiah will come from David's line and rule with justice and righteousness.

This promise is echoed throughout the prophets and fulfilled in Jesus, who is repeatedly called the *"Son of David."* The angel Gabriel tells Mary, *"The Lord God will give him the throne of his father David... and his kingdom will never end."* (Luke 1:32-33). Jesus is the true and eternal King who fulfils the Davidic covenant—not by military conquest, but by laying down His life and rising again.

The Davidic covenant, like the others, is not a detour or a side story—it is a central thread in the whole tapestry of redemption. It reminds us that God's kingdom is not an abstract idea but a tangible reality, which is inaugurated in Christ and is awaiting consummation at His return.

One Story, one Saviour

Though the Bible contains multiple covenants—each with its own context, content, and sign—they are not disconnected. Rather, they form a unified covenant story that moves from promise to fulfilment, from shadow to reality, from law to grace. Each covenant builds upon the previous one, revealing more of God's character and advancing His redemptive plan.

Jesus Christ is the fulfilment of every covenant promise. He is the seed of the woman who crushes the serpent; the true offspring of Abraham through whom the nations are blessed; the obedient Israelite who fulfils the law; the greater David who reigns forever; and the mediator of the New Covenant, which brings forgiveness, transformation, and eternal life.

The Bible is not merely about rules or religion—it is about a relationship. It is about a God Who binds Himself to humanity through covenant, a God Who remains faithful despite our unfaithfulness, and a God Who accomplishes salvation through His Son. To read the Bible without understanding the covenant story is to miss the heartbeat of Scripture. But to see the covenants for what they are—a unified story of divine grace—is to be drawn into the very heart of God.

The progressive revelation of the covenant

The covenant story of Scripture is not a static narrative, but one that unfolds progressively. God's covenantal dealings begin in Eden, but they do not end there. Each successive covenant builds upon the previous one, thereby expanding and deepening our understanding of who God is and how He relates to His people. This progressive revelation is not merely additive—it is also revelatory. In each stage, God discloses more of His nature, His purposes, and His plan for redemption.

The covenant with Noah introduces the concept of divine preservation and mercy in the face of judgment. While humanity deserved destruction, God graciously preserved a remnant and promised stability in the natural order.

With Abraham, the covenant introduces the principle of divine election and promise. Abraham was not chosen because of merit, but because of grace. Through him, God pledged a future filled with blessing, not only for his descendants but for all nations.

The Mosaic covenant provides the structure for a redeemed people to live in relationship with a holy God. It is at Sinai that God reveals the depths of His holiness, the seriousness of sin, and the need for a mediator. Yet, the very laws that expose human sin also point to the One who would perfectly fulfil them. The Mosaic covenant was never meant to be an end in itself but a guardian until Christ came (Galatians 3:24).

The Davidic covenant narrows the focus of redemption to a particular lineage. A king will arise from David's line whose reign will be eternal. This covenant is deeply messianic, pointing forward to Jesus, the Son of David, who will establish a kingdom of justice and peace. Finally, the new covenant, announced by the prophets and inaugurated by Christ, brings fulfilment. It is the covenant of transformation — of new hearts, of forgiveness, of the indwelling Spirit.

The unifying thread of grace

While the covenants differ in content and historical setting, they are united by a single thread: God's grace. Each covenant is an expression of divine initiative. God is always the One Who establishes the covenant, sets its terms, and provides the means for its fulfilment. Human response is necessary, but it is always secondary to divine grace.

Even in the Mosaic Covenant, which emphasizes obedience and includes blessings and curses, grace is present. The Law itself is a gift — it reveals God's will, it protects community life, and it foreshadows the coming Redeemer. Also, the sacrificial system built into the covenant provides atonement for sin, pointing to the ultimate sacrifice of Christ. The unifying message is that God is a covenant-keeping God who relentlessly pursues relationship with His people. At no point does God abandon His purposes.

When His people fail, He provides a way of restoration. When His covenant is broken, He promises a new one. Throughout the narrative, God's faithfulness is unwavering, even when human faithfulness falters.

Covenant and mission

The covenant story is not only about relationship—it is about mission. From the very beginning, God's covenant with His people carried a missional purpose. In Genesis 12:3, God tells Abraham, "*All peoples on earth will be blessed through you.*" This promise is not merely a personal blessing; it is a global commission. Israel was to be a light to the nations, a priestly kingdom through whom God's character and purposes would be revealed to the world.

Unfortunately, Israel often turned inward, viewing the covenant as a mark of superiority rather than a call to servanthood. The prophets repeatedly rebuke this inward focus, calling the people back to their mission. Isaiah declares that Israel is to be "*a light for the Gentiles, that my salvation may reach to the ends of the earth.*" (Isaiah 49:6).

In the New Covenant, this mission is renewed and expanded. Jesus commissions His disciples to "*make disciples of all nations*" (Matthew 28:19). Paul, the apostle to the Gentiles, sees his mission as the outworking of God's covenant promises to Abraham. The covenant people are now defined not by ethnicity or law-keeping, but by faith in Christ. The covenant community is no longer confined to Israel—it now embraces people from every tribe, tongue, and nation.

Covenant and community

Covenant is inherently communal. God's covenant is never merely with individuals in isolation but with a people. Even the covenants that begin with individuals—like Abraham—have communal implications.

The covenant creates a people who are called to live together under God's rule and reflect His character.

The Mosaic covenant is perhaps the clearest expression of this communal aspect. The Ten Commandments and the laws that follow are not just personal ethics; they are communal structures for justice, mercy, worship, and neighbourly love. Covenant life involves mutual accountability, shared worship, and a common mission.

In the church, this communal reality is fulfilled and deepened. The new covenant creates a new people — the body of Christ. We are not merely saved into a private relationship with God, but into a family. The New Testament is replete with *"one another"* commands: love one another, bear one another's burdens, confess your sins to one another, encourage one another. These are covenantal commands. They reflect the kind of life that is birthed and sustained by God's covenant love.

The covenant and the cross

The ultimate expression of God's covenant faithfulness is found at the cross of Christ. All the promises of God find their "Yes" in Christ (2 Corinthians 1:20). At the cross, the demands of the old covenant are met and its curses borne. Jesus, the sinless Son, becomes the covenant-keeper in our place. He fulfils the law, satisfies justice, and offers Himself as the perfect sacrifice.

This is the great and mysterious exchange of the gospel: Christ takes our covenant-breaking upon Himself and gives us His righteousness. The veil is torn. Access to God is granted. The new covenant is ratified in blood — not the blood of animals, but the blood of the Son of God. This covenant is unbreakable, not because of our faithfulness, but because of Christ's. Hebrews 7:22 calls Jesus *"the guarantor of a better covenant."* His priesthood is eternal, His sacrifice sufficient, His intercession unfailing. In Him, we have confidence to draw near to God, in faith not fear.

Living in the light of the covenant

To live under the new covenant is to live in freedom, assurance, and responsibility. We are no longer under the condemnation of the law, but under the transforming power of grace.

This grace does not lead to lawlessness but to love. The moral vision of the covenant is written on our hearts by the Spirit. We obey, not to earn God's favour, but because we already have it.

This covenantal identity shapes every aspect of life. It informs our worship—Christ is our mediator and high priest. It informs our ethics—we are called to reflect the character of our covenant God. It informs our relationships—we are part of a covenant family. It informs our mission—we are ambassadors of the covenant to the world.

To forget the covenant is to lose our spiritual compass. But to remember it is to walk in the joy of belonging, the security of God's promises, and the power of the Spirit. The covenant story is our story. It is the narrative that defines us, sustains us, and sends us.

The covenant and the culmination of God's story

As we follow the golden thread of covenant through the tapestry of Scripture, we arrive at its radiant centre—the cross of Christ. Here, the fullness of God's covenant purposes is not merely explained but embodied. The cross is the covenant writ large in blood and grace, and it is in this moment that we see most clearly how every promise, every shadow, and every sign finds its fulfilment in Jesus.

Jesus as the mediator of the New Covenant

The author of Hebrews makes this truth unmistakably clear: *"For this reason Christ is the mediator of a new covenant, that those who are called may receive the promised eternal inheritance — now that he has died as a ransom to set them free from the sins committed under the first covenant."* (Hebrews 9:15). Christ mediates a new and better covenant, not simply as a spokesman or priest, but as the very sacrifice by which this covenant is ratified. He brings together the promises of God and the deep need of humanity in His person and work. In the Old Covenant, animal sacrifices were offered repeatedly to atone for sin, yet they could never fully cleanse the conscience of the worshipper (Hebrews 10:1-4).

These sacrifices pointed forward to a greater offering. Jesus, the sinless Son of God, offered Himself once for all, providing perfect atonement and inaugurating the eternal covenant.

The blood of the covenant

At the Last Supper, Jesus made a profound statement: *"This is my blood of the covenant, which is poured out for many for the forgiveness of sins."* (Matthew 26:28). This echoes the language used in Exodus when Moses confirmed the Old Covenant by sprinkling the blood of sacrificed animals (Exodus 24:8). But Christ's blood, unlike that of bulls and goats, was efficacious to cleanse, redeem, and reconcile.

This *"blood of the covenant"* was not just symbolic; it was salvific. It marked the definitive turning point in the divine-human relationship. Jesus did not merely update or improve the covenant; He fulfilled its deepest purpose. He bore the curse of covenant-breaking upon Himself and bestowed the blessings of obedience on His people.

The cross as covenant fulfilment

The cross is not simply the place where Jesus died; it is the altar on which the covenant was sealed. Every element of God's covenant story finds its resolution in the cross:

➤ The *promise* to Abraham of a blessing to all nations is realised as Jesus opens the way of salvation to both Jew and Gentile (Galatians 3:14).

➤ The *law* given through Moses finds its righteous requirements met in the obedient life and sacrificial death of Jesus (Romans 8:3–4).

➤ The *Davidic covenant* reaches its climax as the risen Christ ascends to the throne of heaven, ruling as the eternal King in fulfilment of God's promise (Luke 1:32–33).

All these streams flow into the cross, and from the cross they flow outward into the world in rivers of grace.

Covenant and the resurrection

But the covenant story does not end with death. The resurrection of Jesus is the divine affirmation that the covenant has been fulfilled and secured. Paul declares that Jesus *"was delivered over to death for our sins and was raised to life for our justification."* (Romans 4:25). The empty tomb is the Father's "Yes" to the Son's *"It is finished."*

The resurrection also establishes Jesus as the *"firstborn from among the dead"* (Colossians 1:18), the guarantor of the covenant's promises. Because He lives, those united to Him by faith will also live. The new covenant is not merely an agreement written in divine ink; it is a living relationship secured by a living Saviour.

The covenant community formed at Pentecost

Following Jesus' ascension, the Holy Spirit was poured out on the day of Pentecost, marking the birth of the new covenant community — the church. Peter proclaimed, *"The promise is for you and your children and for all who are far off — for all whom the Lord our God will call."* (Acts 2:39). The Spirit not only seals believers in the covenant but empowers them to live as its witnesses.

The church is not a collection of isolated believers but a covenant family. We are the body of Christ, bound together not by common interest or cultural affinity but by the blood of Jesus and the indwelling presence of the Spirit.

Our baptism is the clear sign of this covenantal belonging; our communion table the covenant meal that reminds us of the price paid and the promises given.

Living as covenant people

This covenant is not burdensome; it is liberating. We are not justified by our adherence to the law but by faith in the One who fulfilled the law on our behalf (Romans 3:28). Yet this grace does not lead to lawlessness. The Spirit writes God's law on our hearts, shaping us into the image of Christ.

This covenant shapes every area of life:

➤ In **worship**, we draw near with confidence, knowing our sin has been dealt with once for all (Hebrews 10:19–22).

➤ In **ethics**, we are called to love one another as Christ has loved us (John 13:34).

➤ In **suffering**, we endure with hope, knowing our covenant God is faithful (2 Thessalonians 3:3).

To live as a covenant people is to live with identity, purpose, and security. We are not adrift in a chaotic world; we are part of God's unfolding story, anchored in the unbreakable promises of the cross.

The covenant meal and the covenant hope

Every time we take the bread and the cup in Communion, we proclaim the covenant story. Paul writes, *"For whenever you eat this bread and drink this cup, you proclaim the Lord's death until he comes."* (1 Corinthians 11:26). Communion is not a mere ritual; it is a covenant renewal. It points back to the cross, anchors us in the present grace of Christ, and anticipates the future wedding supper of the Lamb (Revelation 19:9). This forward-looking aspect is crucial. The new covenant is both already and not yet. We experience its blessings now — forgiveness, reconciliation, the indwelling Spirit — but we await its consummation in the return of Christ. The covenant assures us that history is not random; it is headed toward a glorious fulfilment.

The cross is always at the centre

At the heart of God's covenant story stands the cross of Christ. It is there that justice and mercy meet, that wrath and love embrace, that death is defeated and life secured. The cross is not an interruption in the covenant narrative; it is its climax. And from this centre flows the ongoing life of the people of God, called, redeemed, and sent to bear witness to God's faithfulness – the One Who keeps covenant forever. In Jesus, every covenant finds its *yes* and *amen*. And as we live by faith in Him, we become living testimonies to the love, the grace and the glory of our amazing covenant-keeping God.

- 10 -

JESUS, THE APOSTLES AND TWO TESTAMENTS

The living Word meets the written word

At the heart of the biblical story is not just a collection of writings, but a person—Jesus Christ. He is the fulfilment, the centre, and the whole purpose of both the Old and the New Testaments. The relationship between Jesus and all the Scriptures is not merely academic or theological; it is transformative, revelatory, and dynamic. The written word bears witness to the living Word, and the living Word affirms and fulfils the written word.

When we explore how Jesus and the apostles understood, used, and fulfilled the Scriptures, we begin to see the seamless unity between the Old and the New Testaments. Far from being two separate and disconnected volumes, they are actually part of one redemptive narrative that finds its climax in the life, death, and resurrection of Jesus Christ.

This unity is not forced; it emerges naturally from the way Jesus spoke about the Law, the Prophets, and the Psalms. He did not discard the Old Covenant Scriptures; He fulfilled them. He did not abolish the Law; He embodied its righteousness. He did not reject the prophets; He revealed their true message. The apostles, in turn, followed Jesus' lead, interpreting the Old Testament through the lens of His life and ministry and authoring the New Testament as a Spirit-inspired continuation of God's redemptive work.

Jesus and the Old Testament: fulfilment, not abolishment

We must remember that Jesus was born into a Jewish world where the Hebrew Scriptures—the Law, the Prophets, and the Writings—were considered sacred and authoritative. From His earliest days, He was immersed in this scriptural tradition. When tempted in the wilderness, He responded with quotations from Deuteronomy, demonstrating His dependence on the authority of Scripture (Matthew 4:1–11).

When He taught, He often said, *"It is written,"* rooting His message in the Scriptures of Israel. In His Sermon on the Mount, Jesus made a profound statement (Matthew 5:17-18): *"Do not think that I have come to abolish the Law or the Prophets; I have not come to abolish them but to fulfil them. For truly I tell you, until heaven and earth disappear, not the smallest letter, not the least stroke of a pen, will by any means disappear from the Law until everything is accomplished."*

This statement is so critical to our understanding the continuity between the Testaments. Jesus does not treat the Old Testament as obsolete. Instead, He fulfils it—completing its prophecies, embodying its types and shadows, and living out its moral demands with perfect obedience. The word *"fulfil"* here (Greek: *plēroō*) means to complete or bring to full expression. Jesus fulfills the Law by obeying it, by showing its true meaning, and by becoming the sacrificial Lamb to which the Law's sacrificial system pointed. Moreover, He fulfils the Prophets by being the long-awaited Messiah. The prophetic promises of a coming king, a suffering servant, a new covenant, and a restored people all find their realization in Him. Jesus doesn't merely quote the Old Testament to support His claims; He *is* the fulfilment of those very claims.

The Apostles and the Old Testament: A Christ-centred hermeneutic

The apostles, having walked with Jesus and witnessed His resurrection, began to read the Old Testament with new eyes. They came to see that the entire story of Israel pointed to Christ. The Law, the Prophets, and the Psalms were no longer just history or poetry or moral instruction—they were gospel-saturated signposts that led to Jesus.

Peter, in his sermon on the day of Pentecost, quotes extensively from Joel and Psalms to explain the coming of the Holy Spirit and the resurrection of Jesus (Acts 2). Stephen, in his defence before the Sanhedrin, recounts the entire history of Israel to demonstrate that Jesus is the Righteous One foretold by Moses and rejected by the people (Acts 7).

Paul, writing to the Romans, quotes the Old Testament over 60 times to explain the gospel of grace, justification by faith, and the inclusion of the Gentiles. For the apostles, the Old Testament was not a relic of the past. It was the foundation upon which the gospel rested. It provided the theological categories — covenant, sacrifice, kingdom, redemption — through which the life and work of Jesus were understood and proclaimed.

Paul famously wrote: *"All Scripture is God-breathed and is useful for teaching, rebuking, correcting and training in righteousness"* (2 Timothy 3:16). At the time Paul wrote this, "Scripture" primarily referred to the Old Testament. Far from dismissing it, Paul affirmed its ongoing authority and usefulness in the church.

The formation of the New Testament: continuity and authority

While Jesus and the apostles often affirmed the Old Testament, the early church very quickly recognized that the life, teachings, death, and resurrection of Jesus Christ — along with the apostolic witness — demanded a written testimony of their own. Thus, the New Testament emerged, not as a contradiction to the Old, but as its fulfilment and continuation.

The four Gospels provide a portrait of Jesus that is steeped in Old Testament imagery and prophecy. Matthew, for instance, frequently uses the phrase, *"This was to fulfil what the Lord had said through the prophet..."* (e.g., Matthew 1:22; 2:5, 15, 17, 23). He clearly intends his readers to see Jesus as the fulfilment of Israel's story. The Epistles, written by apostles or their close associates, offer theological reflection on the significance of Jesus' work and its implications for the new covenant community. Again and again, the writers turn to the Old Testament to make their case, showing that the New Testament is not a novel invention, but a Spirit-breathed continuation of what God had already begun.

The New Testament's authority, then, is not derived in isolation. It is rooted in the authority of Jesus Himself, who fulfilled the Old Testament, commissioned His apostles, and promised the Spirit would lead them into all truth (John 16:13).

The apostolic writings, inspired by the Spirit, carry the same weight as the prophetic Scriptures before them.

Peter, referring to Paul's letters, writes: "*He writes the same way in all his letters, speaking in them of these matters. His letters contain some things that are hard to understand, which ignorant and unstable people distort, as they do the other Scriptures, to their own destruction*" (2 Peter 3:16). Notice that Peter equates Paul's writings with "the other Scriptures." This early recognition of apostolic authority is key to understanding how the two Testaments function together.

Jesus as the key to understanding the whole Bible

Jesus is not only the fulfilment of the Old Testament; He is also the interpretive key to understanding all of Scripture. On the road to Emmaus, the risen Christ rebuked two disciples for their slowness to believe what the prophets had spoken: "*And beginning with Moses and all the Prophets, he explained to them what was said in all the Scriptures concerning himself.*" (Luke 24:27).

Later, He told the broader group of disciples: "*This is what I told you while I was still with you: Everything must be fulfilled that is written about me in the Law of Moses, the Prophets and the Psalms.*" (Luke 24:44). Jesus taught that the Scriptures are not merely a moral code or a historical record; they are a testimony about Him. This Christ-centred hermeneutic became the lens through which the early church read both the old and emerging Scriptures. It is a lens we must continue to use today.

A unified testimony

They are part of a single, unfolding narrative of redemption. The Old Testament lays the foundation, sets the stage, and raises the questions. The New Testament provides the fulfilment, brings the answers, and reveals the person to whom it all pointed. In both Testaments, we see the same God at work—the God who creates, calls, covenants, judges, redeems, and restores. We see His character, His holiness, His justice, His mercy, and above all, His love. Jesus Christ is the focal point, the lens, and the climax of this divine drama.

The apostles did not invent a new religion. They proclaimed the completion of the old one. They did not reject the Scriptures of Israel; they proclaimed that those Scriptures had reached their intended goal. Remember, that in Christ, all the promises of God are *"Yes"* and *"Amen."* (2 Corinthians 1:20).

To understand either Testament properly, we must read both. To appreciate the fullness of the gospel, we must grasp the weight of the Law. To celebrate the New Covenant, we must see its roots in the Old Covenant. To follow Jesus Christ faithfully, we need to understand the story He came to fulfil.

Apostolic preaching: rooted in the Old Testament

One of the clearest indications of how the apostles viewed the Old Testament is evident in their preaching. The book of Acts, which records the spread of the early church, reveals a consistent pattern: the apostles proclaimed Jesus as the Messiah using the Hebrew Scriptures as their foundation. They did not argue for Christ apart from the Old Testament; rather, they demonstrated how Jesus fulfilled what had already been promised.

Peter's sermon at Pentecost (Acts 2) is a prime example. In addressing a Jewish audience, Peter explains the pouring out of the Holy Spirit as the fulfilment of Joel's prophecy (Joel 2:28–32). He then recounts the life, death, and resurrection of Jesus Christ, appealing to Psalm 16 to show us that King David foresaw the resurrection of the Messiah: *"David said about him: 'I saw the Lord always before me. Because he is at my right hand, I will not be shaken... you will not abandon me to the realm of the dead, you will not let your holy one see decay.'"* (Acts 2:25–27).

This was not a clever appropriation of Scripture; it was a Spirit-led interpretation that aligned with Jesus' own teaching about how the Scriptures pointed to Him. Peter concludes by declaring: *"Therefore let all Israel be assured of this: God has made this Jesus, whom you crucified, both Lord and Messiah"* (Acts 2:36). Later, in Acts 3, Peter again appeals to the prophets: *"Indeed, beginning with Samuel, all the prophets who have spoken have foretold these days"* (Acts 3:24).

He frames Jesus as the prophet like Moses (Deuteronomy 18:15) and reminds the people that the covenant promises made to Abraham are now being fulfilled through Christ.

This pattern is repeated by Stephen, Philip, Paul, and others. The consistent use of the Old Testament to declare the gospel of Jesus demonstrates the apostles' deep conviction that the two Testaments were not in conflict. Rather, the Old provided the foundation and the vocabulary for understanding the New.

Paul's theological use of the Old Testament

Among the apostles, Paul's writings provide the most developed theological engagement with the Old Testament. Far from setting the Law against grace or the Old Testament against the New, Paul engages in a sophisticated interpretation that reveals the unity of God's redemptive purpose.

In Romans, Galatians, and 1 and 2 Corinthians, Paul constantly refers back to the Scriptures of Israel. He interprets Abraham as the father of all who believe, not just Jews, and insists that the promise made to him was not based on the Law but on faith: "*It was not through the law that Abraham and his offspring received the promise... but through the righteousness that comes by faith.*" (Romans 4:13).

He uses the story of Hagar and Sarah in Galatians 4 to illustrate the difference between the old covenant of bondage and the new covenant of freedom. In 1 Corinthians 10, he recounts the failures of Israel in the wilderness to warn the Corinthian church not to repeat their mistakes: "*These things happened to them as examples and were written down as warnings for us, on whom the culmination of the ages has come*" (1 Corinthians 10:11).

Notice that Paul sees the Old Testament not merely as historical record, but as spiritually instructive for the church. These texts, written centuries earlier, still spoke with authority because they bore witness to the same God, the same covenant story, and the same redemptive goal found in Christ.

Paul also affirms the inspiration of all Scripture (2 Timothy 3:16) and urges Timothy to remain faithful to the Scriptures he has known since childhood (2 Timothy 3:15) — a clear reference to the Old Testament. This, again, reinforces that the apostles did not regard the Old Testament as superseded but as foundational and enduring.

The New Testament: completion, not competition

The authority of the New Testament did not arise in competition with the Old Testament but in continuity with it. The writings of the apostles and their associates were recognized as inspired because they bore apostolic authority and the imprint of divine revelation. They also demonstrated a deep connection to the Old Testament narrative and theology.

The Gospels themselves are each saturated with Old Testament references. Matthew alone includes over sixty quotations or allusions, showing how Jesus fulfils specific prophecies. John opens his Gospel with a profound theological statement that recalls Genesis: "*In the beginning was the Word, and the Word was with God, and the Word was God.*"(John 1:1). John's use of *"the Word"* (*logos*) not only reveals Jesus as the eternal Son of God but also connects Him to God's creative and revelatory action throughout the Old Testament.

Hebrews, one of the most theologically rich books in the New Testament, is a masterclass in connecting the old and new covenants. The writer presents Jesus as the final and superior revelation of God, the great high priest, the once-for-all sacrifice, and the mediator of a better covenant. These themes would be unintelligible without the framework provided by the Old Testament.

Consider Hebrews 1:1-3: "*In the past God spoke to our ancestors through the prophets at many times and in various ways, but in these last days he has spoken to us by his Son...*" This contrast is not a dismissal of the former revelation, but an acknowledgment of its culmination. God has never contradicted Himself; He has always completed what He began.

The Apostolic witness to scriptural unity

The apostles consistently demonstrate that the New Testament is not a standalone document but the next chapter in the same book. This is evident not only in their quotations from the Old Testament but in their theological reasoning and pastoral exhortations.

James, writing to Jewish Christians scattered among the nations, appeals to the Law and the Prophets while calling believers to live out the *"royal law"* of love (James 2:8). Peter, in his epistles, draws from Isaiah and the Psalms to remind believers of their identity as God's chosen people — a title once reserved for Israel, now applied to the church (1 Peter 2:9–10).

John, in his epistles and in the book of Revelation, builds heavily on Old Testament imagery. The apocalyptic vision of Revelation cannot be understood apart from the symbols and language of Daniel, Ezekiel, Isaiah, and the Psalms. The final picture of a new heaven and new earth (Revelation 21) echoes Isaiah 65, and the description of the new Jerusalem is drawn from prophetic expectations of restoration.

What becomes abundantly clear is that the apostles did not ever abandon the Scriptures of Israel. They actually embraced them, interpreted them in light of Christ, and affirmed their continuing relevance. Their own writings, now part of our New Testament, were not a rejection of what came before but a Spirit-inspired continuation and fulfilment.

The role of the Holy Spirit in scriptural revelation

One of the key threads uniting the Testaments is the work of the Holy Spirit. The Spirit inspired the prophets of old, empowered the ministry of Jesus, and guided the apostles in the formation of the New Testament canon.

Peter affirms this in 2 Peter 1:21: *"For prophecy never had its origin in the human will, but prophets, though human, spoke from God as they were carried along by the Holy Spirit."*

This same Spirit, Jesus promised, would guide the apostles into all truth (John 16:13). The inspiration of the Old and New Testaments comes from the same divine source. That is why the church has always affirmed the full authority and divine origin of both.

When we speak of the Bible as *"God's Word,"* we do not mean that the New Testament is God's Word while the Old Testament is somehow outdated or inferior. The whole of Scripture is breathed out by God. The same Spirit who spoke through Isaiah and Moses also inspired Paul and John. This shared authorship is the basis for the unity and authority of Scripture.

The Spirit also enables the church to understand Scripture. Paul reminds the Corinthians that *"we have the mind of Christ"* and that spiritual truths are spiritually discerned (1 Corinthians 2:14–16). Without the Spirit, we may miss the connections between the Testaments or misinterpret their meaning. But with the Spirit, we see that the story of redemption from Genesis to Revelation is a single, coherent narrative with Christ at the centre.

Avoiding false dichotomies

Throughout history, some have fallen into the trap of creating a false dichotomy between the Testaments. Marcion, a second-century heretic, rejected the Old Testament and claimed the God of Israel was a different being from the Father of Jesus. The early church rightly condemned this view as heresy, affirming that the God of Abraham, Isaac, and Jacob is the same God Who raised Jesus from the dead.

Even today, a growing number of Christians subtly downplay the Old Testament, viewing it as outdated or irrelevant. They focus exclusively on the New Testament and ignore all the rich theology, history, and revelation which is found in the Hebrew Scriptures. This is a tragic mistake. To truly understand the New Testament, we must be grounded in the Old. The cross only makes sense in light of the sacrificial system. The idea of a covenant community flows from God's relationship with Israel.

Even the title, "Messiah," is meaningless without the prophetic background. So, when we neglect the Old Testament, we cut ourselves off from our very roots. The apostles did not see two disconnected testaments. They saw one story, one revelation, one covenantal movement toward redemption in Christ.

Living and teaching the fulfilment of the scriptures

As Jesus ministered throughout Judea, Galilee, and in the surrounding regions, it became increasingly clear that He did not simply carry a message about the Old Testament Scriptures — He embodied them. His life was the fulfilment of a story which had been unfolding over centuries.

But the fulfilment did not imply replacement. Instead, the continuity between the Old and New Testaments reached its climax in Christ, and from that climax, the apostles were called to proclaim and teach the implications of that fulfilment to the world.

The New Testament writers, particularly the apostles, lived in the dynamic tension of honouring the full authority of the Old Testament while explaining how Jesus transformed its meaning and application. This was not a rejection of the Old, but a Spirit-led reinterpretation through the lens of the crucified and risen Christ. Paul, Peter, John, James, and the others all bore witness to this transformation. The Scriptures of Israel were their foundation, but they understood them now in the light of Christ.

The apostles therefore shaped the early church's understanding of both covenants. The Law and the Prophets continued to instruct, but they did so through the prism of Jesus. The early church, comprised of both Jews and Gentiles, was forced to wrestle with how to handle circumcision, the Sabbath, kosher food laws, temple worship, and other distinctly Jewish practices.

It was not easy. But the Spirit led the apostles to recognise that the heart of God's covenant promise had always been about faith, not rituals; transformation, not tradition; grace, not law-keeping.

Apostolic interpretation of the Old Testament

If there is a consistent pattern in the New Testament, it is that the apostles interpreted the Old Testament Christologically — that is, with Christ at the centre. The Gospels are filled with references to how Jesus' life, death, and resurrection fulfilled what was *"written."* Matthew especially makes extensive use of prophetic fulfilment formulas: *"This was to fulfil what the Lord had said through the prophet..."* (e.g., Matthew 1:22; 2:15, 17, 23).

The apostle Peter followed this same pattern in the book of Acts. When explaining the events of the day of Pentecost, Peter quotes the prophet Joel to show that the outpouring of the Spirit was not a spontaneous novelty, but the fulfilment of God's ancient promise (Acts 2:16–21). When defending the inclusion of the Gentiles, Peter refers to the vision God gave him and connects it with Scripture and the testimony of the Spirit (Acts 10–11, 15).

The apostle Paul's letters are undoubtedly the most detailed theological explorations of this fulfilment. In Galatians 3, he argues that the promise given to Abraham preceded the Law and was fulfilled in Christ. The Law, he writes, *"was our guardian until Christ came that we might be justified by faith."* (Galatians 3:24). Now that Christ has come, we are no longer under that guardian. This is not a dismissal of the Law - it is an explanation of its temporary and preparatory purpose.

In his letter to the Romans, Paul uses Abraham again as a key figure to demonstrate that righteousness has always been by faith, not by works of the Law (Romans 4). In 2 Corinthians 3, he contrasts the *"letter"* of the Old Covenant with the *"Spirit"* of the New Covenant, declaring that the latter brings life. He does not denigrate the old covenant but affirms its role in God's unfolding plan — a role now completed and surpassed in Christ.

The book of Hebrews also gives us an unparalleled theological reflection on the two covenants. Its central claim is that Jesus is the mediator of a better covenant, founded on better promises (Hebrews 8:6).

The old covenant, with its priesthood, sacrifices, and tabernacle, was a shadow of the heavenly reality now revealed in Christ. *"The law is only a shadow of the good things that are coming – not the realities themselves."* (Hebrews 10:1). The Law pointed forward, but now the reality has come.

The unity of the two Testaments

Despite these profound developments, the early church did not divide the Scriptures into two contradictory testaments. Rather, the Old and New Testaments together formed a single, unified narrative – a divine drama which centred on Jesus Christ. The Old was seen as the promise, the New as the fulfilment. The Old revealed the problem of sin and the need for redemption; the New revealed the Redeemer and the means of salvation.

Jesus Himself affirmed this unity. In Luke 24, He explained to the disciples on the road to Emmaus that the whole of the Scriptures pointed to Him: *"Beginning with Moses and all the Prophets, he explained to them what was said in all the Scriptures concerning himself."* (Luke 24:27). Later, with all the disciples present, He said, *"Everything must be fulfilled that is written about me in the Law of Moses, the Prophets and the Psalms."* (Luke 24:44). The three-fold division of the Hebrew Bible – Torah, Prophets, and Writings – was all about Him.

This understanding empowered the apostles to preach Christ from the Scriptures. When Philip met the Ethiopian eunuch in Acts 8, he found him reading Isaiah 53. *"Do you understand what you are reading?"* Philip asked. The man replied, *"How can I...unless someone explains it to me?"* Then, beginning with that very passage, Philip told him the good news about Jesus. This was the normative pattern of apostolic preaching – Jesus from the Scriptures. Thus, the early Christian message was never a departure from Judaism but its fulfilment. The early believers did not throw away the Old Testament; they read it again with new eyes. They saw Christ on every page, in every promise, in every sacrifice, in every king and prophet and psalm. The Law and the Prophets had been waiting for their Messiah – and now He had come.

Apostolic authority and the emergence of the New Testament

As the apostles taught and planted churches, their letters and teachings began to be regarded as having the same authority as the Old Testament Scriptures. Peter refers to Paul's letters as part of *"the Scriptures"* (2 Peter 3:15-16), indicating that even within the lifetime of the apostles, the words of Christ's chosen messengers were being received as divinely authoritative.

The canon of the New Testament did not emerge in isolation from the Old Testament but in continuity with it. The apostles, guided by the Holy Spirit, laid the theological and pastoral foundation for the church, drawing deeply on the Old Testament while proclaiming the gospel of the New.

John's Gospel opens with the breathtaking claim that *"the Word became flesh and made his dwelling among us."* (John 1:14). Here, the eternal Logos who was *"with God"* and *"was God"* (John 1:1) entered the world He made, fulfilling the tabernacle imagery of God's presence among His people. John goes on to say, *"Out of his fullness we have all received grace in place of grace already given. For the law was given through Moses; grace and truth came through Jesus Christ."* (John 1:16-17). This is not a contrast between bad and good, but between partial and complete. The Law was grace — but Christ is greater grace.

Thus, the New Testament writings bear witness not only to the life of Jesus but to the apostolic interpretation of what that life means in light of all that had come before. The two testaments are not rival narratives but a single unfolding story — God's covenant story.

The Testaments as covenant documents

The word "testament" itself is a translation of the Greek *diathēkē*, which can mean either "covenant" or "will." In biblical usage, it carries the weight of a binding agreement between God and His people. The "Old Testament" is, more accurately, the Old Covenant. The "New Testament" is the New Covenant. The content of these testaments reflects that.

The Old is filled with God's covenants with Noah, Abraham, Moses, and David. It details God's laws, promises, warnings, and hopes. The New reveals the new covenant in Jesus' blood (Luke 22:20), a covenant that fulfils the law and the prophets, that writes God's law on our hearts, and that grants forgiveness and transformation through the Spirit. The apostles understood that the cross was the ratification of a new covenant, one foreshadowed by Jeremiah's prophecy (Jeremiah 31:31-34) and anticipated throughout the Scriptures. In Hebrews, this new covenant is described in rich detail as superior, eternal, and based on better promises.

Therefore, the two testaments are not just two parts of a book — they are the records of two covenantal administrations. The old covenant was based on law, the new on grace. The old came through Moses, the new through Christ. The old revealed sin, the new offers forgiveness. The old pointed to a coming Saviour; the new presents Him in full.

A word to today's church

For the contemporary believer, the relationship between the two testaments remains vital. To understand the gospel fully, we must understand the covenant story that gave it birth. We must read the Old Testament with eyes trained on Christ and read the New Testament with an appreciation for all that preceded it.

Far too many Christians either ignore the Old Testament or just misunderstand it. But the Old Testament is not obsolete; it is indispensable. It is the soil from which the gospel grows. Every prophecy, every law, every psalm, and every story points toward Jesus. And the New Testament is not merely a collection of moral teachings or spiritual reflections — it is the climax of a covenantal drama that spans generations and nations. Jesus and the apostles did not offer us a new religion. They fulfilled an ancient promise. They brought to completion what God had begun with Abraham. As Paul puts it in 2 Corinthians 1:20, *"No matter how many promises God has made, they are 'Yes' in Christ."* And so, we too say *"Amen,"* to the glory of God.

- 11 -
THE UNITY OF GOD'S WORD

I have referred to the unity of God's revelation already, but this is so important, I want to dig a little deeper and drive this truth home, so there is no doubt whatsoever that God has only ever told one cohesive story from the beginning. In fact, one of the most remarkable and essential characteristics of the Bible is its profound unity. Spanning more than a thousand years in its composition, written by over forty human authors from diverse backgrounds and professions, and composed in a number of different languages and cultural settings, the Bible remains one cohesive narrative.

This unity is not accidental — it is divinely orchestrated. The Holy Spirit, the true Author of the Bible, superintended the human writers in such a way that, despite their varied individuality, time periods, and circumstances, their contributions form one unified and powerful revelation from God.

At the heart of this unity is God Himself. The Bible does not merely tell stories or offer disconnected moral lessons. It reveals a singular, unfolding drama — the story of God's redemptive plan through Jesus Christ. This chapter will explore the nature of that unity more, how it spans both the Old and New Testaments, how Jesus and the apostles affirmed it, and what it means for how we read, interpret, and apply the Bible today.

One story from beginning to end

The Bible opens with creation, and it ends with a new creation. Genesis 1 and 2 depict the heavens and the earth being created by God, while Revelation 21 and 22 unveil the creation of a new heaven and new earth.

This symmetry is not coincidental; it reflects the overarching storyline of the Bible — a narrative arc that begins with God's perfect design, descends into human rebellion and brokenness, and culminates in restoration through divine grace.

The key moments in this grand narrative include the calling of Abraham, the formation of Israel, the giving of the Law, the ministry of the prophets, the incarnation of Jesus Christ, His atoning death and resurrection, the birth of the church, and the final consummation of all things. These events are not scattered fragments but parts of a carefully woven tapestry. Each thread contributes to the larger picture of God's purposes for humanity and creation.

For example, the covenant promises made to Abraham in Genesis find their fulfilment in Jesus Christ, as Paul explains in Galatians 3:29: *"If you belong to Christ, then you are Abraham's seed, and heirs according to the promise."* The exodus of Israel from Egypt prefigures the ultimate redemption of God's people from sin, led by Christ, the true Passover Lamb (1 Corinthians 5:7). The Law given at Sinai reveals humanity's need for a Saviour, a need answered fully in Jesus Christ (Romans 10:4). The prophets point forward to the coming of a righteous King and suffering Servant, both of whom are fulfilled in Jesus.

Unity in diversity

While the Bible is unified, it is also incredibly diverse. Its many genres include historical narrative, poetry, prophecy, wisdom literature, gospel, epistle, and apocalyptic vision. These forms allow the message of God to be communicated through various lenses, engaging the human heart and mind in multiple ways. Yet, despite this diversity of form and expression, the Bible maintains theological and thematic unity.

One of the key themes running through all Scripture is covenant. From the covenant with Noah, Abraham, and Moses, to the promised New Covenant in Jeremiah and its fulfilment in Christ, covenant serves as the backbone of the biblical storyline. Likewise, the themes of kingdom, temple, sacrifice, holiness, justice, mercy, and grace appear throughout, connecting the various parts of Scripture into one consistent message. The diversity of Scripture does not compromise its unity. Instead, it enriches our understanding by revealing the multifaceted nature of God's character and work.

In His wisdom, God used different voices, cultures, and contexts to communicate timeless truths to every generation.

Jesus and the unity of Scripture

Nowhere is the unity of Scripture more evident than in the ministry of Jesus. Throughout His teaching, Jesus affirmed the authority and coherence of the Old Testament. In Matthew 5:17, He declared, *"Do not think that I have come to abolish the Law or the Prophets; I have not come to abolish them but to fulfils them."* For Jesus, the Hebrew Scriptures were not merely historical artifacts but living, divine testimony pointing to Himself.

In Luke 24, following His resurrection, Jesus walked with two disciples on the road to Emmaus and *"beginning with Moses and all the Prophets, he explained to them what was said in all the Scriptures concerning himself."* (Luke 24:27). Later, He appeared to the larger group of disciples and said, *"This is what I told you while I was still with you: Everything must be fulfilled that is written about me in the Law of Moses, the Prophets and the Psalms."* (Luke 24:44). In this way, Jesus affirmed the tripartite division of the Hebrew Bible and identified Himself as the key to its interpretation.

Jesus did not view the Old and New as separate stories. Rather, He understood His life and mission as the climax of the story the Old Testament was telling. This means that to rightly understand the New Testament, we must know the Old. Likewise, to fully appreciate the Old Testament, we must see its fulfilment in Christ.

The apostolic witness to unity

As outlined in the previous chapter, the apostles recognized and built upon the unity of Scripture. In their preaching and writing, they consistently referenced the Old Testament, not merely to prove points but to show continuity between the ancient promises of God and their realization in Jesus Christ. Peter, in his Pentecost sermon (Acts 2), quotes extensively from Joel and the Psalms to explain the outpouring of the Holy Spirit and the resurrection of Jesus.

Paul, in his various epistles, draws from Genesis, Isaiah, Psalms, Deuteronomy, and more, in order to demonstrate that the gospel he preached was in line with God's long-standing purposes. He writes in Romans 15:4, *"For everything that was written in the past was written to teach us, so that through the endurance taught in the Scriptures and the encouragement they provide we might have hope."*

Paul also instructs Timothy, *"from infancy you have known the Holy Scriptures, which are able to make you wise for salvation through faith in Christ Jesus."* (2 Timothy 3:15). At the time Paul wrote this, the *"Holy Scriptures"* referred to the Old Testament. It is clear that the apostles did not regard the Old Testament as obsolete, but as essential and life-giving when understood in light of Christ.

A unified canon with one divine author

The unity of Scripture is further underlined by the idea of a canon—a recognized, authoritative collection of writings. The development of the biblical canon was not a random or merely human process. The church discerned, rather than decided, the canon. What bound the books together was their apostolic origin or connection, their coherence with the gospel, and their divine inspiration.

In both the Old and New Testaments, we find a consistency in theology, moral vision, and redemptive purpose. Though the literary styles and immediate contexts may vary, the Bible speaks with one voice on the most important matters of human existence—creation, fall, redemption, and consummation.

This consistency is only possible because, behind every human author, there stands the Holy Spirit. As Peter explains, *"For prophecy never had its origin in the human will, but prophets, though human, spoke from God as they were carried along by the Holy Spirit."* (2 Peter 1:21). Likewise, Paul asserts that *"All Scripture is God-breathed"* (2 Timothy 3:16), underscoring the divine source which lies behind every word. Understanding the unity of Scripture is not merely an academic exercise; it profoundly affects how we interpret and apply the Bible.

If the Bible is one cohesive message from God, then we must approach it with interpretive principles that always honour that unity. We do not pit one part of Scripture against another, nor do we disregard sections we may find difficult or culturally distant. Instead, we listen for the harmony that arises when the diverse voices of Scripture sing the same song—each part contributing to a greater whole.

The Bible's unity calls us to a holistic reading. Just as we would not understand a novel by reading a single chapter in isolation, we cannot rightly understand Scripture without considering the flow of redemptive history. This unified story has a beginning, middle, and end—creation, fall, redemption, and restoration. Every text in Scripture sits within this overarching framework, and this awareness keeps us from distorting or fragmenting God's message.

The Old Testament in the New

Nowhere is this unified reading more essential than in our understanding of how the Old Testament relates to the New. A common error among many modern readers is to view the Old Testament as somehow superseded by the New Testament. This perspective ignores the testimony of Jesus, the apostles, and the early church, all of whom affirmed the continued authority and value of the Old Testament.

The New Testament does not replace the Old—it completes it. Jesus Himself declared, *"Scripture cannot be set aside"* (John 10:35), and He repeatedly pointed to the Law, the Prophets, and the Psalms as bearing witness to Him. In Matthew 22:37-40, when asked about the greatest commandment, Jesus referred back to Deuteronomy and Leviticus. His ethical teaching did not abolish the Old Testament but illuminated its true intent. The apostles followed suit.

The book of Hebrews, for instance, is an extended meditation on how Jesus fulfils the Old Covenant, not by abolishing it, but by bringing it to its intended goal. The rich imagery of tabernacle, priesthood, and sacrifice is interpreted in light of Christ's once-for-all atonement.

Similarly, Paul's theology is soaked in Old Testament thought. In Romans, Galatians, and elsewhere, he engages with Abraham, Moses, David, and the prophets to demonstrate that justification by faith, not by works, was always God's way. The gospel he preached was *"promised beforehand through his prophets in the Holy Scriptures."* (Romans 1:2). So, this integrative use of the Old Testament models how we are to read the Bible today—not severing the Testaments from each other, but tracing the threads that connect them and always lead to Jesus Christ.

Typology and promise-fulfilment

One of the ways Scripture demonstrates its unity is through typology—the idea that certain persons, events, and institutions in the Old Testament foreshadow greater realities fulfilled in Christ. These types are not mere symbols; they are real historical elements that point forward to God's ultimate revelation.

For example, Adam is a type of Christ (Romans 5:14). Just as Adam represented humanity in the fall, Christ represents redeemed humanity in salvation. The exodus from Egypt serves as a type of spiritual liberation. The Passover lamb finds its fulfilment in Christ, *"our Passover lamb [who] has been sacrificed."* (1 Corinthians 5:7). The tabernacle and temple represent God's presence with His people, a reality fully realized in Christ, who *"tabernacled"* among us (John 1:14), and in the church, which is now God's dwelling place through the Spirit (Ephesians 2:22).

This pattern of promise and fulfilment reinforces the Bible's cohesiveness. It shows that God's plan was not improvised but deliberately executed over time. It encourages us to read with expectation, knowing that what was once concealed has now been revealed in Christ.

The moral and theological continuity

In addition to narrative and typological unity, the Bible exhibits moral and theological consistency. The attributes of God—His holiness, justice, mercy, patience, and love—are the same throughout both Testaments.

The God Who delivered Israel from Egypt is the same God who raised Jesus from the dead. His character does not change, nor does His redemptive purpose.

Some critics argue that the God of the Old Testament appears harsh and wrathful, while the New Testament reveals a God of love and grace. This dichotomy is false. The Old Testament abounds in declarations of God's love and compassion: *"The Lord, the Lord, the compassionate and gracious God, slow to anger, abounding in love and faithfulness."* (Exodus 34:6). Likewise, the New Testament contains sober warnings of judgment and calls to repentance.

God's moral vision is also consistent. While ceremonial laws tied to Israel's temple worship and national identity may no longer be binding under the New Covenant, the ethical commands rooted in God's character remain unchanged. The call to love God and neighbour, to practice justice and mercy, to reject idolatry and immorality—these are as central to the New Testament as they were to the Old.

Jesus affirms this continuity when He says, *"Anyone who sets aside one of the least of these commands and teaches others accordingly will be called least in the kingdom of heaven."* (Matthew 5:19). The Sermon on the Mount, far from dispensing with the Law, deepens its demands by addressing the heart.

The unity of the gospel message

Perhaps the greatest evidence of the Bible's unity is the consistency of its gospel message. From Genesis to Revelation, the Bible tells the story of salvation by grace through faith. Adam and Eve were clothed by God's grace after the fall. Abraham believed God, and it was credited to him as righteousness. Israel was saved from Egypt not by merit but by the blood of the lamb. The sacrificial system taught the need for atonement. The prophets called people to trust in God, not themselves. All of this culminates in the life, death, and resurrection of Jesus. The New Testament does not introduce a new plan of salvation—it reveals its fulfilment.

The good news is that what was promised long ago has now been accomplished. Paul writes, *"This righteousness is given through faith in Jesus Christ to all who believe. There is no difference... for all have sinned and fall short of the glory of God, and all are justified freely by his grace."* (Romans 3:22–24).

This unity of message is crucial. It means that the entire Bible is relevant to the believer. We do not segment the Scriptures into useful and outdated sections. Instead, we affirm: *"all Scripture is God-breathed and is useful for teaching, rebuking, correcting and training in righteousness."* (2 Timothy 3:16). This conviction then guards us against selective reading and ensures that our faith is rooted in the full counsel of God.

Reading the Bible with unity in mind

Embracing the unity of Scripture also affects how we approach specific texts. We learn to interpret Scripture with Scripture — allowing clearer passages to illuminate more difficult ones and reading each passage in light of the whole. We learn to ask, *"How does this text fit within the broader story of redemption?"* and *"What does this teach me about God's character and purposes?"*

This approach fosters humility. It reminds us that we are not the centre of the story — God is. It guards against moralism, where we reduce the Bible to a set of rules or life tips. Instead, we see the Bible as a revelation of God's grace, unfolding over time and culminating in Christ.

Moreover, it teaches us patience. Not every passage yields its riches immediately. But when we study with the awareness of Scripture's unity, we are more equipped to trace the connections, discern the themes, and discover the treasures hidden in both familiar and obscure places.

Reading with unity in mind also builds our confidence. If the Bible is truly one message, then it speaks with authority and clarity. It may be complex, but it is not contradictory. It may be challenging, but it is coherent. This gives us a firm foundation for faith and practice.

Implications for the church

For the church today, the unity of Scriptures has profound implications. It shapes our preaching, our discipleship, and our worship. It calls us to proclaim the whole counsel of God, not just our favourite portions. It invites us to disciple people with the full story of Scripture, helping them see how every part fits together and points to Jesus.

It also enriches our worship. When we sing psalms, we join with the worship of ancient Israel. When we read the prophets, we hear the voice of God calling His people to repentance and hope. When we gather around the Lord's Table, we participate in the same covenantal meal that Christ instituted as the fulfilment of the Passover.

Furthermore, it unites the global church across time and space. Believers in every generation and culture are shaped by the same Word. We may have different languages and traditions, but we share the same story — the story of a God who creates, redeems, and restores.

The living and enduring Word

The unity of Scripture is not merely conceptual or structural; it is also dynamic and living. The Word of God is not static ink on a page — it is *"alive and active,"* (Hebrews 4:12). It continues to speak with relevance and authority to every generation. This vitality arises not from human cleverness but from the breath of God Himself, for *"all Scripture is God-breathed"* (2 Timothy 3:16). It is this divine breath that binds together the many human authors, styles, contexts, and centuries into a single, coherent, Spirit-inspired message.

The enduring power of Scripture is seen in its ability to transcend time and culture. Unlike human documents, which fade with relevance and require reinterpretation, the Bible retains its central truths through the ages. Psalm 119:89 proclaims, *"Your word, Lord, is eternal; it stands firm in the heavens."* This eternal nature of God's Word reinforces its unity.

The same Word that established the heavens in Genesis is the Word made flesh in John 1. The promises spoken through the prophets are fulfilled in Christ. The commands given in ancient covenant contexts still call us to holiness and reverence. The Word is not bound by historical limits; it carries forward the purposes of God from creation to new creation.

The living quality of the Word also means that it continues to interpret and transform us. As we read Scripture, we are not standing above it, analysing it as a neutral observer might dissect a text. Rather, Scripture reads us. It pierces the soul, reveals the heart, confronts sin, and comforts the broken. The transformative power links both Testaments. The same Spirit who inspired the prophets of old now illuminates the mind of the believer to understand and respond to the Word. In this way, the Word is unified not just in content, but in effect. It is a living, active agent of divine grace across both Testaments.

The unity of divine revelation

The unity of God's Word is most clearly seen when we recognize the unified purpose behind it—God revealing Himself to His people. From Genesis to Revelation, Scripture is the record of divine self-disclosure. God speaks, God acts, God intervenes, God redeems. He does not remain silent or hidden but makes Himself known. This revelation is progressive, not because God changes, but because His people needed to grow in their capacity to receive it.

In the Old Testament, God revealed Himself through creation, through covenant, through the law, and through the prophets. These revelations were real, true, and authoritative. They were also preparatory. They laid the foundation for the full unveiling of God's character and purposes in Jesus Christ.

Each of the New Testament writers understood themselves not as replacing the old revelation, but as bearing witness to its fulfilment. Hebrews 1:1-2 declares, *"In the past God spoke to our ancestors through the prophets at many times and in various ways, but in these last days he has spoken to us by his Son."*

The Son is not a different message, but the ultimate expression of the same message: God is holy, just, gracious, and redemptive. This unified purpose of revelation gives coherence to the Bible. Every story, every psalm, every prophecy, every epistle is part of a single unfolding drama—the drama of God making Himself known so that we might know Him and be reconciled to Him. The Scriptures are not just a record of religious history; they are the Word of the living God, inviting us into fellowship with Him.

Reading the whole Bible with a Christ-centred lens

One of the most practical ways the unity of Scripture comes to life for the believer is through reading the whole Bible with a Christ-centred lens. This is not to force Christ into every passage, but to recognize that He is the climax and fulfilment of God's redemptive plan. Jesus Himself taught His disciples to read the Scriptures this way. On the road to Emmaus, He explained to them (Luke 24:27) *"what was said in all the Scriptures concerning himself."* Again in verse 44, He tells the disciples, *"Everything must be fulfilled that is written about me in the Law of Moses, the Prophets and the Psalms."*

This interpretive approach honours the integrity of the Old Testament while acknowledging its fulfilment in the New. We do not discard the earlier chapters of a novel once we reach the final chapter. In the same way, the Old Testament enriches our understanding of Christ, and Christ clarifies and deepens our appreciation of the Old Testament. The sacrificial system, for example, makes sense in the light of Jesus' once-for-all sacrifice. The kingly line of David culminates in the eternal reign of the Messiah. The covenant promises to Abraham are realized in the global church. Every thread finds its convergence in Christ.

Reading the Bible with this lens also guards us from fragmenting Scripture or mishandling it. It keeps us from moralizing Old Testament narratives without gospel context or reducing the New Testament to isolated doctrines without their redemptive-historical roots. It reminds us that the Bible is not about us—it is about God, and specifically, about His saving work in Christ.

The role of the Holy Spirit in unifying understanding

This clear unity of the Scriptures also demands a unified reading community — a people indwelt by the same Spirit who inspired the text. It is the Spirit Who guides believers into all truth, Who opens our minds to understand the Scriptures, and Who also illuminates the heart to respond in faith. Without the Spirit, the Bible becomes a closed book — capable of being read but not truly understood.

Throughout all of church history, the Spirit has preserved and clarified the unity of the biblical message through the faithful interpretation of the church. While a multitude of disagreements and distortions have arisen over time, the core truths have remained remarkably consistent: creation, fall, redemption, and restoration; the triune nature of God; salvation by grace through faith; the centrality of Christ. These are not merely theological propositions but the Spirit-breathed core of Scripture's unified witness.

Moreover, the Spirit enables the church today to interpret the Scriptures correctly, not through novel revelation, but through humble submission to the text and its true Author. This involves prayerful study, communal discernment, and a willingness to be shaped by the Word rather than to shape it to our preferences. The same Spirit who spoke through the prophets and apostles continues to speak today through the Scriptures, bringing clarity, conviction, and comfort.

The practical implications of unity

If the Bible is truly one unified Word from God, then this has profound implications for how we approach it. First, we must read all of it. We cannot treat the Old Testament as a dusty preamble or the New Testament as a detached epilogue. Both are essential to understanding God's redemptive plan. The whole counsel of God is needed to form mature, discerning, Spirit-filled believers. Second, we must interpret each part in light of the whole. This means we avoid proof-texting — isolating verses out of context to support preconceived ideas.

It also means that we study Scripture with theological depth and canonical awareness. Whether a proverb, a psalm, or a parable, each have meaning in their own right, but they also gain fuller meaning when seen within the grand story of Scripture.

Third, we must teach the Bible in a way that reflects its unity. Preachers, teachers, and disciplers must avoid presenting the Testaments as contradictory or God as inconsistent. Instead, they should highlight the continuity, the fulfilment, and the divine faithfulness that runs throughout. This builds trust in the Word and deepens faith in the God who speaks through it.

Finally, we must live as people shaped by the whole Word. This means embracing both the commands and the promises of God, both the justice and the mercy, both the warnings and the hope. It means being biblically saturated, not just in knowledge, but in obedience and devotion.

The beauty of the unified Word

There is a beauty to the Bible that becomes increasingly radiant the more we grasp its unity. It is the beauty of divine coherence, of truth woven across time and culture, of a God who is the same yesterday, today, and forever. It is the beauty of one story with many voices—like a symphony composed over centuries but perfectly harmonized. It is the beauty of the gospel echoing through every page, the heartbeat of grace pulsing through the law, the prophets, the psalms, and the epistles.

To read the Bible as a unified Word is to hear the voice of our Shepherd with increasing clarity. It is to know His ways more deeply, to trust His promises more fully, to love His Son more passionately. It is to be swept up into the great narrative of redemption that continues to unfold even now as the Spirit calls and gathers a people for God's glory. And it is to await the final chapter—not yet written in ink but promised in blood—when the unity of God's Word will be perfectly fulfilled in the unity of God's people gathered before His throne, singing, *"Great and marvellous are your deeds, Lord God Almighty. Just and true are your ways, King of the nations."* (Revelation 15:3).

- 12 -

WALKING IN NEW COVENANT FREEDOM

Freedom with a purpose

Freedom is one of the most celebrated and misunderstood concepts in the modern world. It evokes images of personal autonomy, breaking shackles, and casting off restraint. Yet when Scripture speaks of freedom — particularly the freedom found in the New Covenant — it presents something far richer and more purposeful than the mere absence of restrictions. New Covenant freedom is not an escape from responsibility - it is actually an empowerment for righteousness. It is not liberty to serve the self, but liberty to serve God in love and truth.

Paul writes in Galatians 5:1, "*It is for freedom that Christ has set us free. Stand firm, then, and do not let yourselves be burdened again by a yoke of slavery.*" This is not a vague or philosophical concept; it is a tangible reality that changes the life of the believer. The New Covenant liberates us from the legalism and futility of self-righteousness under the old system. Yet this liberation is not aimless. It is *for* something — for holiness, for love, for life in the Spirit. Christian freedom is never lawlessness - it is Spirit-filled obedience. It moves us from an external conformity to an internal transformation, from obligation to joyful surrender.

This transformation is rooted in the person and work of Jesus Christ. He fulfilled the law, bore its curse, and inaugurated a new era by His death and resurrection. In Him, we are not merely forgiven; we are renewed. We are no longer bound to sin or enslaved to fear. Instead, we are fully adopted into God's family, indwelt by His Spirit, and invited into a glorious life of intimate communion.

That is the essence of New Covenant freedom: we are free to walk with God, not merely live for Him from a distance. This communion is marked by joy, peace, and a sense of divine purpose that reshapes every area of our lives. Christian freedom is not self-directed independence but a radical dependence upon Christ.

The paradox of Christian liberty is that we are freest when we are most surrendered. Jesus taught, *"Whoever wants to be my disciple must deny themselves and take up their cross daily and follow me."* (Luke 9:23). This kind of freedom does not enslave but liberates us from the tyranny of our own sinfulness. It aligns our will with God's, transforming duty into delight and burden into blessing.

The burden of the Law removed

Before we can fully grasp what we are set free *for,* we must understand what we are free *from.* Under the Old Covenant, the law of Moses functioned as a covenantal framework that governed the life of Israel. It was holy, righteous, and good — yet it became a burden when approached as a means of justification or identity. Paul makes this clear in Romans 7:10 when he says, *"I found that the very commandment that was intended to bring life actually brought death."*

The problem was never with the law itself. It was with the human heart — our inability to meet its righteous demands. The law exposed sin but could not conquer it. It revealed the standard of holiness but offered no power to attain it. It demanded obedience but could not produce it. Instead of bringing freedom, the law became a tutor, a guardian, even a prison warden, until Christ came (Galatians 3:23-25). The law prepared the way for grace but could not itself impart it.

In the New Covenant, this burden is lifted. Hebrews 8:13 tells us that by calling the covenant *"new,"* God has made the first one obsolete. Christ, the mediator of the New Covenant, has now rendered the old system unnecessary for salvation and spiritual vitality. This does not mean that God's moral standards have changed, but the way those standards are fulfilled has been transformed.

No longer do we offer animal sacrifices or live under ceremonial regulations to remain in covenant with God. The veil has been torn. The final sacrifice has been offered. The law's demands have been met in Christ.

This freedom is not merely theological; it is intensely practical. We are free from the relentless cycle of guilt and sacrifice. We are free from the anxiety of never measuring up. We are free from the fear of condemnation. As Romans 8:1 proclaims, *"Therefore, there is now no condemnation for those who are in Christ Jesus."* This truth liberates the heart and mind to live with confidence, not insecurity. It gives the believer the courage to pursue holiness, not as a way to earn acceptance, but as a joyful response to already being accepted.

Moreover, this freedom brings a new kind of rest. The Sabbath rest foreshadowed in the Old Covenant becomes a living reality in Christ. Hebrews 4:9–10 says, *"There remains, then, a Sabbath-rest for the people of God; for anyone who enters God's rest also rests from their works, just as God did from his."* In Christ, we cease from striving and begin abiding. Our identity is no longer tied to performance but to grace. This rest is not inactivity — it is Spirit-empowered living.

Life in the Spirit

New Covenant freedom is inseparable from the indwelling presence of the Holy Spirit. The Spirit is the distinguishing mark of the New Covenant and the empowering agent of Christian freedom. Paul writes in 2 Corinthians 3:17, *"Where the Spirit of the Lord is, there is freedom."* This freedom is not abstract; it is intensely personal and transformational. It changes how we think, how we live, and how we relate to God and others.

The Spirit takes up residence in the believer, writing God's law on our hearts (Jeremiah 31:33), producing in us the fruit of righteousness (Galatians 5:22–23), and empowering us to walk in holiness. Romans 8:2 affirms, *"Through Christ Jesus the law of the Spirit who gives life has set you free from the law of sin and death."* This is the new dynamic of obedience — not legalistic observance but Spirit-empowered devotion.

This life in the Spirit brings with it a fresh capacity to love, to serve, and to discern. The Spirit equips us with gifts for ministry, empowers us to overcome sin, and leads us in truth.

John 16:13 tells us, *"But when he, the Spirit of truth, comes, he will guide you into all the truth."* This guidance is not limited to theological understanding; it encompasses every facet of life — relationships, decisions, character formation, and even suffering.

The Spirit's presence assures us that we are not alone. He is our Comforter, Advocate, and Teacher. He convicts us of sin but also assures us of grace. He challenges us to grow but also empowers us to do so. In every way, the Spirit transforms the Christian life from a burdensome duty into a living relationship. This is the heartbeat of New Covenant freedom.

Walking in the Spirit also means walking in community. The New Covenant creates not just individual believers but a Spirit-filled people. As members of the one body, we encourage one another, bear one another's burdens, and spur one another on toward love and good deeds (Hebrews 10:24). Freedom in Christ is never isolated. It thrives in fellowship and accountability. It is a shared journey into deeper grace.

This freedom is not fragile; it is resilient. It stands firm in trials, holds fast in temptation, and rejoices in hope. It is the kind of freedom that sings in prison cells, forgives enemies, and lives generously. It is the kind of freedom that can never be legislated or taken away because it is rooted in Christ Himself. This is New Covenant freedom — unshakable, glorious, and alive.

Our identity is now in Christ

As mentioned earlier, one of the most profound transformations brought about by the New Covenant is the complete redefinition of our identity. In the old system, identity was tied to lineage, nationhood, ritual observance, and adherence to the law. Under the New Covenant, however, identity is rooted in Jesus Christ Himself. We are not who we are because of what we have done or where we come from, but because of who Christ is and what He has done for us. Paul emphasizes this radical shift in 2 Corinthians 5:17: *"Therefore, if anyone is in Christ, the new creation has come: The old has gone, the new is here!"*

This is not mere metaphor; it is spiritual reality. In Christ, we are no longer defined by our failures, our sins, or our inadequacies. We are no longer strangers to God or slaves to sin. We are sons and daughters, heirs of promise, and members of the body of Christ.

This new identity comes with both privilege and responsibility. We are free from condemnation (Romans 8:1), but we are also called to live as those who have been made new. This freedom is not a license to indulge the flesh, but a summons to walk in the Spirit. Galatians 5:13 makes this tension clear: *"You, my brothers and sisters, were called to be free. But do not use your freedom to indulge the flesh; rather, serve one another humbly in love."*

When we embrace our new identity, we begin to see ourselves and others through the lens of grace. We are empowered to forgive as we have been forgiven, to love as we have been loved, and to extend mercy because we have received mercy. Our value is no longer derived from performance or status but from the unchanging love of God.

A New Covenant community is strikingly diverse, transcending the barriers that often divide humanity — race, class, gender, nationality. Paul famously declared, *"There is neither Jew nor Gentile, neither slave nor free, nor is there male and female, for you are all one in Christ Jesus."* (Galatians 3:28).

This unity does not erase our differences, it actually redeems them. Within the covenant community, diversity becomes a strength. It reflects the manifold wisdom of God, who delights to gather a people *"from every nation, tribe, people and language."* (Revelation 7:9).

The church is called to live out this unity in practical, tangible ways. That means bearing with one another in love, pursuing reconciliation, and rejecting the tribalism that characterizes so much of the world. It means welcoming the outsider, embracing the weak, and giving voice to those who are often silenced. The New Covenant community is not marked by uniformity, but by unity rooted in Christ.

As Paul wrote to the Ephesians, we are to *"make every effort to keep the unity of the Spirit through the bond of peace."* (Ephesians 4:3). Yet this unity is not automatic. It must be cultivated and guarded. The early church faced conflicts over food laws, circumcision, and cultural traditions — issues that threatened to fracture the community. But through prayer, teaching, and the work of the Spirit, they found unity in the gospel.

Today, we face different challenges — political divisions, theological disputes, generational tensions — but the call remains the same: to be one as the Father and Son are one (John 17:21).

Freedom from sin's dominion

One of the most liberating aspects of the New Covenant is the freedom from sin's dominion. While believers still wrestle with sin, we are no longer its slaves. The power of sin to control, define, and condemn us has been broken by the finished work of Christ. This is a foundational truth of the gospel.

Romans 6:6-7 declares, *"For we know that our old self was crucified with him so that the body ruled by sin might be done away with, that we should no longer be slaves to sin — because anyone who has died has been set free from sin."* This does not mean that sin ceases to exist in the believer's life, but rather that it no longer reigns. We are not helpless victims; we are Spirit-empowered overcomers.

This freedom demands a response. Paul exhorts us, *"In the same way, count yourselves dead to sin but alive to God in Christ Jesus. Therefore, do not let sin reign in your mortal body so that you obey its evil desires."* (Romans 6:11-12). Christian freedom is active, not passive. It involves reckoning with the truth of our new position in Christ and resisting the pull of the old nature.

Spiritual disciplines, such as prayer, Scripture meditation, worship, and fellowship, are not legalistic obligations but means of grace through which we grow in our freedom. They help us fix our eyes on Jesus and walk in step with the Spirit. Freedom from sin is not merely about avoiding wrong; it is about living rightly, reflecting the holiness and character of God.

Serving in the power of grace

New Covenant freedom redefines the way we serve God and others. Under the Old Covenant, service was often seen as duty — a response to command, a fulfilment of law, or an offering to appease. In the New Covenant, service becomes a joy, an act of love, and a reflection of grace.

Paul captures this beautifully in 1 Corinthians 15:10: *"But by the grace of God I am what I am, and his grace to me was not without effect. No, I worked harder than all of them - yet not I, but the grace of God that was with me."* Grace does not negate effort; it empowers it. Grace is not opposed to striving, but to earning. It transforms our labour from a burden into a blessing.

Serving in the power of grace means that our motivation changes. We no longer serve to earn God's favour but because we already have it. We do not strive for acceptance but from acceptance. This shift is crucial because it guards us from both pride and despair. When we succeed, we give glory to God. When we fail, we return to grace.

Moreover, serving in grace means that we can extend grace to others. We serve not only out of gratitude but also out of compassion. We become conduits of God's love, instruments of His peace, and agents of His kingdom. We serve the church, our communities, and the world not because we must, but because we are compelled by love.

Living in community

Freedom in the New Covenant is deeply relational. We are not set free to live in isolation but to live in community. The New Testament consistently emphasizes the communal nature of the Christian life. We are members of one body, stones in one temple, branches on one vine. Hebrews 10:24-25 urges us, *"And let us consider how we may spur one another on toward love and good deeds, not giving up meeting together, as some are in the habit of doing, but encouraging one another — and all the more as you see the Day approaching."*

True freedom includes the freedom to love, encourage, challenge, and support one another. True community provides accountability, encouragement, and opportunity. It is within a community context that we can practice forgiveness, patience, generosity, and hospitality.

It is in community that we discover our spiritual gifts and use them to build up the body. It is in community that our freedom becomes visible and fruitful.

The early church exemplified this reality. In Acts 2:42-47, we see a community devoted to teaching, fellowship, prayer, and the breaking of bread. They shared their possessions, met each other's needs, and praised God together. Their freedom was not self-centred but Christ-centred and other-focused.

Hope for the future

Finally, New Covenant freedom anchors us in a hope that transcends this world. While we experience genuine spiritual liberty now, the fullness of our freedom is yet to come. We live in the tension of the "already" and the "*not yet.*"

Romans 8:21 speaks of the creation itself being liberated from its bondage to decay and brought into the freedom and glory of the children of God. Our freedom is a foretaste of a greater liberation—when Christ returns, sin is no more, and we dwell with God in unbroken fellowship. This future hope empowers present faithfulness.

We endure trials, resist sin, and serve diligently because we know that our labour in the Lord is not in vain. We are pilgrims with a purpose, sojourners with a destination, ambassadors with a message. New Covenant freedom gives us confidence for today and courage for tomorrow.

We are not defined by our past, nor confined by our present. We are shaped by the promise of what is to come. And that promise is sure, because it is anchored in the finished work of Jesus Christ.

Freedom to love and serve

New Covenant freedom is not only a deliverance from the weight of the law and the bondage of sin; it is a liberation unto something glorious—love. Paul makes this startlingly clear in Galatians 5:13: *"You, my brothers and sisters, were called to be free. But do not use your freedom to indulge the flesh; rather, serve one another humbly in love."* Freedom in Christ is not self-catered autonomy. It is self-giving love. It enables us to live not for ourselves but for others, because we have already been fully loved and accepted by God.

This Christ-centred freedom should totally remove the anxiety of performance. Because we are secure in God's grace, we are released from the compulsion to prove our worth. No longer do we serve others to earn God's favour; we serve from the fullness of having already received it. This creates the possibility for genuine, sacrificial love. It also transforms Christian community. Instead of comparison and competition, there is mutual edification. Instead of striving for approval, there is contentment in identity. Freedom becomes fertile ground for fellowship.

This was Paul's point in Romans 13:8–10, where he writes, *"Let no debt remain outstanding, except the continuing debt to love one another, for whoever loves others has fulfilled the law... Love does no harm to a neighbour. Therefore, love is the fulfilment of the law."* In this statement, we find one of the great paradoxes of New Covenant freedom: by setting us free from the law, Christ empowers us to fulfil the very heart of it. Not through legalism, but through love. Not through external compulsion, but through internal transformation.

Freedom from condemnation

Another critical facet of New Covenant freedom is our release from all condemnation. Romans 8:1 is triumphant, *"Therefore, there is now no condemnation for those who are in Christ Jesus."* This is not merely a theoretical statement; it is a life-altering truth. The enemy of our souls, Satan, is called the accuser of the brethren. He thrives on guilt and shame.

Under the Old Covenant, the weight of guilt was heavy, and the sacrifices were a constant reminder of sin (Hebrews 10:3). But in the New Covenant, Jesus' once-for-all sacrifice puts away sin entirely (Hebrews 9:26).

This freedom from condemnation means that even when we fail, we do not fall back under judgment. We are disciplined as children, not punished as criminals. The cross absorbed the wrath that we deserved, and now, in Christ, we are declared righteous. This allows believers to walk in confidence rather than fear, in joy rather than anxiety. It fosters a boldness in prayer, a resilience in hardship, and a humility in success.

But this liberty is not license. Paul anticipates this concern in Romans 6:15: *"What then? Shall we sin because we are not under the law but under grace? By no means!"* Grace is not soft on sin—it is powerful against it. Condemnation breeds hiding and hypocrisy. Grace brings freedom to confess and change. A person who knows they are forgiven is more likely to pursue holiness than one who lives under threat. This is the strange power of gospel freedom—it makes obedience a joy rather than a burden.

Freedom to bear fruit

The imagery of fruit is a favourite in Scripture when describing the Spirit-filled life. Jesus said, *"I am the vine; you are the branches. If you remain in me and I in you, you will bear much fruit"* (John 15:5). In the New Covenant, we are no longer striving to manufacture righteousness from within ourselves. We are abiding in Christ, and as we do, His life flows through us to produce fruit. This fruit is not only personal but communal.

The fruit of the Spirit—(Galatians 5:22–23) love, joy, peace, patience, kindness, goodness, faithfulness, gentleness, and self-control—are not just internal virtues; they shape how we engage with others.

A community of believers walking in New Covenant freedom will be marked by these traits. There will be relational harmony, spiritual vitality, and a compelling witness to the world.

Legalism stifles fruit. It turns the Christian life into a checklist of do's and don'ts. But the Spirit gives life. He does not merely call us to bear fruit—He enables it. And the fruit that grows in this environment of freedom is lasting. It is not the temporary behaviour modification of outward religion; it is the inward renewal of a transformed heart.

Moreover, fruitfulness in the New Covenant includes ministry and mission. We are freed to serve, freed to witness, freed to invest in the lives of others. The Spirit equips every believer with gifts for the building up of the body (1 Corinthians 12:7). Freedom is not passive; it is productive. We are set free not only from sin, but for good works prepared in advance for us to do (Ephesians 2:10).

Freedom from fear

Fear is a cruel master. Whether it is fear of failure, fear of man, fear of the future, or fear of God's wrath, it cripples and enslaves. The Old Covenant, while holy, often left people afraid. Mount Sinai was shrouded in thunder and smoke. The Holy of Holies was inaccessible. The high priest entered it only once a year, and not without blood. The message was clear: approach with caution, lest you perish.

But the New Covenant ushers in a different atmosphere. Hebrews 12:22–24 paints a beautiful contrast: *"You have come to Mount Zion, to the city of the living God... to Jesus the mediator of a new covenant."* Under this covenant, we do not cower at a distance; we draw near with confidence (Hebrews 4:16). The Spirit we have received is not one of fear but of adoption, by whom we cry, *"Abba, Father"* (Romans 8:15).

Freedom from fear is not recklessness; it is security. It is knowing that our standing with God does not fluctuate with our performance. It is resting in the finished work of Christ. This does not make us complacent; it makes us courageous. We can take risks in faith. We can confess our sins. We can speak truth in love. We can endure suffering. Perfect love drives out fear (1 John 4:18), and in the New Covenant, we are perfectly loved.

Freedom to worship

One of the most glorious expressions of New Covenant freedom is worship. The old system restricted access to God through priests and sacrifices. Worship was largely mediated and confined to specific locations and rituals. But Jesus told the woman at the well, *"A time is coming and has now come when the true worshipers will worship the Father in the Spirit and in truth"* (John 4:23). That time has arrived.

In the New Covenant, every believer is a priest (1 Peter 2:9). We no longer go to a temple; we are the temple. Worship is no longer confined to a place—it is a posture of the heart, a life lived in response to grace. This means that worship is not just a Sunday activity; it is a daily reality. It happens in song, in service, in stillness, and in sacrifice.

This freedom to worship also brings diversity. Because we are not bound to a single form or culture, the church can express praise in manifold ways. Liturgical and spontaneous, solemn and celebratory, traditional and contemporary—what matters is not the style but the sincerity. Worship in the New Covenant is Spirit-empowered and Christ-exalting. It flows from hearts made alive by grace. Furthermore, this freedom invites intimacy.

Under the Old Covenant, the veil separated the people from the presence of God. But in Christ, the veil is torn. We behold the glory of the Lord with unveiled faces and are transformed into His image (2 Corinthians 3:18). Worship is not performance; it is communion. It is not obligation; it is delight.

Freedom with responsibility

While New Covenant freedom is glorious, it comes with responsibility. Paul urges the Galatians to stand firm and not return to the yoke of slavery (Galatians 5:1). This implies that freedom can be forfeited, or at least hindered, by wrong choices. Grace is not fragile, but it can be frustrated (Galatians 2:21). Therefore, believers are called to steward their freedom wisely.

This includes resisting legalism on one hand and licentiousness on the other. Legalism adds to the gospel and enslaves through man-made rules. Licentiousness cheapens grace and indulges the flesh. Both are distortions. True freedom is the narrow road of grace-fuelled holiness. It is a freedom that bows joyfully to the lordship of Christ.

It also includes accountability within the body. Freedom does not mean isolation. In fact, it flourishes in community. We are called to carry one another's burdens (Galatians 6:2), to spur one another on toward love and good deeds (Hebrews 10:24), and to submit to one another out of reverence for Christ (Ephesians 5:21). Freedom is not individualistic; it is relational.

Moreover, freedom must be protected. In every generation, the church must guard against attempts to reintroduce legalism or minimize sin. We must keep returning to the gospel, keep proclaiming the finished work of Christ, and keep living in the power of the Spirit. Only then will we experience the fullness of what it means to walk in New Covenant freedom.

A life worth living

Ultimately, New Covenant freedom is a call to live the life we were always meant to live—a life of holiness, love, peace, and purpose. It is a freedom that reflects the character of Christ and advances the mission of His kingdom. It is the freedom of the children of God, walking in the Spirit, resting in grace, and bearing fruit for eternity. This freedom cost Jesus everything. It was not won cheaply, and it must not be taken lightly. But it is ours. It is real. It is transformative. And it is glorious.

- 13 -

COVENANT AND THE CHURCH

A people set apart by grace

The New Covenant does not only transform individual hearts; it creates a people. From the beginning of God's dealings with humanity, covenant has always been about relationship—not merely between individuals and God, but among those who belong to Him.

When God called Abraham, He promised to make him a great nation. When He redeemed Israel from Egypt, He formed them into a covenant people. Now, under the New Covenant, this redemptive pattern continues, but it is fulfilled in a deeper, broader, and more spiritual way. The church is the covenant community of the New Covenant—a people redeemed by the blood of Christ, united by faith, and empowered by the Spirit.

This community is not defined by ethnicity, geography, or external observance, but by shared life in Christ. The Apostle Peter describes the church as *"a chosen people, a royal priesthood, a holy nation, God's special possession."* (1 Peter 2:9). These are not empty titles; they reflect the church's identity and calling. As a covenant community, we are not a collection of spiritual consumers or religious individuals—we are the body of Christ, a spiritual household, a holy temple being built together to reflect the glory of our covenant-keeping God.

A Spirit-filled fellowship

The New Covenant community is also a Spirit-filled fellowship. The same Spirit who indwells individual believers also binds them together into one body. At Pentecost, when the Spirit was poured out, the immediate result was not only bold preaching and miraculous signs but the formation of a new kind of community. Acts 2:42-47 describes a people who were daily devoting themselves to the apostles' teaching, to fellowship, to the breaking of bread, and to prayer. They shared their possessions, met one another's needs, and praised God with glad and sincere hearts.

This was not a utopian experiment or a temporary enthusiasm—it was the natural outworking of the Spirit's presence among them. Where the Spirit is at work, community flourishes. Relationships deepen. Generosity increases. Forgiveness flows. The church becomes a foretaste of the kingdom of God. Paul describes the church as the temple of the Holy Spirit a dwelling place for God among His people. This spiritual reality should shape our expectations of church life. We are not simply attending events or consuming spiritual 'products'—we are participating in a supernatural fellowship, knit together by the Spirit of Christ.

Such fellowship requires intentionality. It involves showing up, opening up, and committing to walk with others through the highs and lows of life. It means using our spiritual gifts not for personal recognition but solely for the building up of the body of Christ (1 Corinthians 12:7). It means praying for one another, confessing sins to one another, and bearing one another's burdens. These are not optional extras—they are the lifeblood of the covenant community.

A holy and missional people

The New Covenant community is called to holiness. Just as Israel was to be a holy nation, so the church is to reflect the character of God. This holiness is not primarily about separation from the world in a physical sense, but about moral and spiritual distinction. We are called to be in the world but not of it, to shine as lights in a dark place, to be salt that preserves and purifies. As Paul exhorted the Philippians, we are to *"live lives worthy of the gospel of Christ."* (Philippians 1:27).

Holiness begins in the heart, but it must be expressed in community. It affects how we speak to one another, how we handle conflict, how we use our resources, and how we treat the vulnerable. The church is to be a refuge for the broken, a sanctuary for the weary, and a training ground for discipleship. Our life together should bear witness to the reality of God's kingdom—a kingdom of righteousness, peace, and joy in the Holy Spirit (Romans 14:17).

At the same time, the New Covenant community is missional. We are not called to retreat into holy huddles or form spiritual ghettos. We are sent out as ambassadors of Christ, ministers of reconciliation, and proclaimers of the good news. Jesus said, *"As the Father has sent me, I am sending you"* (John 20:21).

The church exists not only to nurture believers but to reach the lost. Evangelism, justice, mercy, and advocacy are not peripheral activities — they are central to our identity as a covenant people. Every local church is a mission outpost. Every believer is a missionary. The Spirit who unites us also sends us. He gives boldness to speak, wisdom to engage, and compassion to serve. The church must always resist the temptation to become inward-focused or self-protective. We are stewards of a message the world desperately needs. And we are witnesses to a kingdom that cannot be shaken.

Living as the covenant community

To live as the New Covenant community is to embrace a different vision of life — a vision shaped not by individualism but by mutuality, not by consumerism but by sacrificial love. It means valuing the gathered church, committing to a local body, and investing in relationships. It means seeing church not as an event to attend but a people to belong to. This kind of life is countercultural, but it is deeply biblical.

Hebrews 10:24-25 exhorts us, *"Let us consider how we may spur one another on toward love and good deeds, not giving up meeting together, as some are in the habit of doing, but encouraging one another."* This is the heartbeat of covenant life. We need one another. We grow through one another. We reflect Christ to one another. In a world of isolation and division, the church offers something radical: a community formed by grace, sustained by the Spirit, and oriented toward God's glory.

This covenant community is not perfect — far from it. But it is precious. It is the bride of Christ, the household of God, the pillar and foundation of the truth. And it is through this community that God is making Himself known to the world.

Mutual responsibility and loving accountability

Life within the covenant community is not individualistic; it is deeply communal. The New Covenant transforms not only our relationship with God but also our relationships with one another.

At the heart of this transformation is mutual responsibility. Believers are called to bear one another's burdens, to encourage one another daily, and to spur one another on toward love and good deeds (Galatians 6:2; Hebrews 3:13; 10:24). This shared responsibility creates a culture of loving accountability — where grace does not excuse sin but empowers godly living.

Paul, writing to the church in Galatia, says, *"Brothers and sisters, if someone is caught in a sin, you who live by the Spirit should restore that person gently. But watch yourselves, or you also may be tempted."* (Galatians 6:1). This passage exemplifies the balance between grace and truth. Accountability in the New Covenant is not about condemnation but restoration. It is the loving act of helping a brother or sister realign with the truth of the gospel, always mindful of our own vulnerability and dependence on grace.

In this context, church discipline is not punitive but redemptive. It aims to reclaim the straying believer and reaffirm the holiness of the community. The goal is always restoration, not exclusion. In 2 Thessalonians 3:15, Paul instructs the church regarding a disobedient member: *"Do not regard them as an enemy, but warn them as you would a fellow believer."* Even in correction, the underlying tone is one of familial love.

The practice of forgiveness

One of the defining features of the covenant community is its commitment to forgiveness. Jesus taught that forgiveness must be limitless: *"I tell you, not seven times, but seventy-seven times."* (Matthew 18:22). This is not merely a matter of arithmetic but of attitude. The community of believers is a forgiven people, and they are called to be a forgiving people.

Forgiveness is not optional—it is essential. In Colossians 3:13, Paul writes, *"Bear with each other and forgive one another if any of you has a grievance against someone. Forgive as the Lord forgave you."* The standard is daunting: as the Lord forgave us. And yet, it is precisely because we have been forgiven so fully and freely in Christ that we are empowered to forgive others.

Forgiveness becomes both a testimony to the gospel and a means of maintaining unity in the body. This does not mean that forgiveness is easy. It often involves deep pain and great cost.

But the New Covenant provides the resources to forgive: the assurance that God is just, the promise that vengeance belongs to Him, and the example of Jesus who, while suffering unjustly, prayed, *"Father, forgive them."* (Luke 23:34). In forgiving, we imitate Christ and walk in the freedom He secured for us.

Generosity and shared resources

Another mark of the covenant community is generosity. The early church in Acts is a striking example of this. In Acts 2:44-45, we read, *"All the believers were together and had everything in common. They sold property and possessions to give to anyone who had need."* This was not communism or forced redistribution, but voluntary, Spirit-led generosity born of love and shared purpose.

In the New Covenant, our possessions are no longer our own—they are resources entrusted to us by God for the blessing of others. Generosity becomes a tangible expression of covenant love. Paul commends the Macedonian churches because of their generosity, saying, *"In the midst of a very severe trial, their overflowing joy and their extreme poverty welled up in rich generosity."* (2 Corinthians 8:2). They gave beyond their ability, motivated not by compulsion but by grace.

This kind of generosity is not limited to financial support; it extends to time, hospitality, service, and emotional investment. The covenant community is one where needs are met—not just because it is the right thing to do, but because it reflects the heart of God.

Paul reminds us in 2 Corinthians 9:7, *"God loves a cheerful giver,"* and the cheerful giver reflects the character of a God who gave us His Son.

Unity in diversity

One of the greatest testimonies of the New Covenant community is its unity in diversity. The gospel breaks down the walls that divide us — ethnic, social, economic, and cultural — and creates one new humanity in Christ. Paul writes, *"There is neither Jew nor Gentile, neither slave nor free, nor is there male and female, for you are all one in Christ Jesus."* (Galatians 3:28).

This unity does not erase diversity but redeems it. The body of Christ is composed of many parts, each with unique gifts, perspectives, and roles. In 1 Corinthians 12, Paul describes the church as a body made up of different members, all essential and interdependent. *"The eye cannot say to the hand, 'I don't need you!'"* (v. 21). In the covenant community, every person matters, every gift is valued, and every member is needed.

Diversity is not a threat to unity — it is its beauty. But maintaining unity amid diversity requires humility, patience, and love. Paul exhorts the Ephesians to *"make every effort to keep the unity of the Spirit through the bond of peace."* (Ephesians 4:3). Unity is not automatic; it must be pursued. And it is only possible through the power of the Spirit and the centrality of Christ.

Worship as a community identity

Worship is both the heartbeat and the lifeblood of the covenant community. It is in worship that we remember who we are and whose we are. Corporate worship is not just a weekly ritual but a formative act that reorients our hearts, renews our minds, and strengthens our bonds.

The psalmist says, "I rejoiced with those who said to me, 'Let us go to the house of the Lord'" (Psalm 122:1). Worship is a shared joy. In the New Covenant, worship is no longer tied to a specific place like the temple in Jerusalem.

Jesus told the Samaritan woman that *"a time is coming when you will worship the Father neither on this mountain nor in Jerusalem... true worshipers will worship the Father in the Spirit and in truth."* (John 4:21-23). Worship becomes a spiritual act, empowered by the Spirit and grounded in the truth of the gospel.

Nevertheless, corporate worship remains vital. Hebrews 10:25 warns us not to give up meeting together, as some are in the habit of doing, *"but encouraging one another – and all the more as you see the Day approaching."* The church gathers to sing, pray, hear the Word, partake in the sacraments, and encourage one another. In these gatherings, the presence of Christ is made manifest in unique and powerful ways.

Leadership and servanthood

Leadership in the covenant community reflects the values of the New Covenant itself – grace, humility, and service. Jesus turned worldly ideas of leadership upside down when He told His disciples, *"Whoever wants to become great among you must be your servant."* (Matthew 20:26). In the New Covenant, leadership is not about status or control but about shepherding and sacrifice.

Elders and pastors are called to be examples to the flock, not domineering but serving willingly (1 Peter 5:2-3). They are to equip the saints for the work of ministry, to teach sound doctrine, and to guard the church from false teaching (Ephesians 4:11-13; Titus 1:9). But leadership is not limited to formal roles.

Every believer is gifted by the Spirit and called to exercise influence within the body, whether that is through teaching, hospitality, encouragement, or service.

At the same time, the community is called to respect and support its leaders. *"Have confidence in your leaders and submit to their authority,"* the writer of Hebrews says, *"because they keep watch over you as those who must give an account."* (Hebrews 13:17). This mutual relationship of loving leadership and joyful submission fosters trust and spiritual maturity.

A people on mission

The covenant community is not an inward-focused club but an outward-reaching movement. Jesus commissioned His disciples to *"go and make disciples of all nations."* (Matthew 28:19), and that commission belongs to the whole church. The New Covenant community is called to proclaim the true gospel, embody the kingdom, and bear witness to the reign of Christ.

This mission is local and global. It involves personal evangelism, social justice, mercy ministries, and cross-cultural outreach. It means we are living as salt and light in our neighbourhoods, workplaces, and schools. It means supporting missionaries, praying for all unreached peoples, and engaging in acts of compassion and reconciliation. The mission of the church is not an optional add-on — it is intrinsic to its identity. Jesus said, *"As the Father has sent me, I am sending you."* (John 20:21). The covenant community is a sent people, empowered by the Spirit and anchored in the gospel. Our message is one of hope, our motive is love, and our model is Christ.

Enduring together in hope

Throughout redemptive history, God's covenant community has been marked not only by its privileges but by its perseverance. From the wilderness wanderings of Israel to the persecution of the early church, the people of God have never been strangers to hardship.

What distinguishes the New Covenant community is not merely its endurance but the hope that fuels its endurance — a hope grounded in the promises of God, fulfilled in Christ, and sealed by the Spirit.

Romans 5:1-5 reminds us, *"Therefore, since we have been justified through faith, we have peace with God through our Lord Jesus Christ... Not only so, but we also glory in our sufferings, because we know that suffering produces perseverance; perseverance, character; and character, hope."* This is not mere stoicism or blind optimism. It is the supernatural resilience that flows from being rooted in the eternal covenant of grace.

The church only endures because God's promises endure. We persevere because we are held fast by the One who covenanted Himself to us. The church is not a collection of individuals trying to survive spiritual battles. It is a body, a household, a city on a hill. When one member suffers, the others suffer with them; when one rejoices, the others share that joy (1 Corinthians 12:26). This is the power of covenantal life—it binds us together not in mere sympathy but in spiritual solidarity. We carry one another's burdens (Galatians 6:2), we pray for each other (James 5:16), we spur one another on toward love and good deeds (Hebrews 10:24). This is not optional; it is our identity. The covenant community exists as a living testimony to the truth that God is faithful, even in suffering.

Such perseverance is never passive. It is a Spirit-empowered determination to press on when everything in us cries out to give up. Hebrews 12:1-2 exhorts us, *"Let us run with perseverance the race marked out for us, fixing our eyes on Jesus, the pioneer and perfecter of faith."* The covenant community is not marching toward defeat but toward victory—because Christ has already overcome. Every trial, setback and heartbreak is reframed in the light of eternity. The church is not being dismantled by the world's hostility; it is being refined, prepared, and purified for her Bridegroom.

A pilgrim people

One of the most poignant themes in the New Testament is that of the church as a pilgrim people. The covenant community lives in the tension of the *"now"* and the *"not yet."* We have already received the promises of God in Christ, but we have not yet seen their full consummation. Hebrews 11 gives us a sweeping portrait of the saints who lived by faith, *"longing for a better country—a heavenly one. Therefore, God is not ashamed to be called their God, for he has prepared a city for them."* (v. 16).

This pilgrim identity shapes the way we live in the world. We are not settlers; we are sojourners. We do not put our hope in earthly systems, governments, or institutions.

Though we are called to be salt and light, to work for the good of our cities and nations, we remember that our citizenship is in heaven (Philippians 3:20). Our true home is not here. We are exiles whose compass always points homeward.

Yet this longing does not make us passive or disengaged. On the contrary, it gives our lives urgency and focus. Because we are not living for this world's fleeting pleasures, we can invest our time, resources, and energy in things that will last.

We build for eternity. We disciple, we evangelize, we serve, and we sacrifice because we know that this present world is passing away. As Peter writes, *"Since everything will be destroyed in this way, what kind of people ought you to be? You ought to live holy and godly lives... looking forward to the day of God."* (2 Peter 3:11–12).

The covenant community is not a people without roots; we are rooted in Christ. But our roots reach beyond this age into the soil of the age to come. We live as those who await the return of the King, the resurrection of the dead, and the restoration of all things. That vision compels us to live differently, to walk by faith and not by sight, to endure the scorn of the world with joy, knowing that our inheritance is secure.

Worship as a covenant response

At the heart of the covenant community is worship — true, Spirit-filled, Christ-exalting worship. The New Covenant has reoriented worship away from the temple in Jerusalem to the gathered body of believers. Now we worship the Father in the Spirit and in truth. Worship is no longer confined to sacred places or ritual forms. It is the living expression of a redeemed people offering themselves to God.

Romans 12:1 captures the covenantal nature of New Testament worship: *"In view of God's mercy, offer your bodies as a living sacrifice, holy and pleasing to God — this is your true and proper worship."* We do not worship to earn covenant status; we worship because we are already His. Our worship is response, not performance. It is gratitude, not obligation. It is delight, not duty.

This worship is communal. Though each believer can worship privately, there is a unique glory in the church's corporate voice rising as one before the throne of God. This worship is more than singing or liturgy. It is the total orientation of our lives toward God. It is seen in how we treat one another, how we steward our gifts, how we respond to trials, and how we proclaim the gospel.

In the covenant community, every act of love, every expression of faith, every moment of obedience becomes an offering of worship. This is why the church gathers — not to check a religious box but to recalibrate our hearts around the beauty of Christ and the reality of our shared covenant.

The mission of the covenant community

God's covenant with His people was never meant to be inward-focused or self-contained. From the beginning, God's promise to Abraham included all the nations: *"All peoples on earth will be blessed through you."* (Genesis 12:3). The New Covenant does not erase that mission; it fulfils it. Jesus sent His disciples into the world to make disciples of all nations... teaching them to obey everything Jesus had commanded them. The church exists not just to worship and fellowship, but to witness.

The covenant community is a missionary community. We are sent people. Every believer, whether across the globe or across the street, is called to be a witness to the grace and truth of Jesus. This is not a secondary feature of church life — it is central to our identity. We are ambassadors of the King, heralds of the New Covenant, bearers of light in a world of darkness.

Mission is not a burden but a joy. It is not about human strategy but about divine power. We proclaim a message that is not ours but God's — a message that has the power to raise the dead, heal the broken, and reconcile the lost. The gospel is not a suggestion; it is a summons. It calls every person to repentance and faith and offers the free gift of covenant relationship with God through Jesus Christ. This mission must shape everything we do as a covenant people. It must infuse our worship with urgency, our fellowship with purpose, and our structures with flexibility.

The early church understood this. They met daily in homes and temple courts, shared everything they had, and preached boldly despite persecution. Why? Because they believed the risen Christ had entrusted them with the greatest news the world would ever hear.

We are entrusted too. Our context differs, but our commission does not. The New Covenant community exists to know Christ and to make Him known. This is not optional. It is who we are.

The glory of the covenant fulfilled

In the final book of the Bible, we see the full consummation of God's covenant purposes. Revelation 21:3 declares, *"Now the dwelling of God is with men, and he will live with them. They will be his people, and God himself will be with them and be their God."* This is covenant language. It echoes the refrain of Scripture from Genesis to Revelation: *"I will be your God, and you will be my people."*

What began in Eden, was distorted by sin, and progressively restored through covenant history, will finally reach its glorious fulfilment in the new creation. The covenant community will no longer be threatened by sin, death, or sorrow. We will see God face to face, and His name will be on our foreheads. No temple will be needed, for the Lord God Almighty and the Lamb will be our temple. No sun or moon will be required, for the glory of God will be our light.

In that moment, the church will fully become what she has always been destined to be: the Bride of Christ, radiant and without blemish, dwelling in eternal union with her Lord. The New Covenant will reach its final crescendo, and the people of God will rejoice in unbroken communion forever.

This is not a dream; it is our destiny. It is the guaranteed outcome of a covenant sealed in blood, sustained by grace, and secured by divine promise. Until that day, we live in anticipation. We love, we serve, we endure, and we proclaim. We do not shrink back; we press on.

The covenant community may be battered by history, maligned by culture, and flawed by weakness—but it is precious to God. It is the vessel of His purposes, the theatre of His glory, the first fruits of the new creation.

Let us therefore embrace our identity, cherish our calling, and live as those who truly belong to the covenant community of the living God.

COVENANT AND KINGDOM

The divine framework

From Genesis to Revelation, two great themes form the backbone of God's amazing redemptive work with humanity: covenant and kingdom. These are not isolated theological concepts but interconnected dimensions of the same divine narrative. The covenant is God's chosen means of establishing relationship, while the kingdom is the outworking of His sovereign reign through those very relationships. Understanding the harmony between covenant and kingdom is essential for grasping the overarching story of Scripture and the life God calls us to in Christ.

When we speak about *covenant*, we refer to God's faithful commitment to His people—a binding agreement initiated by divine grace. God has covenanted with humanity not out of obligation, but out of love and purpose. These covenants define the relationship between God and His people and progressively unfold throughout the biblical storyline. From Noah, Abraham, Moses, and David to the New Covenant in Christ, each covenant builds on the last, revealing more of God's redemptive intent.

The *kingdom*, on the other hand, speaks to God's rule and reign. It is not merely a geographical or political entity but the dynamic reality of God's authority manifesting on earth as it is in heaven. The kingdom comes wherever God's will is done, and God's purposes are advanced. This rule is exercised through covenant partners—individuals and communities bound to Him by grace and called to live under His lordship.

Thus, covenant and kingdom are not two parallel lines but deeply entwined. The covenant establishes the relationship, and the kingdom defines the mission. God's people are not just saved *from* something (sin, judgment, death), they are also saved *for* something—namely, to represent and extend God's rule and reign on the earth.

Kingdom mandate from the beginning

The interplay between covenant and kingdom is not just a New Testament innovation—it begins in Eden. In Genesis 1:26-28, God creates humanity in His image and commands them to *"be fruitful and increase in number; fill the earth and subdue it. Rule over the fish in the sea and the birds in the sky and over every living creature."* This is the first expression of the kingdom mandate. Human beings are commissioned as vice-regents, tasked with stewarding creation under God's sovereign rule.

This mandate was always relational. Adam and Eve were not autonomous rulers; their authority flowed from their covenant relationship with God. They were to reflect His character, implement His will, and walk in intimacy with Him. But the fall in Genesis 3 fractured this harmony. Adam and Eve violated the covenant, and as a result, the kingdom expression of God's rule through humanity was distorted. Sin brought alienation, chaos, and a struggle for power divorced from divine authority.

Yet even in judgment, God's covenant purpose was never abandoned. The promise of Genesis 3:15, that the seed of the woman would crush the serpent's head, set the trajectory for the reestablishment of God's kingdom through covenant renewal. From this point forward, the rest of Scripture unfolds as the outworking of that promise—the restoration of covenant relationship and kingdom rule through divine initiative.

The Abrahamic Covenant: Blessing for the nations

The call of Abraham in Genesis 12 marks a significant development in God's plan. Here, the covenant and kingdom become explicitly missional. God tells Abram: *"I will make you into a great nation, and I will bless you; I will make your name great, and you will be a blessing... and all peoples on earth will be blessed through you."* (Genesis 12:2-3)

The covenant is not merely personal; it is global in its scope. Through Abraham, a family will arise—a covenant people—who will carry the blessings of God's reign to all nations.

This blessing is not only material but spiritual: to know the living God, to be reconciled to Him, and to live under His lordship. In Genesis 15, we see God formalizing this promise with a covenant ceremony, and in Genesis 17, He adds the sign of circumcision. Abraham's descendants, through Isaac and Jacob, will become the nation of Israel — a people uniquely chosen to embody God's covenant and display His kingdom to the world.

But Israel's vocation was always *representative*, not exclusive. They were chosen not instead of the nations, but *for* the sake of the nations. As Exodus 19:5-6 says, *"Although the whole earth is mine, you will be for me a kingdom of priests and a holy nation."* The kingdom mission is reaffirmed: Israel is to be a priestly people, mediating God's presence and rule to the world.

The Mosaic Covenant and theocratic kingdom

With the Exodus, God redeems His people from slavery and brings them into a covenantal relationship at Mount Sinai. Here, the themes of covenant and kingdom are joined in a powerful way. God declares in Exodus 19:4, *"I carried you on eagles' wings and brought you to myself."* The covenant is once again rooted in grace — God initiates, rescues, and then invites Israel into a life of obedience as His treasured possession.

The giving of the law was not a means of salvation but a charter for living as God's kingdom people. The Torah set Israel apart, not to elevate them above others, but to display a different way of life under God's rule. The law was meant to shape their national identity as a theocracy — God Himself as King, ruling through His Word and His appointed leaders.

However, Israel struggled to live faithfully within this covenant. They frequently rebelled, chasing after other gods, violating justice, and resisting God's commands. The covenant curses described in Deuteronomy 28 were the natural consequence of rejecting the King's rule. But even then, God's faithfulness endured. He repeatedly sent prophets to call His people back, reminding them of both the covenant and their kingdom calling.

The Davidic Covenant and kingdom foreshadowed

A significant turning point comes with the establishment of the monarchy. Though God allowed Israel to have a king, the true intent was that the king would be a servant under God's supreme rule. Saul failed to fulfil this calling, but David became the model of a covenantal king – imperfect, yet after God's own heart.

In 2 Samuel 7, God makes a covenant with David, promising that his lineage would endure and that his throne would be established forever. This is not merely about politics or dynastic succession; it is about the convergence of covenant and kingdom in a messianic hope. A future king from David's line would rule with justice and righteousness, restoring the blessings of Eden and fulfilling the promises to Abraham.

The prophets build upon this expectation. Isaiah speaks of a child born to us, a son given, whose government will be on His shoulders and who will reign on David's throne forever (Isaiah 9:6–7). Jeremiah declares, *"The days are coming... when I will make a new covenant with the people of Israel and with the people of Judah."* (Jeremiah 31:31), and in the same breath speaks of a righteous Branch from David's line who will reign as King (23:5–6).

Thus, the Old Testament concludes with a growing sense of anticipation: God will restore His people, renew His covenant, and reestablish His kingdom through a coming Messiah.

Jesus: The fulfilment of covenant and kingdom

Jesus arrives on the scene declaring, *"The time has come... The kingdom of God has come near. Repent and believe the good news!"* (Mark 1:15). This is not a generic call to spirituality – it is the announcement that God's kingdom is breaking in, and that the long-awaited covenant promises are being fulfilled in Him.

Jesus is the true Son of David, the righteous King, the faithful Israelite, and the perfect covenant partner. In His life, He embodies the obedience Israel failed to render. In His death, He bears the covenant curse for our unfaithfulness.

In His resurrection, He inaugurates a new creation and secures the blessings of the kingdom for all who trust in Him. At the Last Supper, Jesus declares, *"This cup is the new covenant in my blood, which is poured out for you."* (Luke 22:20). With these words, He binds together the themes of covenant and kingdom. His blood secures the new relationship, and His resurrection guarantees the new reign. Those who belong to Him are not only forgiven — they are made citizens of the kingdom, ambassadors of His reign, and partakers of His divine nature.

The kingdom is not merely future. It is now — present wherever Jesus is acknowledged as Lord, and His Spirit empowers obedience, justice, love, and mercy. Yet it is also not fully realized. We live in the "already/not yet" tension, awaiting the day when Christ will return to consummate His kingdom and dwell with His covenant people forever.

Living as covenant people in a kingdom world

Having explored the theological foundations of covenant and kingdom, the natural progression is to consider the practical outworking of this divine framework in the life of the believer and the church. What does it mean to live as people of the New Covenant under the reign of the risen King? How do covenant and kingdom shape our identity, our mission, and our daily walk with God? The answers are not abstract or philosophical — they are profoundly tangible and deeply transformative.

In the New Covenant, the believer is not only covenant-bound, but also kingdom-sent. These are not two separate callings but two interwoven aspects of exactly the same divine purpose. The covenant provides the relational security: we are God's children, redeemed, forgiven, and sealed by His Spirit. The kingdom provides the missional urgency: we are God's ambassadors, sent to proclaim His reign and demonstrate His righteousness in a broken world. This dual identity finds its roots in the life and teachings of Jesus. He was the perfect covenant partner, living in unbroken intimacy with the Father. He was also the perfect kingdom representative, preaching the good news, healing the sick, and confronting the forces of evil.

As followers of Christ, we are called to walk in His steps, empowered by His Spirit, anchored in His love, having been commissioned for His work.

Who we are

Understanding our covenant identity is actually foundational to kingdom living. Before we can serve, proclaim, or confront, we must know who we are. The covenant answers that question: we are God's beloved. We are His children, adopted into His family, cleansed by the blood of Christ, and indwelt by the Spirit. This identity is not achieved but received. It is not earned by merit but granted by grace.

Romans 8:15-16 declares, *"The Spirit you received does not make you slaves, so that you live in fear again; rather, the Spirit you received brought about your adoption to sonship. And by him we cry, 'Abba, Father.' The Spirit himself testifies with our spirit that we are God's children."* This relational reality transforms everything. We no longer serve God to earn His approval—we serve because we already have it. We do not strive to secure love—we act out of the abundance of love already given.

Covenant identity also shapes how we view sin and failure. In the old covenant framework, disobedience often led to exile, punishment, and broken fellowship. In the New Covenant, while sin grieves the Spirit and disrupts our communion, it does not alter our status as sons and daughters.

Hebrews 10:14 affirms, *"For by one sacrifice he has made perfect forever those who are being made holy."* We are secure even as we are being sanctified. This gives us the freedom to confess, repent, and rise again—not in shame, but in faith. Living out this identity also cultivates humility and gratitude. We recognize that everything we have—life, forgiveness, purpose, hope—is a gift. Covenant people are thankful people. They live with open hands and soft hearts, knowing that they belong not because of their performance but because of God's promise. This security frees us from the fear of man and the need to prove ourselves. It liberates us to love boldly and serve generously.

Why we are here

If covenant tells us who we are, the kingdom tells us why we are here. The believer is not only saved from sin but saved for mission. We are called to extend the reign of Christ in every sphere of life—to embody His values, announce His gospel, and confront injustice wherever it exists. The church is not merely a worshiping community; it is a kingdom outpost, a colony of heaven in the midst of a fallen world.

This mission is rooted in Jesus' Great Commission: *"All authority in heaven and on earth has been given to me. Therefore go and make disciples of all nations..."* (Matthew 28:18–19).

Here we see the overlap: the King with all authority sends His covenant people into the world to make disciples, baptizing them into the covenant and teaching them to obey everything He commanded. This is kingdom work flowing from covenant grace.

But the mission is not limited to evangelism. It encompasses the holistic transformation of lives, communities, and cultures. In Luke 4, Jesus reads from Isaiah and declares His mission: to preach good news to the poor, proclaim freedom for the prisoners, recovery of sight for the blind, and to set the oppressed free.

This is not mere rhetoric—it is the blueprint for kingdom engagement. It calls us to social justice, to healing ministries, to reconciliation efforts, and to advocacy for the marginalized.

Kingdom mission also means living counter-culturally. We do not conform to the patterns of this world but are transformed by the renewing of our minds (Romans 12:2). In a culture obsessed with power, we serve. In a world driven by greed, we give. In an age of polarization, we forgive.

In a society of self-promotion, we walk in humility. These actions are not just good morals—they are kingdom demonstrations. They reveal what God is like and draw others to His reign.

The church as a covenant kingdom community

The church is where covenant and kingdom converge most clearly. It is the gathered people of God — redeemed by grace and commissioned for mission. It is the community of the New Covenant, bound by love, shaped by the Word, and empowered by the Spirit. It is also the primary vehicle through which God's kingdom advances in the world.

Acts 2 offers a vivid picture of this reality. After Pentecost, the early believers *"devoted themselves to the apostles' teaching and to fellowship, to the breaking of bread and to prayer… All the believers were together and had everything in common… And the Lord added to their number daily those who were being saved."* (Acts 2:42-47). This is a covenant community living out a kingdom vision. They worship, grow, serve, and multiply — all under the lordship of Christ.

The church is the visible expression of God's covenant and kingdom on earth. It is not merely an organization, but an organism — a living, breathing community indwelt by the Spirit, formed by grace, and sent on mission. The church is both the bride of Christ and the body of Christ, bound to Him in covenant love and commissioned by Him to carry forward the kingdom.

In Ephesians 2:19-22, Paul paints a picture of the church as *"a holy temple in the Lord,"* built together into a dwelling place for God by the Spirit. This image fuses covenant and kingdom. We are God's people, chosen and cherished, but we are also God's dwelling, a launch point for His reign to extend into the world.

This dual identity shapes everything the church does. Worship is not just covenant response; it is kingdom declaration. Fellowship is not just community; it is formation for mission. Discipleship is not mere information transfer; it is kingdom training. Evangelism is not a sales pitch; it is a royal announcement: *"Jesus is King. Come and follow Him."* Tragically, many churches lose sight of this dual calling. Some emphasize covenant at the expense of kingdom, retreating into a safe but passive spirituality.

Others chase kingdom action without covenant grounding, leading to burnout or compromise. But when both are held together, the church becomes what it was meant to be: a prophetic, priestly people called to declare and demonstrate the reign of God in every sphere of life. Today, the church is called to embody the same dynamic. It must be a place of radical grace and also radical obedience. A people where racial, social, and economic barriers are torn down. A people who love one another deeply, forgive readily, and serve sacrificially. A people who proclaim the gospel, heal the sick, and confront evil with the authority of Christ. In short, the church is not a building or a program—it is a covenant family on a kingdom mission.

This also means that discipleship must be holistic. It is not merely about learning doctrine or attending services. It is about forming people who know God deeply, live in authentic community, and engage the world with courage and compassion. Discipleship is the process by which covenant identity and kingdom mission are internalized and practiced over a lifetime.

Challenges to living in the tension

Yet we must be honest—living in the intersection of covenant and kingdom is not easy. There are dangers on both sides. Some believers emphasize the covenant to the neglect of the kingdom. They enjoy the security of salvation but have little passion for mission.

Others emphasize the kingdom and lose sight of the covenant. They become activists without intimacy, workers without worship. This imbalance leads to burnout, legalism, or apathy. The only remedy is to continually return to the gospel—the good news that God has invited us into a relationship (covenant) and a purpose (kingdom) through Jesus Christ.

We must drink deeply of grace and then rise to extend that grace to others. We must rest in our identity and then engage our world with boldness. This rhythm of abiding and going, receiving and giving, defines the Christian life.

There is also the challenge of opposition. Kingdom people will face resistance—spiritual, cultural, and personal. Jesus warned that His followers would be misunderstood, persecuted, and hated. But He also promised His presence: *"Surely I am with you always, to the very end of the age."* (Matthew 28:20). Covenant loyalty sustains kingdom faithfulness. Knowing that we are loved and chosen enables us to endure and press on.

The kingdom in action: Ambassadors of the covenant

The convergence of covenant and kingdom is not meant to be a lofty theological construct locked in academia or church pulpits—it is the foundation for daily Christian living. When we grasp that we are covenant partners with the King of kings and that we bear His authority to represent Him in the world, everything changes. The Christian life is not passive. It is an active participation in the unfolding mission of God, empowered by the Spirit, grounded in grace, and directed by divine purpose. Jesus made this dynamic explicitly clear when He said to His disciples in John 20:21, *"As the Father has sent me, I am sending you* In the same breath with which He affirms their security in His resurrection, He commissions them.

Kingdom people are always sent people. Covenant people are commissioned people. We are not called to merely enjoy the blessings of salvation but to embody and extend them. This calling takes on tangible expression in our relationships, vocations, choices, and worship. We do not live for ourselves, because we were bought at a price (1 Corinthians 6:19-20). We live under the reign of a gracious King who empowers us to bring His kingdom to bear in the world—through justice, mercy, truth, and love.

The Apostle Paul captures this beautifully in 2 Corinthians 5:20 when he writes, *"We are therefore Christ's ambassadors, as though God were making his appeal through us."* Ambassadors operate with authority, but it is delegated authority. They represent not themselves, but the King who sends them. As ambassadors of the New Covenant, our identity is wrapped in grace, but our purpose is inseparable from mission.

Covenant obedience and kingdom responsibility

The life of faith under the New Covenant is marked by loving obedience – not as a means to secure our relationship with God, but as its natural outworking. This obedience is not rigid legalism nor unthinking servitude. It is the response of covenant love to the rule of a worthy King. Jesus links love and obedience in profound simplicity in John 14:15, *"If you love me, keep my commands."* The commands of Christ are not external laws chiselled in stone; they are now written on our hearts by the Spirit (Jeremiah 31:33). This transformation from within is what makes New Covenant living so radically different from the religious striving of the old system. It is not a burden we carry – it is a life we live.

At the same time, kingdom responsibility demands that we take seriously our role in advancing God's purposes in the world. The parable of the talents in Matthew 25 underscores this: the King entrusts His servants with resources, expecting them to use and multiply them for His glory. Those who bury their gifts or neglect their calling are not commended. Faithfulness is not just about preservation; it's about fruitfulness.

Covenant and kingdom together form the crucible in which this fruitfulness is forged. The covenant secures our relationship with God, ensuring that we labour from acceptance, not for it. The kingdom gives us the context in which our labour matters, as we live out the reality of God's reign in a world that desperately needs His justice, peace, and truth.

Suffering, struggle, and sovereignty

Living as kingdom ambassadors in covenant relationship does not exempt us from suffering. In fact, it often increases it. Jesus warned His followers, *"In this world you will have trouble. But take heart! I have overcome the world."* (John 16:33). Paul echoes this truth in Romans 8:17, saying that we are *"heirs of God and co-heirs with Christ, if indeed we share in his sufferings in order that we may also share in his glory."* The tension between the *now* and the *not yet* of the kingdom ensures that suffering and struggle remain part of the Christian life.

The kingdom is inaugurated, but not yet consummated. Christ reigns, but every knee has not yet bowed. We live in this in-between time as witnesses to a kingdom that is present but still unfolding. The covenant sustains us in this tension. Because our relationship with God is not dependent on our circumstances but on His faithfulness, we can endure hardship with hope. Kingdom citizens are not promised comfort, but they are always promised victory. This is not necessarily victory in the temporal sense—but ultimate, eternal, spiritual triumph.

The sovereignty of God undergirds both covenant and kingdom. We do not serve a King who is scrambling to respond to world events. He sits enthroned in the heavens, unshaken by the chaos of nations. His purposes are sure. As Psalm 103:19 proclaims, *"The Lord has established his throne in heaven, and his kingdom rules over all."* That rule includes both the grand sweep of redemptive history and the intimate details of our personal journeys.

The hope of consummation

The story of covenant and kingdom is moving toward a climactic fulfilment. Revelation gives us a breathtaking glimpse of this hope: *"Now the dwelling of God is with men, and he will live with them… They will be his people, and God himself will be with them and be their God."* This is covenant in its ultimate form—which is unmediated, uninterrupted fellowship with God. And it is kingdom in its consummate expression—every knee bowed, every power subdued, every tear wiped away. No more rebellion, injustice, or death.

Until that day, we live in anticipation. We pray, as Jesus taught us, *"Your kingdom come, your will be done, on earth as it is in heaven."* (Matthew 6:10). And we labour, empowered by the Spirit, to live as faithful covenant partners and courageous and as kingdom ambassadors. Our calling is not easy, but it is glorious. We walk in grace, but we also stand in authority. We rest in the promises of God, but we also run with the purpose of God. This is the life of the Christian under the New Covenant—deeply loved, radically sent, and joyfully engaged in the unfolding drama of God's kingdom.

- 15 -

COVENANT AND THE CROSS

The cross at the heart of the covenant

The cross of Jesus Christ stands as the central, and unshakable foundation of the New Covenant. Without the cross, there is no covenant of grace, no forgiveness of sins, no reconciliation with God. The crucifixion is not an incidental moment in God's redemptive plan; it is the climactic fulfilment of all that the Old Covenant foreshadowed and the definitive revelation of God's covenantal love and justice. At the cross, the covenant was not merely renewed or revised — it was sealed in blood, fulfilled in Christ, and opened to all who would believe.

When Jesus lifted the cup during the Last Supper and declared, *"This cup is the new covenant in my blood, which is poured out for you."* (Luke 22:20), He was intentionally drawing His disciples into the cosmic significance of what He was about to endure. He was not simply referring to the shedding of blood in general; He was speaking of *His* blood — innocent, sinless, and sacrificial. That blood would become the sign and substance of the New Covenant, fulfilling the prophetic expectation of Jeremiah 31 and Ezekiel 36 and replacing the temporary sacrifices of the Old Covenant with one perfect offering.

The cross is where covenant meets kingdom, mercy meets judgment, and love meets justice. It is where God's faithfulness to His promises intersects with His righteous requirement for sin to be punished. In short, the cross is where God kept His covenant with Himself — for our sake.

The need for atonement

To fully appreciate the centrality of the cross in the New Covenant, we must understand the problem it solves: sin. Sin is not merely the breaking of a rule — it is the betrayal of a relationship. It is a covenantal breach, a cosmic act of treason against a holy God who created us for communion with Himself.

From Genesis onward, the Scriptures make it clear that the consequence of sin is death—both physical and spiritual. This death is not arbitrary; it is the just result of rebellion against the Author of life. The Old Covenant system, with its sacrifices and rituals, acknowledged the severity of sin. Blood had to be shed for atonement, not because God is bloodthirsty, but because sin corrupts life and demands justice. Hebrews 9:22 states, *"Without the shedding of blood there is no forgiveness."* Yet those sacrifices, as the author of Hebrews makes clear, were not sufficient in themselves. They were symbolic, temporary, and anticipatory. They pointed to a better sacrifice, a final offering, a once-for-all act of redemption that only the Messiah could accomplish.

Jesus, the spotless Lamb of God, fulfils this need completely. His death is not a tragedy—it is a triumph. It is not the sad end of a noble life—it is the glorious fulfilment of God's eternal covenant plan. As Paul writes in Romans 3:25–26, "God presented Christ as a sacrifice of atonement, through the shedding of his blood—to be received by faith... so as to be just and the one who justifies those who have faith in Jesus." In other words, the cross is where God upheld His justice and extended His mercy in one unparalleled act.

Covenant love displayed

One of the most breathtaking aspects of the cross is that it was not primarily an act of wrath, but an act of love. As Paul writes, *"God demonstrates his own love for us in this: While we were still sinners, Christ died for us."* (Romans 5:8). This is covenant love—not conditional, not reactive, but deliberate and costly. Unlike human love, which often depends on worthiness or reciprocity, divine love takes the initiative. It moves toward the undeserving. It bears the full weight of rejection, suffering, and death in order to bring about reconciliation.

The cross reveals a covenant love that goes far beyond sentiment. This is agape love—self-giving, sacrificial, unyielding. It is the love of a covenant-keeping God who, despite humanity's repeated unfaithfulness, remained faithful to His promise.

As Isaiah prophesied centuries before, *"He was pierced for our transgressions, he was crushed for our iniquities... and by his wounds we are healed."* (Isaiah 53:5). This love is the very foundation of the New Covenant. In contrast to the conditionality of the Mosaic Covenant, the New Covenant is based on divine grace, not human performance. We do not enter into it through our obedience, but through faith in the One who obeyed perfectly on our behalf — even to the point of death on a cross.

The cross as the end of the Old Covenant

I chose the title, *'From Sinai to Calvary'* for this book because, in a very real sense, the cross marks the end of the Old Covenant declared on Mount Sinai, and the inauguration of the New Covenant in the death of Jesus on Mount Calvary. Jesus Himself affirmed this in His dying words: *"It is finished."* (John 19:30). With those three words, He declared the completion of His whole redemptive mission. The law had been fulfilled. The final sacrifice had been offered. The curtain of the temple was torn in two, signifying that the way into the Most Holy Place was now open — not through animal blood or priestly mediation, but through the once-for-all sacrifice of Christ (Hebrews 10:19–20).

The tearing of the temple curtain was not only symbolic — it was seismic. It signified that the old system, with its layers of separation and ceremonial boundaries, was now obsolete. Access to God was no longer restricted to priests or limited to sacred places. The cross had changed everything. The barrier of sin was removed. The covenant of works had given way to the covenant of grace. The external regulations had been superseded by internal transformation. As Paul writes in 2 Corinthians 3:6, *"He has made us competent as ministers of a new covenant — not of the letter but of the Spirit; for the letter kills, but the Spirit gives life."*

Blood of the covenant

The shedding of Jesus' blood is the ratifying act of the New Covenant. Just as the Old Covenant was sealed with blood (Exodus 24:8), so too the New Covenant is inaugurated with blood — but not the blood of bulls and goats.

The blood of Christ is infinitely superior, not only because of His divinity, but because of His sinless humanity. Hebrews 9:12 tells us, *"He did not enter by means of the blood of goats and calves; but he entered the Most Holy Place once for all by his own blood, thus obtaining eternal redemption."*

This blood does not merely cover sin — it removes it. It does not merely postpone judgment — it satisfies it. It cleanses the conscience, not just the flesh. It provides a basis for lasting forgiveness, not temporary pardon. As Hebrews 10:14 says, *"By one sacrifice he has made perfect forever those who are being made holy."* Importantly, the blood of Christ also binds us to a new identity and a new destiny. In ancient times, covenant partners would often mingle blood as a sign of unbreakable union.

By faith in Christ, we are brought into such a bond with the Son of God. His blood secures our adoption, our justification, our sanctification, and our future glorification. We are not merely followers of Jesus; we are covenant-partners in His redemptive mission.

The cross and covenant identity

As I have stressed already in this study, the cross doesn't only secure our forgiveness; it actually redefines who we are. In the Old Covenant, identity was largely based on ethnicity, ritual observance, and external markers such as circumcision and dietary laws. In the New Covenant, our identity is rooted in the cross. We are defined not by what we do or where we come from, but by what Christ has done for us. Galatians 2:20 captures this transformative truth: *"I have been crucified with Christ and I no longer live, but Christ lives in me."*

This cruciform identity means that our past no longer defines us. The guilt of sin, the shame of failure, the bondage of addiction — all were nailed to the cross and left in the tomb. We are now new creations (2 Corinthians 5:17), not just patched-up versions of our old selves. The cross did not simply improve us; it recreated us. Moreover, this new identity is corporate as well as individual. We are not only reconciled to God but also to one another.

Ephesians 2:14-16 declares that Christ, by His cross, *"has destroyed the barrier, the dividing wall of hostility,"* making peace between Jew and Gentile and creating "one new humanity." The cross is therefore not only the foundation of personal salvation but the basis for a new community—the church—defined by grace, not law; unity, not division.

The cross as the mediator of the New Covenant

At the very centre of the biblical narrative stands the cross of Jesus Christ. It is not merely the instrument of Roman execution—it is the hinge upon which the entire covenantal story of God turns. If the Old Covenant was mediated through Moses with tablets of stone and sacrificial blood, the New Covenant is mediated through Jesus with His own broken body and shed blood. This is not just symbolic. The cross is the legal and spiritual instrument through which the New Covenant is enacted, empowered, and eternally secured.

Hebrews 9:15 states it clearly: *"For this reason Christ is the mediator of a new covenant, that those who are called may receive the promised eternal inheritance – now that he has died as a ransom to set them free from the sins committed under the first covenant."* The death of Christ was not simply the end of His earthly life—it was the legal ratification of a covenant that superseded and fulfilled all that came before.

A mediator is one who stands between two parties, establishing the terms for peace and for a reconciliation. In ancient covenantal practices, the mediator was often the guarantor of the covenant's integrity. Jesus, fully God and fully man, occupies that role in a way no one else could. As man, He represents humanity's obligation to keep covenant with God. As God, He upholds the divine side of the covenant.

At the cross, He bore the penalty due to covenant breakers and offered the obedience and righteousness that fulfils the covenant's demands. Therein lies the stunning beauty of the gospel: we are welcomed into covenant with God not because of our performance but because of Christ's perfection.

This understanding of Christ as the mediator reshapes our understanding of salvation. It is not merely that Jesus died for our sins — though that is gloriously true — it is that His death established a binding, eternal relationship between God and His people. The New Covenant is not fragile, it's not temporary, and it's not contingent upon our ongoing merit. It is as secure as the resurrected life of the One who enacted it.

The blood of the covenant

When Jesus instituted the Lord's Supper on the night He was betrayed, He echoed the words Moses had spoken centuries earlier during the inauguration of the Old Covenant: *"This is the blood of the covenant that the Lord has made with you."* (Exodus 24:8). The echo is deliberate. Jesus was not only referencing a sacred history; He was revealing its fulfilment.

Blood has always been central to covenant. In ancient Israel, blood was sprinkled on the altar and on the people as a solemn sign that covenant obligations were sealed in life and death. The shedding of blood meant that the covenant was no longer merely theoretical — it was enacted with the highest possible stakes. In the New Covenant, the blood is not that of animals but of the Son of God. This raises the stakes infinitely higher. The cost of our redemption is not symbolic — it is sacrificial.

This is not a primitive demand of a bloodthirsty deity, but a theological truth rooted in the gravity of sin and the justice of God. Sin ruptures covenant. It creates a huge debt. It demands satisfaction. Yet God, in His mercy, provides the satisfaction Himself through Jesus. At the cross, divine justice and mercy meet. The blood of Christ doesn't merely cleanse — it covenants. It seals a relationship that is irrevocable, because it is not based on our merit but on His mercy. This is why Paul can write with such confidence in Romans 8: *"There is now no condemnation for those who are in Christ Jesus."* The cross has settled the terms. The blood has been shed. The covenant is complete. No further sacrifice is needed. No additional work is required. The table is set; the invitation is issued; the covenant is secure.

The cross and the end of the Law

One of the most profound implications of the cross is its relationship to the law. The Old Covenant, as we've seen, was built upon a framework of laws — moral, civil, and ceremonial. These laws defined Israel's relationship to God and to each other. But they also highlighted a fundamental problem: humanity's inability to keep them. The law exposed sin but could not save from it. It demanded righteousness but could not produce it. Enter the cross.

Paul writes in Romans 10:4, *"Christ is the end of the law so that there may be righteousness for everyone who believes."* This statement is staggering in its scope. Christ is the end — not the abolition but the fulfilment — of the law. The Greek word used here, *telos*, denotes both goal and termination. The law pointed forward to Christ. He is its completion, its goal, its perfect embodiment.

What does this mean practically? It means that the believer is no longer under the law as a covenantal system. We do not relate to God on the basis of our adherence to commandments but on the basis of Christ's obedience. This does not render us lawless; rather, it liberates us into Spirit-led living. The moral vision of the law is not discarded — it is fulfilled in love (Romans 13:10). But the law's power to condemn has been broken. The law's burden to prove ourselves righteous has been lifted. The believer walks in the freedom of grace, not the fear of failure.

Colossians 2:14 describes this freedom in vivid terms: *"Having cancelled the charge of our legal indebtedness, which stood against us and condemned us; he has taken it away, nailing it to the cross."* This is not just courtroom language — it is covenant language. The charges of covenant unfaithfulness have been erased. The penalties have been borne. The records have been destroyed. In Christ, we are declared righteous — not hypothetically, but covenantally.

This reality is liberating, but it also calls us to a new kind of obedience — not one driven by fear or ritual, but one rooted in love and gratitude. The cross does not make holiness optional; it makes holiness possible.

Living under the shadow of the cross

The cross is not just a past event; it is a present power and a future hope. The Christian life is lived under the shadow of the cross, and the covenant it enacted shapes every dimension of our existence. We are a people of the cross—a people marked by sacrificial love, enduring grace, and radical forgiveness.

Paul writes in Galatians 2:20, *"I have been crucified with Christ and I no longer live, but Christ lives in me."* This is not metaphorical fluff. It is covenantal reality. To belong to Christ is to be united with Him in His death and resurrection. It is to live not for ourselves but for Him who died and was raised. The covenant changes not just our status before God but our daily walk with God.

This means that every trial we endure, every temptation we face, every sin we fight must be seen through the lens of the cross. The cross tells us that God is for us, not against us. The cross tells us that sin has been defeated, not coddled. The cross tells us that suffering is not meaningless, but redemptive. The covenant forged at Calvary is not just a doctrine—it is the heartbeat of the Christian life.

Moreover, the cross invites us into a community defined by covenant. Just as God bound Himself to us through Christ, so we are bound to one another. The New Covenant creates not just individual believers but a covenant people—a church that is the body of Christ. This people is called to embody the values of the cross: humility, service, reconciliation, love. We are to be cross-shaped in our relationships, not just in our theology.

The cross and covenant hope

The covenant enacted at the cross is not the end of the story—it is the beginning of a new creation. The cross not only addresses our past sin and present struggle; it secures our future glory. This is a covenant with eschatological weight. The cross inaugurated a kingdom that will one day be fully revealed. The blood that was shed at Calvary purchased not only our forgiveness but our inheritance.

Jesus Himself spoke of this in Matthew 26:29: *"I tell you, I will not drink from this fruit of the vine from now on until that day when I drink it new with you in my Father's kingdom."* This covenant meal is not just a memorial — it is a preview. The cross points forward to the wedding supper of the Lamb, where the covenant community will gather in eternal joy.

Revelation 21:3-4 gives us a glimpse of this hope: "God's dwelling place is now among the people, and he will dwell with them. They will be his people, and God himself will be with them and be their God… there will be no more death or mourning or crying or pain." This is covenant language brought to completion. What was begun at Sinai, fulfilled at Calvary, will be consummated in the New Jerusalem.

In this hope we live. In this hope we endure. In this hope we proclaim the message of the cross — not as an artifact of the past, but as the living power of God for the salvation of everyone who believes.

The cross and the covenantal identity of God's people

The cross of Jesus Christ does more than redeem individual sinners; it redefines an entire people. The New Covenant inaugurated through the cross establishes a new community — a covenant people drawn not from one ethnic lineage, but from every tribe, tongue, and nation. Whereas the Old Covenant community was bound by ancestry, circumcision, and temple rituals, the New Covenant community is bound by faith, sealed by the Spirit, and identified by the cross.

The apostle Peter proclaims this new identity in 1 Peter 2:9-10: *"But you are a chosen people, a royal priesthood, a holy nation, God's special possession… Once you were not a people, but now you are the people of God."* The church is the new covenantal people of God, not as a replacement of Israel in a dismissive sense, but as the fulfilment of what God always intended — one united people under one Saviour, in one Spirit, worshipping one Lord. At the cross, Jesus tore down the wall that separated Jew from Gentile, slave from free, male from female.

Paul writes in Ephesians 2:14-16, *"For he himself is our peace... His purpose was to create in himself one new humanity out of the two, thus making peace... through the cross."* The cross does not just reconcile us to God—it reconciles us to each other. The covenant of the cross forges a community of grace, marked by humility, service, forgiveness, and love.

This is not just theoretical. It is deeply practical. The local church becomes the living outpost of the covenant—a place where the values of the cross are embodied and shared. In a world which is defined by competition, self-interest, tribalism, and division, the covenant community becomes a radical alternative: a people who are shaped by sacrificial love, bear each other's burdens, confess their sins to one another, and pursue holiness together. This is why Paul relentlessly exhorts believers to maintain unity, forgive as Christ forgave, and love sacrificially. These are not suggestions; they are covenant obligations—responses to grace, not requirements for merit.

The sacraments of the New Covenant—baptism and the Lord's Supper—are not mere rituals, but covenantal signs. Baptism marks our initiation into the covenant community, symbolizing our union with Christ in His death and resurrection (Romans 6). The Lord's Supper is the covenantal meal, a regular participation in the benefits of Christ's ultimate sacrifice, a remembrance and proclamation of the cross, and a foretaste of the banquet to come (1 Corinthians 11:26).

When we participate in these signs, we declare not only our individual faith but our corporate identity. We are not isolated recipients of grace—we are members of a body. The cross not only saves—it gathers. It not only reconciles vertically—it binds us horizontally. To walk in the New Covenant is to walk in community, not in isolation.

The ongoing power of the cross

One of the great dangers in the Christian life is to relegate the cross to the past. We know Christ died for our sins. We celebrate that fact on Good Friday and remember it at Communion.

But the power of the cross is not confined to a moment in history — it is a present, living reality. The covenant it enacted continues to shape, empower, and direct our lives daily. Paul speaks of this ongoing power in 1 Corinthians 1:18: *"For the message of the cross is foolishness to those who are perishing, but to us who are being saved it is the power of God."* Notice the tense — *"are being saved."* Salvation is not merely a past event; it is a present process and a future hope. The cross is the power of God not only to forgive but to transform.

This is vital for our understanding of our sanctification. Many believers begin the Christian life at the foot of the cross, receiving forgiveness, but then seek to live the Christian life through their own strength. They strive, they labour, they attempt to earn what they've already been given. But Paul reminds us in Galatians 3:3, *"After beginning by means of the Spirit, are you now trying to finish by means of the flesh?"* The cross is not just the starting line — it is the ongoing source of strength and direction.

To live under the cross means to embrace a lifestyle of daily dying to self. Jesus said, *"Whoever wants to be my disciple must deny themselves and take up their cross daily and follow me."* (Luke 9:23). The cross was not just Christ's instrument of obedience — it is ours as well. This is not a call to self-hatred but to self-surrender. The covenantal life is a cruciform life — a life shaped by the cross, in posture, in priorities, and in power.

This ongoing crucifixion applies to our sins, our idols, our ambitions, and even our religious pride. As Paul says in Galatians 6:14, *"May I never boast except in the cross of our Lord Jesus Christ, through which the world has been crucified to me, and I to the world."* The cross cuts the cord between us and the world's value system. It reorients our lives toward God's kingdom. It delivers us not only from guilt but from the grip of self-rule. This is why the preaching of the cross must remain central in the life of the church. It is not merely for evangelism — it is for discipleship. It is not only the gate — it is the path. Every sermon, every worship service, every act of ministry must be shaped by the cross. To drift from the cross is to drift from the covenant.

The cross and the glory of God

Ultimately, the covenant enacted at the cross is not about us — it is about the glory of God. Yes, we benefit immensely. Yes, our sins are forgiven, our lives are transformed, our future is secured. But the ultimate purpose of the cross is the glorification of God's justice, mercy, holiness, and love. The cross is the place where God's attributes converge in perfect harmony. His justice is upheld — sin is punished. His mercy is extended — the sinner is pardoned. His love is demonstrated — Christ dies for the ungodly. His faithfulness is proven — the covenant is fulfilled. No other event in history displays the character of God so clearly and completely.

This is why the cross must remain central not only in our theology but in our worship. The songs we sing, the prayers we pray, the lives we lead should all echo the melody of Calvary. As the old hymn declares, *"In the cross of Christ I glory, towering o'er the wrecks of time."* The cross is not a relic — it is a revelation. Revelation 5 gives us a picture of eternal worship, and at the centre of it stands a Lamb *"looking as if it had been slain."* The covenant community in heaven sings, *"You are worthy... because you were slain, and with your blood you purchased for God persons from every tribe and language and people and nation."* The cross is not only the foundation of earthly salvation — it is the theme of heavenly adoration.

When we live under the cross, we live for God's glory. We do not merely seek comfort, blessing, or success. We seek to magnify the One who bore our curse and gave us life. Every act of obedience becomes an offering. Every trial becomes a testimony. Every moment becomes sacred. The covenant of the cross calls us to live doxologically — to see our entire lives as worship.

The cross and the coming kingdom

The New Covenant enacted through the cross also points us forward — to the consummation of all things. The cross inaugurated a kingdom that is already present but not yet fully revealed.

It guarantees a future in which the covenant community will dwell with God forever in a new heavens and a new earth. Jesus linked the covenant to the future when He said, *"I will not drink again from the fruit of the vine until the kingdom of God comes."* (Luke 22:18). The cross was not the end — it was the beginning of the end. It was the down payment on a future where righteousness dwells, where every tear is wiped away, and where the Lamb reigns on the throne.

This eschatological dimension of the covenant gives the church both hope and mission. We live in the "already" and the "not yet." The victory has been won, but the battle still rages. The kingdom has come, but its fullness awaits. In this in-between time, we are called to be ambassadors of the covenant — proclaiming the cross, embodying its values, and pointing forward to its consummation.

Paul captures this tension beautifully in Philippians 3:20-21: *"But our citizenship is in heaven. And we eagerly await a Saviour from there, the Lord Jesus Christ… who will transform our lowly bodies so that they will be like his glorious body."* The cross secures not only our forgiveness but our final transformation. The covenant promises not only redemption but resurrection.

This forward-looking faith will shape our endurance, so that when suffering comes, we look to the cross and the crown. When temptation entices, we remember the price paid and the glory to come. When the world seems dark, we cling to the light of the Lamb who was slain. We are a people of the cross — and of the kingdom.

- 16 -

COVENANT AND DISCIPLESHIP

The call to follow

From the earliest pages of Scripture, covenant has always been tied to relationship. God's covenant with Abraham called him to leave his homeland and follow a divine promise into the unknown. When Jesus Christ inaugurated the New Covenant, He likewise extended a call — not merely to believe, but to follow. This call is central to Christian discipleship. It is a summons to reorient our lives, to forsake all and embrace the way of Christ. The New Covenant, while rooted in grace, issues a radical call to discipleship that transforms every part of our existence.

In Matthew 4:19, Jesus says to Simon Peter and Andrew, *"Come, follow me, and I will send you out to fish for people."* This simple yet profound invitation embodies the very heart of New Covenant discipleship. It is personal *("come")*, it demands an immediate response *("follow me")*, and it carries purpose *("I will send you")*. Discipleship is not optional for the believer; it is the natural and necessary response to covenantal grace. Grace draws us in — but it does not leave us unchanged.

The covenant Jesus offers is not a contract for minimal religious observance. It is an all-consuming relationship of trust, loyalty, and transformation. He bids us come and die — die to self, to the world, to sin — and rise to newness of life in Him. Luke 9:23 echoes this theme: *"Whoever wants to be my disciple must deny themselves and take up their cross daily and follow me."* Covenant and discipleship are inseparable.

Covenant identity and discipleship

As we know, under the Old Covenant, Israel's identity was bound to the Law and national heritage. Under the New Covenant, identity is shaped by union with Christ. This identity is not static; it compels a lifelong journey of transformation. Romans 8:29 declares that God's purpose is to conform us *"to the image of his Son."*

Discipleship, then, is not about achieving religious performance but about living out our new identity in Christ. To be in covenant with God is to belong to Him. This belonging changes how we see ourselves and how we live in the world. Paul often describes himself not merely as a believer, but as a *"servant of Christ Jesus."* (Romans 1:1). This is not a title of drudgery but of devotion. The New Covenant binds us to Jesus Christ, and that binding then produces movement—obedient, loving, and joyful movement toward Christlikeness.

Such identity is deeply relational. Jesus does not call us into solitary discipleship but into community. The New Covenant establishes the church as the covenant people of God. Together, we will learn to follow Jesus. Together, we will wrestle with His teachings, bear each other's burdens, and reflect His love to the world. Discipleship in isolation is always incomplete. The New Testament epistles continually call believers to *"one another"* commands: love one another, serve one another, bear with one another. Covenant identity includes covenant community.

Costly grace and true discipleship

Although it is misunderstood too often, Dietrich Bonhoeffer's distinction between *"cheap grace"* and *"costly grace"* has never lost its prophetic power. Cheap grace assumes forgiveness without transformation, salvation without surrender. Costly grace, on the other hand, is the grace that calls us to follow Jesus with our whole lives. Bonhoeffer writes, *"When Christ calls a man, he bids him come and die."*

The New Covenant does not reduce discipleship to legalism or performance. But neither does it allow complacency. Grace is free, but it is not cheap. It cost Jesus His life, and it will cost us ours—not in the sense of earning salvation, but in surrendering to its implications. Romans 12:1 urges believers, *"Offer your bodies as a living sacrifice, holy and pleasing to God—this is your true and proper worship."* The New Covenant reorients our desires and redefines what is valuable. The things we once pursued—status, success, security—lose their grip. In their place, we find the surpassing worth of knowing Christ (Philippians 3:8).

Discipleship means trading what is temporary for what is eternal. It means living not for the approval of man, but for the pleasure of God. It is not easy — but it is liberating.

Obedience from the heart

One of the hallmarks of the New Covenant is the internalization of obedience. Jeremiah 31:33 speaks of God writing His law on our hearts. This heart-level obedience is a defining characteristic of discipleship. Under the Old Covenant, obedience was very often reduced to external compliance. Under the New Covenant, obedience flows from transformed desires.

This is why Jesus speaks so extensively about the heart in the Sermon on the Mount. He is not interested in outward performance alone. He wants purity of heart, integrity of motive, and wholeness of life. The disciple is not one who merely avoids sin but one who hungers and thirsts for righteousness. Paul affirms this in Romans 6:17: *"Though you used to be slaves to sin, you have come to obey from your heart the pattern of teaching that has now claimed your allegiance."*

Obedience in the New Covenant is relational. It is not fear-based conformity but love-driven faithfulness. Jesus said, *"If you love me, keep my commands."* (John 14:15). This is not a burdensome requirement but a joyful expression of our covenant bond. The disciple delights to do the will of the Master — not to earn favour, but because favour has already been given.

Daily surrender and spiritual growth

Discipleship is not a moment but a movement — a daily journey of surrender and growth. Jesus called His disciples to take up their cross *"daily."* This daily surrender is not glamorous. It involves small, hidden acts of faithfulness. It means forgiving those who hurt us, loving those who oppose us, serving when we feel empty, trusting when we are afraid. Spiritual growth under the New Covenant is organic. It is not driven by duty but by delight. The Spirit nurtures fruit in us over time — love, joy, peace, patience, and more.

This fruit cannot be forced. It is the natural result of abiding in Christ. As Jesus says in John 15:5, *"If you remain in me and I in you, you will bear much fruit; apart from me you can do nothing."*

This abiding is the very essence of discipleship. It is not about accomplishing various spiritual tasks but remaining in relational connection. It is living in continual dependence on the grace of God. It is learning to hear His voice, trust His promises, and follow His lead. In this, we grow—not through striving, but through surrender.

The end goal: Christlikeness

The destination of discipleship is not merely heaven, but Christlikeness. Romans 8:29 reveals God's eternal purpose: *"to be conformed to the image of his Son."* This transformation is both positional and progressive. In Christ, we are already holy. Yet we are also being made holy. Discipleship bridges this gap—it is the Spirit-led journey from who we are in Christ to how we live in Christ.

This Christlikeness touches every part of our lives. It reshapes our relationships, our ethics, our ambitions, and our affections. It aligns us with the heart of God and prepares us to represent Him in the world. The disciple does not ask, *"What do I want to do with my life?"* but *"What does Christ want to do through me?"*

The New Covenant makes this transformation possible. It is not the product of human effort, but of divine power. Paul assures us, *"It is God who works in you to will and to act in order to fulfil his good purpose."* (Philippians 2:13). Discipleship, then, is not a solo endeavour. It is a grace-empowered journey into the likeness of Christ, through the covenant love of God.

The church as a discipleship community

Discipleship is not a private journey of faith, detached from others. From the beginning, God has called a people to Himself, not isolated individuals. This communal aspect of faith is deeply embedded in the New Covenant.

Jesus did not merely call individual disciples to follow Him independently—He formed them into a community, a group of learners and followers shaped by their relationship with Him and with one another. This model continues in the church today, which is not a passive audience but an active discipleship community.

The church is where disciples are made, formed, corrected, encouraged, and sent. It is where the gifts of the Spirit are exercised, and the fruit of the Spirit is cultivated. Paul's letters to the churches are filled with exhortations that only make sense in a relational context. Discipleship is forged in the fire of real relationships—where grace is needed, forgiveness is extended, and love is put into practice. Hebrews 10:24-25 exhorts us, *"Let us consider how we may spur one another on toward love and good deeds, not giving up meeting together... but encouraging one another."*

This encouragement is not limited to moral support. It is deeply theological and transformational. The community reminds us of who we are in Christ, challenges us to live accordingly, and bears witness to the power of the gospel. The New Covenant church becomes a living demonstration of discipleship in motion—a people marked by truth, unity, holiness, and love.

Discipleship through teaching and obedience

Jesus' final command in the Great Commission underscores the centrality of teaching in the life of a disciple: *"Therefore go and make disciples of all nations... teaching them to obey everything I have commanded you."* (Matthew 28:19-20). Teaching is not simply passing on information; it is shaping lives. It involves careful instruction in the Word of God and modelling obedience to that Word in daily life.

The teaching ministry of the church is critical in shaping disciples who are not merely informed but transformed. In the New Covenant, teaching is empowered by the Spirit and rooted in Scripture. It is not authoritarian control, but relational guidance. Paul instructs Timothy to *"preach the word... with great patience and careful instruction."* (2 Timothy 4:2).

Discipleship thrives when teaching is patient, clear, and focused on application—not just intellectual understanding but heart-level transformation. Obedience, then, becomes the fruit of good teaching. It is the echo of grace working within. As James 1:22 says, *"Do not merely listen to the word, and so deceive yourselves. Do what it says."* In New Covenant discipleship, learning and living go hand in hand. The Word is not just heard—it is practiced. The disciple who follows Jesus listens attentively, reflects deeply, and responds actively.

Discipleship in the face of opposition

Jesus never promised that following Him would be easy. In fact, He promised the opposite. *"If the world hates you, keep in mind that it hated me first."* (John 15:18). Discipleship in a fallen world inevitably invites resistance. The values of the Kingdom of God stand in stark contrast to the values of the world. Faithfulness to Christ often means rejection by others. Yet in this opposition, the disciple is refined and strengthened. Suffering becomes a crucible for maturity. *"We also glory in our sufferings, because we know that suffering produces perseverance; perseverance, character; and character, hope."*(Romans 5:3-4). The hardships we face as disciples—whether through persecution, disappointment, or personal struggle—are not obstacles to growth but means of grace. They remind us of our dependence on God and our identification with Christ, who also suffered.

In this, we follow in the footsteps of countless disciples before us. Hebrews 11 and 12 recount the stories of those who endured opposition for the sake of faith. The call to discipleship is not a call to comfort but to courage. As we persevere through trials, we are being shaped into the likeness of Christ. This kind of discipleship is not for the faint of heart—but it is for those who have found something worth dying for.

The role of spiritual disciplines

New Covenant discipleship doesn't occur accidentally. While transformation is the work of the Spirit, it is cultivated through intentional practices—often called spiritual disciplines.

These are habits of grace that position us to receive and respond to God's transforming work. They include Scripture reading, prayer, fasting, worship, solitude, confession, and service. These disciplines are not means of earning God's favour; rather, they are ways of drawing near to Him who has already drawn near to us in Christ. They are tools of alignment—helping us tune our hearts to God's voice and align our lives with His will.

Paul urges young Timothy in 1 Timothy 4:7, to *"train yourself to be godly."* This spiritual training is not about striving in the power of the flesh but cooperating with the Spirit.

Scripture becomes our daily bread. Prayer becomes our lifeline. Worship becomes our atmosphere. These practices are not legalistic duties but lifegiving rhythms. As we engage in them consistently, the Spirit works in us deeply.

Our character is shaped, our discernment sharpened, and our love for God and others expanded. These disciplines become the trellis on which the vine of grace can grow.

Mission as an outflow of discipleship

Discipleship and mission are two sides of the same coin. To be a disciple is to be sent. Jesus did not merely gather followers to form a private spiritual club—He commissioned them to go and make more disciples. This sending is not limited to pastors or missionaries; it is the calling of every believer. We are witnesses, ambassadors, light in the darkness. Disciples are not consumers of religious goods but co-labourers in the gospel.

Mission flows from identity. The disciple understands that their life is not their own. They have been bought with a price and are now agents of reconciliation. Paul writes in 2 Corinthians 5:20, *"We are therefore Christ's ambassadors, as though God were making his appeal through us."* This ambassadorship is not optional—it is the natural outflow of a life shaped by covenant and discipleship. Whether through acts of compassion, words of truth, or lives of integrity, disciples bring the presence of Christ into every sphere of our life and ministry.

The workplace, the neighbourhood, the classroom, and the home all become mission fields. This is not an added burden, but a joyful privilege. Discipleship lifts our eyes from self to service, from maintenance to mission.

Discipleship as a lifelong journey

There is no graduation from the school of discipleship. It is a lifelong journey of becoming more like Jesus every day. Or, to be more accurate, being transformed by the Spirit into the image of Jesus. While the New Covenant secures our salvation, it also sets us on a daily path of sanctification.

This journey includes both mountaintops and valleys, victories and setbacks. But through it all, the Spirit remains faithful. Philippians 1:6 offers this hope: *"He who began a good work in you will carry it on to completion until the day of Christ Jesus."*

Each season of life brings new challenges and new opportunities for growth. In youth, we learn dependence. In adulthood, we learn responsibility. In suffering, we learn endurance. In ageing, we learn hope.

Discipleship adapts but it never, ever ends. It deepens over time, refining us through trials, celebrations, relationships, and the quiet daily faithfulness of walking with God.

The goal is not perfection but progress. Discipleship is not a linear ascent but a dynamic relationship. There are times of great growth and times of slow refinement. But the promise of the New Covenant is that God Himself is committed to our transformation. He does not leave us to wander alone. His Spirit leads, convicts, comforts, and empowers.

As we continue this journey, we discover that discipleship is not a burden but a blessing. It is the path to joy, peace, and eternal significance. To walk as a disciple of Jesus is to walk in the fullness of the covenant—to live the life we were always meant to live, in fellowship with the One who loves us perfectly.

The church's prophetic role in discipleship

The church is not only a community of mutual encouragement and accountability; it is also a prophetic community — one that embodies and declares the truth of the gospel in a world marred by sin and rebellion. In the context of covenant and discipleship, this prophetic dimension is indispensable.

Disciples are not shaped only by what happens within the community, but by how the community engages with the world around it. The church is called to speak truth to power, to live counter-culturally, and to bear witness to the transforming reign of Christ.

This prophetic calling was evident in Jesus' ministry. He confronted religious hypocrisy, He challenged injustice, and He welcomed the marginalized. He called people to repentance and to a new way of life under God's rule. His disciples are to do the same — not as moralists, but as covenant people who reflect the heart of God.

The New Covenant calls the church to boldly proclaim not only salvation, but also the implications of that salvation in every area of life — justice, mercy, family, economics, and ethics.

This prophetic witness often invites resistance, but it also opens hearts to transformation. When the church models integrity, love, and truth, it becomes a living critique of the world's broken systems and a beacon of hope. Discipleship that embraces this prophetic edge is both courageous and compassionate. It does not conform to the world but is transformed by the renewing of the mind (Romans 12:2).

Community and accountability in discipleship

One of the defining characteristics of New Covenant discipleship is its communal accountability. While each believer has a personal relationship with God, that relationship is nurtured, challenged, and enriched in the context of community. *"As iron sharpens iron, so one person sharpens another."* (Proverbs 27:17). The Christian life was never intended to be lived in isolation.

Accountability is not about control or surveillance; it is about love. It is rooted in mutual care and a shared desire to see one another grow in Christ. In Galatians 6:1–2, Paul urges believers, *"If someone is caught in a sin, you who live by the Spirit should restore that person gently... Carry each other's burdens, and in this way you will fulfil the law of Christ."* This kind of restoration is central to discipleship. It reflects the covenant heart of God, who is always seeking the restoration of His people.

One-on-on mentoring relationships, intentional discipleship partnerships and small groups, are all practical ways to cultivate this accountability. In these spaces, believers can be honest about their struggles, receive wise counsel, and be reminded of their identity in Christ. Accountability fosters maturity, guards against spiritual drift, and encourages perseverance.

Discipleship and the Word of God

At the core of New Covenant discipleship is the centrality of Scripture. God has revealed Himself through His Word, and it is through the Word that all His disciples are fed, guided, and transformed. Psalm 119:105 declares, *"Your word is a lamp for my feet, a light on my path."* The Bible is not merely a textbook or a rulebook — it is the living voice of God, speaking into the lives of His people.

Under the New Covenant, the Spirit writes God's law on our hearts (Jeremiah 31:33). This internalization of the Word means that Scripture is not external to the disciple but embedded in their very being. It shapes the conscience, informs the mind, and fuels obedience. As Hebrews 4:12 states, *"The word of God is alive and active. Sharper than any double-edged sword... it judges the thoughts and attitudes of the heart."*

Effective discipleship involves both the study and application of Scripture. Teaching and preaching must be grounded in the text, and personal devotion must be a daily rhythm. Memorization, meditation, and reflection allow the Word to dwell richly within the disciple (Colossians 3:16).

This immersion in Scripture equips believers to discern truth from error, to resist temptation, and to align their lives with the purposes of God.

Leadership in discipleship

Leaders in the church have a unique role in cultivating discipleship. Their task is not merely to manage programs or deliver sermons but to shepherd souls. Paul highlighted the purpose of leadership: *"to equip his people for works of service, so that the body of Christ may be built up... attaining to the whole measure of the fullness of Christ."* (Ephesians 4:11-13). Leaders are disciple-makers, equippers, and examples.

Paul's relationship with Timothy is a prime example of this kind of discipleship leadership. He not only instructed Timothy in doctrine but modelled a life of integrity, sacrifice, and mission. He called Timothy to follow his example as he followed Christ. This relational, intentional, and Spirit-empowered leadership is what the church needs today. Leaders who invest in people—not just programs—create a culture where discipleship flourishes.

Leadership in discipleship also means creating space for others to grow and lead. It is not about control, but about release. Jesus entrusted His disciples with significant responsibilities and then sent them out.

Similarly, leaders today must entrust others, coach them, and celebrate their growth. This multiplication mindset ensures that discipleship does not stop with one generation but continues and expands.

Discipleship in a digital age

In our contemporary world, discipleship is facing both new challenges and new opportunities. The digital age has reshaped how people communicate, learn, and form relationships. While technology can be a good tool for discipleship—through online teaching, virtual groups, and digital resources—it also presents significant distractions and dangers.

The constant stream of information, entertainment, and social media can fragment attention, foster comparison, and promote superficiality. Discipleship, by contrast, requires depth, focus, and intentionality. It calls for slowing down, listening, and engaging in real relationships. In this environment, the church must be countercultural — which means offering not just content but community, not just information but transformation.

Discipleship in the digital age must also address the questions and issues that arise from this context. Issues of identity, sexuality, justice, and truth are shaped by digital narratives. Disciples need a biblical worldview that equips them to engage thoughtfully and faithfully. This requires robust teaching, open dialogue, and a safe space to wrestle with complex issues.

The hope of glory

Discipleship is not only about the present journey — it is also about the future hope. The New Covenant points us to the ultimate fulfilment of God's promises. Colossians 1:27 speaks of *"Christ in you, the hope of glory."* This hope sustains the disciple through trials, energizes obedience, and anchors the soul.

One day, the journey will be complete. We will see Him face to face, and we will be like Him. Revelation 21:3-4 offers a glorious vision: *"God's dwelling place is now among the people... He will wipe every tear from their eyes. There will be no more death or mourning or crying or pain."* This is the destiny of every disciple — a life forever with the One we have followed.

Until that day, we press on. We walk by faith, empowered by grace, surrounded by a cloud of witnesses, and strengthened by the Spirit. Discipleship is therefore our calling, our joy, and our preparation for eternity. As we walk in covenant with God and one another, we participate in His redemptive story — a story that will culminate in the restoration of all things.

COVENANT AND MISSION

The Missional heart of God

The story of the Bible is, at its core, a story of mission. From Genesis to Revelation, we see a God who is not passive or distant but actively working to redeem, restore, and renew a broken world.

This mission begins with the call of Abraham, which we read about in Genesis 12, where God promises to make him into a great nation and to bless all peoples on earth through him. This promise is not merely about privilege but about purpose. Abraham and his descendants were to be a light to the nations, a conduit of divine blessing.

The Old Covenant established Israel as God's chosen people, a nation set apart to reveal God's holiness and justice. Yet Israel's calling was always outward-facing. Isaiah 49:6 makes this clear: *"I will also make you a light for the Gentiles, that my salvation may reach to the ends of the earth."* This missional thread weaves through the Old Testament, culminating in the New Covenant inaugurated by Jesus Christ.

Jesus is the ultimate expression of God's missional heart. He is the incarnate Word, sent by the Father into the world not to condemn it but to save it (John 3:17). His ministry, death, and resurrection are the central acts of God's redemptive plan. The New Covenant established through His blood (Luke 22:20) is not only the fulfilment of Old Testament prophecy but also the launching pad for a global mission that continues to this day.

In Christ, the scope of God's covenant expands. What was once centred on a single ethnic people now opens to all nations. The dividing wall between Jew and Gentile is broken down (Ephesians 2:14), and a new humanity is created in Christ. This is the church—a multi-ethnic, global body united by faith and called to embody the gospel in word and deed.

Mission flows from covenant identity

Understanding the mission to which we are each called, requires us to understand the covenant identity of the people of God. We are not a volunteer organisation or a social movement. We are a covenant people—called, chosen, redeemed, and sent. Our mission flows not from mere obligation but from who we are in Christ. As 1 Peter 2:9 declares, *"But you are a chosen people, a royal priesthood, a holy nation, God's special possession, that you may declare the praises of him who called you out of darkness into his wonderful light."*

This covenant identity reorients everything. We are no longer defined by nationality, social status, or personal ambition. We are defined by our relationship with God through Christ. And this relationship carries with it a divine mandate: to declare His praises, to live as His witnesses, to make disciples of all nations. Mission is not a program of the church; it is the very essence of the church.

Jesus' commissioning of His disciples in Matthew 28:18–20 is grounded in His authority and presence. *"All authority in heaven and on earth has been given to me. Therefore, go and make disciples of all nations... And surely I am with you always, to the very end of the age."* This Great Commission is both a command and a promise. It is not dependent on our strength but on His. It is not optional but essential. Every covenant blessing carries a covenant responsibility.

The church as a missionary people

The early church understood itself as a missionary community. The book of Acts records the Spirit-empowered expansion of the gospel from Jerusalem to Judea, Samaria, and the ends of the earth (Acts 1:8).

Persecution did not stop the mission; it often accelerated it. Believers scattered by opposition carried the message of Jesus Christ wherever they went. They preached in synagogues, homes, marketplaces, and public courts. They planted churches, discipled converts, and challenged the idols of their age.

This missionary impulse was not reserved for a professional elite. Ordinary believers, filled with the Holy Spirit and shaped by the gospel, became extraordinary witnesses. Their lives were marked by courage, compassion, and conviction. They crossed cultural boundaries, embraced suffering, and lived with eternal purpose. They were living proof that the New Covenant had created a new kind of people — a people on mission with God.

Today, the church is still called to be this kind of people. The methods may change, but the mandate remains. Whether through church planting, global missions, social justice, or personal evangelism, the church is to embody and proclaim the good news of the kingdom. Every local church is a mission outpost, every believer a missionary.

Empowered by the Holy Spirit

The mission of Christ cannot be fulfilled in human strength. It requires divine empowerment. This is why the coming of the Holy Spirit at Pentecost is so pivotal to all that we do. Jesus instructed His disciples to wait in Jerusalem until they were *"clothed with power from on high."* (Luke 24:49). When the Spirit came, He filled them with boldness, wisdom, and supernatural ability to speak the gospel in ways that transcended language and culture.

The Holy Spirit is the missional engine of the church. He convicts hearts, opens doors, empowers speech, and guides strategy. In Acts, we see the Spirit directing missionary journeys, raising up leaders, and confirming the message with signs and wonders. Paul writes in Romans 15:18-19, *"I will not venture to speak of anything except what Christ has accomplished through me... by the power of signs and wonders, through the power of the Spirit of God."*

Under the New Covenant, every believer has access to this same Spirit. The mission is not limited to those with special training or titles. It belongs to the whole body of Christ, empowered by the Spirit and equipped through the Word. The Spirit does not replace our effort but empowers it. He leads us into the mission field and gives us what we need to bear fruit there.

Holiness and mission

One of the great tensions in the Christian life is the balance between being set apart and being sent out. Holiness and mission must walk hand in hand. In the Old Covenant, Israel was called to be holy as God is holy (Leviticus 19:2). This call remains in the New Covenant, but now it is fulfilled through the sanctifying work of the Spirit (1 Thessalonians 5:23).

Holiness is not withdrawal from the world but distinction within it. The church is not meant to mirror the culture but to contrast it. Our lives should provoke questions, stir curiosity, and reflect the character of Christ. As Jesus prayed in John 17:15-18, "*My prayer is not that you take them out of the world but that you protect them from the evil one... As you sent me into the world, I have sent them into the world.*"

This holiness is itself missional. A holy life is a compelling witness. When the church embodies the love, truth, justice, and mercy of God, it shines like a city on a hill. Our conduct becomes part of our message. Integrity in business, kindness in speech, purity in relationships, and generosity in need—these are all powerful apologetics. The gospel is not only heard; it is seen. In this way, covenant and mission are inseparably linked. We are a holy people, not for our own sake, but for the sake of the world. We are blessed to be a blessing, called out to be sent in, set apart to be poured out. This is the pattern of the gospel and the rhythm of the New Covenant life.

The mission of Christ in a fractured world

We live in a world marked by fragmentation. Social, political, economic, and religious divides dominate the global landscape. Yet into this fractured world, God sends His church—not merely as spectators or survivors, but as agents of reconciliation and restoration. This is not a new idea; it is a continuation of the covenantal mission established long ago. The church is not merely a gathering of individuals seeking personal spiritual fulfilment—it is the covenant community sent into the world with a divine mandate.

Paul captures this missional identity in 2 Corinthians 5:18-20, where he writes: *"All this is from God, who reconciled us to himself through Christ and gave us the ministry of reconciliation... We are therefore Christ's ambassadors, as though God were making his appeal through us."*

We are ambassadors of a kingdom not of this world. Our message is reconciliation, and our ministry is driven by covenantal love. The church, as the people of the New Covenant, carries the call to bridge the divides of sin, hatred, and injustice by proclaiming and embodying the gospel.

This requires courage. It requires presence. And it requires a deep understanding of our covenant identity. We are not called to mimic the values of the culture but to challenge them with the truth and grace of Christ. In doing so, we become salt and light (Matthew 5:13-16), preserving what is good and illuminating what is true.

The Great Commission and the covenant mandate

The Great Commission (Matthew 28:18-20) is often viewed as a standalone command, yet it is best understood as the outworking of God's covenant purposes. Jesus begins with a declaration of authority — *"All authority in heaven and on earth has been given to me"* – before commissioning His followers to make disciples of all nations. This reflects the global vision first given to Abraham: that through him, all peoples on earth would be blessed.

The covenant God made with Abraham finds its fulfilment in Christ and its expansion through the church. The command to *"make disciples of all nations"* is the direct continuation of the covenant mission to bless the nations.

It is not only about evangelism, but about forming communities of obedience and transformation under the lordship of Christ. Baptising, teaching, and discipling are covenantal acts—they bring people into the covenant family and shape them according to the covenant way.

Importantly, Jesus concludes the Commission with a covenant promise: "*Surely I am with you always, to the very end of the age.*" God's presence with His people has always been the hallmark of covenant relationship. From the tabernacle to the temple to the indwelling Spirit, God dwells with His people. In mission, we do not go alone — we are accompanied by the covenantal presence of Christ.

A kingdom people on mission

The church is not just a covenant people but a kingdom people. These two realities are inseparable. The covenant establishes the relationship; the kingdom defines the rule. To be in covenant with God is to live under His reign. And where God reigns, His will is done on earth as it is in heaven. Therefore, every act of mission — whether it is proclamation, or service, or justice, or compassion — it's a declaration that the kingdom of God is near.

Jesus' ministry was filled with demonstrations of the kingdom. He healed the sick, He cast out demons, He raised the dead, and He preached good news to the poor. These were not random acts of kindness; they were signs of the inbreaking kingdom. And now, as the covenant community, we are called to continue this kingdom work — not by our own power, but through the presence of the Spirit.

Mission, therefore, is not confined to pulpits or platforms. It happens in homes, workplaces, schools, and streets. Every believer is a kingdom ambassador, and every context is a mission field. The church does not wait for the world to come in; it goes out to where people live and suffer and hope. This is not a programme but a posture — a way of life shaped by covenantal loyalty to the King.

Justice and compassion as covenant expressions

God's covenant with His people has always included a call to justice and compassion. In the Old Testament, Israel was commanded to care for the widow, the orphan, and the stranger (Deuteronomy 10:18–19).

These commands were not ancillary but central to the covenant. To belong to God was to reflect His character—and He is a God of justice, mercy, and compassion. Under the New Covenant, this mandate continues. James writes, *"Religion that God our Father accepts as pure and faultless is this: to look after orphans and widows in their distress."* (James 1:27).

Likewise, Jesus' parable of the Good Samaritan (Luke 10:25–37) challenges us to redefine neighbour-love as the active, costly care of those in need. This is not optional charity; it is covenantal faithfulness.

Mission, therefore, is holistic. It includes proclaiming the gospel, but it also includes feeding the hungry, welcoming the stranger, advocating for the oppressed, and building systems that reflect God's justice. When the church engages in acts of justice and compassion, it does so not as an NGO, but as a covenant people bearing witness to a just and compassionate God.

In this way, the mission of the church becomes a foretaste of the kingdom. We do not bring the kingdom in its fullness—that is God's work—but we live as signs of its reality. Every healed relationship, every restored dignity, every act of generosity speaks of the covenant God who is making all things new.

Suffering and mission

The covenantal mission of the church does not shield it from suffering. In fact, suffering is often the crucible in which mission is forged. Jesus was a suffering servant, and His followers are called to take up their cross. The early church faced persecution, imprisonment, and martyrdom—not because they failed in mission, but because they were faithful to it.

Paul wrote from prison: *"I want to know Christ—yes, to know the power of his resurrection and participation in his sufferings..."* (Philippians 3:10). He saw suffering not as a hindrance to mission but as a pathway to deeper union with Christ and greater gospel impact.

In many parts of the world today, the church continues to suffer. Believers are mocked, marginalised, and martyred for their faith. Yet even in suffering, the mission continues. In fact, the blood of the martyrs is often the seed of the church. Faithful witness in the face of opposition is a powerful testimony to the reality of the covenant and the lordship of Christ.

For those in more comfortable settings, the call is still to embrace sacrificial mission. This may mean giving generously, leaving familiar surroundings, crossing cultural divides, or standing for truth in hostile environments. The covenant demands our whole lives. Mission is not safe—but it is worth it.

The role of the local church

While the church is a global body, its mission is firmly rooted in local expression. Each local church is a microcosm of the New Covenant community. It is a training ground for mission and a launchpad for outreach. The health of the broad, global church depends on the faithfulness of local churches.

The local church is where believers are discipled, gifts are developed, and community is cultivated. It is where the gospel is preached, sacraments are celebrated, and mutual care is practised. But it is also where mission begins. A church that is inward-focused is a contradiction of its covenant calling.

Healthy local churches embrace their neighbourhoods. They seek the peace and prosperity of the cities where they dwell (Jeremiah 29:7). They become known not only for their regular gatherings but for their love, service, and presence. Whether through food pantries, counselling ministries, evangelistic outreach, or creative arts, the mission of God finds feet and hands in the local church.

Pastors and leaders must constantly cast vision for mission—not as an add-on, but as the lifeblood of the church. Every sermon, every small group, every ministry opportunity must be tied back to the covenant call: we are a people on mission with God.

The global scope of the New Covenant mission

The New Covenant mission is inherently global. This is not a modern invention or an add-on to the gospel. From the very beginning, God's redemptive purpose has encompassed every nations. The promise to Abraham was that *"all peoples on earth will be blessed through you."* (Genesis 12:3). This promise did not expire with the Old Covenant. Rather, it found its full expression in Jesus Christ, who commissioned His followers to *"go and make disciples of all nations."* (Matthew 28:19).

The global scope of the mission reflects the heart of a God who desires that none should perish (2 Peter 3:9). It also reflects the fulfilment of prophetic vision. Isaiah foresaw a day when *"the nations will come to your light, and kings to the brightness of your dawn."* (Isaiah 60:3). Revelation gives us a glimpse of that fulfilled mission: *"a great multitude that no one could count, from every nation, tribe, people and language"* standing before the throne and before the Lamb (Revelation 7:9).

This global vision drives the church beyond comfort zones and cultural boundaries. It compels us to cross oceans and streets, to learn languages and customs, to preach the gospel and plant churches in every corner of the earth. The church cannot be parochial or provincial. It must be global in heart and action, because the gospel is for all people.

Global mission includes more than geographic expansion. It also involves cultural engagement. We are called not only to translate the Scriptures but also to contextualize the message—to make the gospel intelligible and compelling in every culture. This requires humility, sensitivity, and deep theological grounding. We do not change the message, but we learn to speak it faithfully in different tongues.

Justice and compassion as missional imperatives

Mission is not limited to proclamation. It also includes demonstration. The gospel of the kingdom touches every aspect of life, including the social, economic, and political dimensions.

In the ministry of Jesus, healing the sick and feeding the hungry went hand in hand with preaching the Word. He proclaimed good news to the poor, freedom for the prisoners, and recovery of sight for the blind (Luke 4:18).

The New Covenant mission continues this holistic pattern. As we proclaim salvation through Christ, we also seek justice for the oppressed, care for the vulnerable, and advocate for the marginalised. Micah 6:8 reminds us of God's requirements: *"To act justly and to love mercy and to walk humbly with your God."* James 1:27 declares that *"religion that God our Father accepts as pure and faultless is this: to look after orphans and widows in their distress."*

Mission that ignores suffering is incomplete. We must be people of both truth and compassion. The church must engage in works of mercy — not as a distraction from the gospel but as a visible expression of it. Whether through building hospitals, running orphanages, defending the unborn, or feeding the hungry, these acts are missional acts. They point to the coming Kingdom where justice and peace will reign.

Such engagement requires wisdom. Compassion must be discerning. The church must resist the temptation to replace the gospel with social activism. But it must also resist the temptation to preach a gospel devoid of love. True mission holds word and deed together in harmony, reflecting the heart of the One who *"went around doing good and healing all who were under the power of the devil."* (Acts 10:38).

The role of every believer in the mission

One of the revolutionary aspects of the New Covenant is the priesthood of all believers. No longer is mission the exclusive task of priests or prophets. Every believer is called, gifted, and sent. As Peter writes, *"You are a royal priesthood... that you may declare the praises of him who called you."* (1 Peter 2:9). Paul echoes this in Ephesians 4, where he says that Christ gave leaders to the church *"to equip his people for works of service."* This means that mission is not just for the pulpit but for the pew. It belongs in the boardroom, classroom, living room, and neighbourhood.

The Spirit equips each member of the body for ministry. Teachers, engineers, nurses, artists, farmers, and students all have a place in God's mission. The church must affirm and equip the laity, not as helpers of professional ministers, but as co-labourers in the harvest field.

This decentralised model of mission increases the reach and resilience of the church. When every member sees themselves as a missionary, the gospel spreads exponentially. Evangelism is no longer an event; it becomes a lifestyle. Discipleship is no longer confined to classrooms; it happens in the rhythms of daily life. This also challenges us to rethink success in mission. Faithfulness becomes more important than fame. Quiet obedience is as valuable as public proclamation. The mother who disciples her children, the retiree who visits the sick, the teenager who shares Christ with a friend — these are all frontline missionaries in the New Covenant age.

Suffering and the cost of mission

Mission is glorious, but it is not glamorous. The call to follow Christ into the world is a call to suffer. Jesus made this clear: *"Whoever wants to be my disciple must deny themselves and take up their cross daily and follow me."* (Luke 9:23). Paul's life certainly exemplified this. He endured imprisonment, beatings, hunger and shipwrecks — all for the sake of the gospel.

In many parts of the world today, to follow Jesus publicly is to invite persecution. churches are burned, pastors are jailed, believers are ostracised. And yet, the gospel continues to spread — often most powerfully in places of greatest opposition. Tertullian famously wrote, *"The blood of the martyrs is the seed of the church."* Suffering, when it is embraced for Christ's sake, becomes a strong witness. It testifies to the surpassing worth of knowing Him. It strips away superficial faith and reveals the depth of covenant commitment. The New Covenant gives us not only a mission but also the power to endure its cost. *"We are hard pressed on every side, but not crushed... struck down, but not destroyed."* (2 Corinthians 4:8-9).

Western churches must learn from their persecuted brothers and sisters. While we may not face imprisonment, we do face the subtle pressures of secularism—mockery, marginalisation, and indifference. Our response must be faithful, not fearful. The cost of mission is real, but so is the reward. Jesus promised, *"Everyone who has left houses or brothers or sisters... for my sake will receive a hundred times as much and will inherit eternal life."* (Matthew 19:29).

The consummation of the mission

The mission of the church is not endless. It has a destination. One day, the work of witness will be complete, the harvest gathered, and the King will return. Jesus said, *"This gospel of the kingdom will be preached in the whole world... and then the end will come."* (Matthew 24:14). The completion of the mission precedes the consummation of the Kingdom.

This eschatological vision fuels urgency. We simply do not have unlimited time. Every generation is responsible for its moment in history. The church today stands on the shoulders of all the missionaries and martyrs who went before us. Now the baton passes to us. We are stewards of the gospel for this time and this place. But, as we will see in the next chapter, there is a final and glorious consummation.

The end of the mission is not merely the end of effort; it is the beginning of glory. The Lamb who was slain will receive the reward of His suffering. The nations will bow, and every tongue will confess that Jesus Christ is Lord. The new heavens and new earth will be filled with worshippers from every tribe and tongue. And the church will rest from her labours, rejoicing in the eternal presence of her Lord.

Until that day, we labour on. Not in despair, but in hope. Not in fear, but in faith. The New Covenant mission is unstoppable because it is upheld by the promise of God, the power of the Spirit, and the victory of Christ.

- 18 -

COVENANT AND THE CONSUMMATION

The grand story of redemption

As we have already noted in this study, the Bible is not a random collection of religious texts. It is one unified, divinely inspired story — a narrative that begins in a garden, crescendos at a cross, and concludes in a glorious city. This grand story is held together by the theme of covenant. From Eden to the New Jerusalem, the covenants of God reveal His heart, His purposes, and His relentless faithfulness. At every stage of redemptive history, God's covenantal dealings with humanity point forward to a final, glorious consummation — the full and eternal realization of His promises.

When we speak of consummation in theological terms, we are referring to the ultimate fulfilment and final completion of God's redemptive plan. This is not merely about the end of time, but about the goal of all time. It is not only about the return of Christ, but the restoration of all things. It is the moment when the kingdom of God is fully and visibly established, when the dwelling of God is again with His people, and when the New Covenant reaches its glorious climax.

Understanding the consummation through the lens of covenant allows us to grasp the depth of what God is doing in history. The promises made to Abraham, the Law given through Moses, the kingdom established under David, and the prophecies spoken by Isaiah and Jeremiah all find their ultimate fulfilment in Jesus Christ and the world to come. The New Covenant is not the end of the story — it is the beginning of the final chapter, the inauguration of a new age that will culminate in glory.

Covenant hope in a groaning creation

As you know, we live in what theologians call the *"now but not yet."* The New Covenant has been inaugurated through Christ's death and resurrection.

The Spirit has been poured out. The kingdom of God is here, but not yet fully realised. We still live in a world which is marked by suffering, sin, death, and decay. Paul captures this tension in Romans 8:22-23: *"We know that the whole creation has been groaning as in the pains of childbirth right up to the present time. Not only so, but we ourselves...groan inwardly as we wait eagerly for our adoption to sonship, the redemption of our bodies."*

This groaning is not a sign of hopelessness; it is a sign of great expectation. Like a mother in labour, creation is not dying—it is giving birth. The New Covenant gives us the assurance that redemption is not partial but complete. Christ's work has dealt with sin's penalty and power, and one day it will remove sin's presence entirely. The resurrection of Jesus is the first fruits of what is to come (1 Corinthians 15:20). Just as He was raised, we too will be raised. Just as He reigns, we too will reign with Him.

Our covenantal hope is not escapism. We are not waiting to be plucked from the earth, leaving it to burn. Rather, we are looking forward to a renewed heaven and a renewed earth—a place where righteousness dwells (2 Peter 3:13). God is certainly not abandoning His creation; He is redeeming it. The same Creator who called the world into being will one day declare, *"I am making everything new!"* (Revelation 21:5).

The return of the covenant king

At the centre of the consummation is the promised return of Jesus Christ. The first advent of Christ was marked by humility, suffering, and apparent defeat. The second advent will be marked by glory, triumph, and visible vindication. Revelation 19 presents Christ as the rider on the white horse, faithful and true, coming to judge and make war in righteousness. He wears many crowns and bears the *name "King of kings and Lord of lords."*

This is not a different Jesus—it is the same Jesus in the fullness of His revealed glory. The covenant King who came to serve will come again to reign. His return is not a footnote in Christian theology; it is the climactic event.

Titus 2:13 calls it, *"the blessed hope – the appearing of the glory of our great God and Saviour, Jesus Christ."* The church therefore lives in anticipation of this appearing, not as a distant fantasy, but as a concrete future that shapes our present. When Christ returns, He will consummate the New Covenant by fully establishing the kingdom He inaugurated. The dead in Christ will rise. The living will be transformed. Justice will roll like a river. Every knee will bow, and every tongue confess that Jesus is Lord, to the glory of God the Father. The covenant people, purified and glorified, will finally become what they were always meant to be – a spotless bride, presented to the Bridegroom in splendour and joy.

The marriage supper of the Lamb

One of the most beautiful images of the consummation is the marriage supper of the Lamb. Revelation 19:6-9 describes a heavenly celebration where God's people are united with Christ in eternal fellowship: *"Blessed are those who are invited to the wedding supper of the Lamb!"* This is the fulfilment of covenant language that runs throughout Scripture.

In the Old Testament, God often refers to His relationship with Israel in marital terms. When Israel strayed into idolatry, it was described as adultery (Hosea 2:2; Jeremiah 3:20). Yet God promised a glorious day of reconciliation and restoration – a new covenant in which His people would be betrothed to Him forever in righteousness and faithfulness (Hosea 2:19-20).

In Ephesians 5:25-27, the church is described as the bride of Christ. The covenant relationship is intimate, loving, and exclusive. The marriage supper of the Lamb is not just symbolic; it is eschatological. It signifies the full and final union between Christ and His people. No more sin. No more distance. No more waiting. Face to face communion, joy unending, and love that will never fade. This vivid imagery also reinforces the truth that the consummation is not the end of our story – it is the beginning of the real story. Just as a wedding day marks not an ending but a glorious new beginning, so the return of Christ and the final establishment of His kingdom will launch us into the eternal purposes of God.

Life in the age to come will be neither static nor monotonous but rather dynamic and overflowing with purpose, joy, worship, and discovery.

The judgment of the wicked

While this consummation will bring joy and vindication for the covenant people, it will also bring judgment for those who have rejected God's covenant offer. The final judgment is not a very popular topic, but it is a necessary one. A covenant implies relationship, responsibility, and consequence. God is patient and merciful, but He is also holy and just. Those who persist in rebellion, who reject His grace, and who refuse His rule will face the righteous judgment of the covenant King.

Revelation 20 describes the great white throne judgment, where the dead are raised and judged according to what they have done. Those whose names are not found in the book of life are thrown into the lake of fire. This is sobering, but it is also just. God will not allow evil to have the final word. The enemies of righteousness will be defeated. The accuser will be silenced. The oppressors will be overthrown. Every injustice that was overlooked on earth will be dealt with in heaven's court.

This judgment is part of the consummation of the covenant. The New Covenant offers forgiveness, transformation, and eternal life—but it must be received. It is not forced upon anyone. God does not send people to hell against their will; He simply honours their decision to reject Him. As C.S. Lewis once wrote, *"There are only two kinds of people – those who say to God, 'Your will be done,' and those to whom God says, in the end, 'Your will be done.'"*

The reality of judgment heightens the urgency of mission. If the consummation is coming—and it is—then we must be about the Father's business. We proclaim the gospel not as religious opinion but as eternal truth. We invite others into the covenant not out of fear, but out of love. We long for the day when every tribe and tongue will gather before the throne—not just because it is glorious, but because it means our task is complete.

Living in light of the end

The doctrine of consummation is not merely about the future – it profoundly shapes how we live in the present. The New Covenant is not an abstract theological idea confined to ancient scrolls or academic texts. It is a living reality that calls us to embody its promises in the here and now.

The early Christians lived with an acute awareness that they were citizens of a coming kingdom. Their ethics, priorities, and decisions were formed not by the pressures of the age but by the hope of glory.

This exhortation from Paul captures this beautifully: *"But our citizenship is in heaven. And we eagerly await a Saviour from there, the Lord Jesus Christ, who...will transform our lowly bodies so that they will be like his glorious body."* (Philippians 3:20-21). Living in covenant with God means living with the end in view. The consummation may seem distant, but it is nearer now than ever before (Romans 13:11). And because the end is certain, our calling in the present is clear: to walk in faithfulness, holiness, and readiness.

The church is not a people in retreat, anxiously waiting for rescue. We are a people advancing, pressing forward in the power of the Spirit, anchored in covenant hope. The future is not an unknown abyss – it is the fulfilment of every promise. Christ is returning. The kingdom will come. Justice will prevail. And because of that certainty, we can live with courage, joy, and purpose today.

The 'now' and the 'not yet'

The theological tension of the 'now' and the 'not yet' is central to New Covenant life. The kingdom of God has already broken into history through the death and resurrection of Jesus. The powers of the age to come are already at work through the Holy Spirit. We are already justified, adopted, indwelt, and commissioned. But we are not yet glorified. Sin still clings. Death still stalks. Creation still groans. This tension is not a flaw in God's plan – it is a feature. It keeps us watchful, humble, and hopeful.

The church currently lives between the inauguration and the consummation of the kingdom, between the cross and the crown. This in-between time is not a waiting room – it is a mission field. It is a time for sowing, for building, for proclaiming, and for living out the values of the coming age.

The writer to the Hebrews captures this dynamic very well when he said, *"Let us hold unswervingly to the hope we profess, for he who promised is faithful...and all the more as you see the Day approaching"* (Hebrews 10:23,25). Covenant hope does not lead to passivity but to perseverance. The Day is approaching. That is not just an eschatological truth – it is pastoral comfort and motivational fire.

The consummation and the renewal of all things

One of the most breathtaking aspects of biblical consummation is the promise of cosmic renewal. The scope of redemption is not merely personal or ecclesial – it is universal. The New Covenant does not end with the salvation of souls; it culminates in the restoration of all things.

Peter declares in Acts 3:21 that Christ must remain in heaven *"until the time comes for God to restore everything, as he promised long ago through his holy prophets."* Isaiah envisioned this when he prophesied of new heavens and a new earth (Isaiah 65:17). Paul speaks of all creation being liberated from its bondage to decay (Romans 8:21). And Revelation concludes with the descent of the New Jerusalem – a city where God dwells with His people in a renewed creation (Revelation 21:1-3).

This eschatological vision is profoundly covenantal. In Eden, God walked with humanity in perfect fellowship. Sin shattered that communion, but the story of Scripture is about God restoring what was lost – and more. The consummation is not merely a return to Eden; it is the unveiling of something greater than Eden. It is the eternal union of heaven and earth. It is the place where righteousness dwells, where tears are wiped away, where the curse is no more. This shapes how we treat creation today. If God intends to renew the earth, then our stewardship matters.

If the material world is not destined for destruction but transformation, then our work, our culture, our creativity — they all have eternal significance. The consummation redeems not only our souls but our calling as image-bearers and caretakers of God's world.

The resurrection and the body

Central to the Christian vision of this consummation is the resurrection of the body. Too often, believers have absorbed unbiblical ideas of disembodied bliss, floating on clouds or escaping the material realm. But the New Testament hope is bodily. Just as Jesus was raised physically, so shall we be. Paul devotes an entire chapter — 1 Corinthians 15 — to this truth. *"The trumpet will sound, the dead will be raised imperishable, and we will be changed" (v. 52).* The resurrection body is not a return to our current frailty. It is a glorified, imperishable, spiritual body — suited for the new creation. It will be free from pain, sin, and death. It will be like Christ's resurrection body — recognisable, tangible, and yet transcendent (Philippians 3:21).

This truth has profound implications. It affirms the goodness of creation and the dignity of the human body. It gives comfort in grief, strength in suffering, and purpose in the present. Our labour is not in vain (1 Corinthians 15:58) because it is not lost in death. The resurrection means that nothing done for Christ is wasted. Every act of love, justice, faithfulness, and witness will echo in eternity.

The resurrection is the covenantal victory over death — the last enemy (1 Corinthians 15:26). It is the seal of God's promise, the vindication of the gospel, and the doorway into the age to come.

The glory of the Lamb and the light of the city

In the final vision of Revelation, the glory of God fills the new creation. There is no temple, for the Lord God Almighty and the Lamb are its temple (Revelation 21:22). There is no sun, for the glory of God gives it light, and the Lamb is its lamp (v. 23). This is the consummation of all covenant worship.

From the tabernacle of Moses to the temple of Solomon, from the prophetic visions of Ezekiel to the final descent of the heavenly city, God's covenant promise has always been: *"I will dwell among them and be their God" (Ezekiel 37:27; Revelation 21:3)*. The final fulfilment of this promise is not a building, but a Person—the Lamb slain, now glorified.

Worship in the age to come is not ritualistic—it is relational. It is not confined to times and places—it is unending and all-encompassing. The presence of God will saturate every aspect of life. There will be no more separation, no more veils, no more longing—only communion.

This vision sustains us in the wilderness. It reminds us that we were made for glory, and glory is our destiny. The Lamb who was slain is the Light that will never be extinguished. His wounds have become our healing. His reign will be our joy. And His presence will be our home.

The covenant people and eternal reward

The consummation brings with it not just judgment, but reward. Jesus frequently spoke of reward in the age to come: treasures in heaven, crowns of righteousness, commendation from the Master, and eternal inheritance. While salvation is by grace alone, the Scriptures are clear that our faithfulness matters. What we do with our lives in the body has eternal consequences.

Jesus said, *"Look, I am coming soon! My reward is with me, and I will give to each person according to what they have done"* (Rev. 22:12). Paul speaks of a *"crown of righteousness"* laid up for those who long for Christ's appearing (2 Timothy 4:8), and Peter speaks of an *"inheritance that can never perish, spoil or fade – kept in heaven for you."* (1 Peter 1:4).

These promises are not about earning salvation—they are about recognising covenant faithfulness. The New Covenant believer, empowered by the Spirit, lives a life of obedient love, and God, in His grace, chooses to reward that obedience eternally.

Every hidden act of service, every sacrifice made in love, every faithful endurance through trial—none of it is forgotten. This reward is not only individual but corporate. The church will reign with Christ (Revelation 20:6), inherit the earth (Matthew 5:5), and judge angels (1 Corinthians 6:3). We are heirs with Christ, and we will share in His glory (Romans 8:17). The final reward is not just the absence of pain—it is the fullness of joy in God's presence and participation in His reign forever.

The New Covenant and eternal security

A vital aspect of the New Covenant is its permanence. The Old Covenant could be broken, but the New Covenant, sealed by the blood of Christ and written on the hearts of believers, cannot be broken and it cannot be undone. This covenant brings with it the assurance of eternal security.

Jesus said, *"I give them eternal life, and they shall never perish; no one will snatch them out of my hand"* (John 10:28). The writer to the Hebrews affirms that by one sacrifice Christ has perfected forever those who are being made holy (Hebrews 10:14). Paul assures us in Romans 8:38–39 that nothing in all creation can separate us from the love of God that is in Christ Jesus. This eternal security is not a license for complacency but a foundation for confident living. It frees us from the fear of condemnation and empowers us to live boldly for the kingdom. We can persevere because we are preserved. We can fight the good fight because the victory is secure.

In the consummation, this security becomes sight. Faith gives way to fulfilment. The trials of the present are eclipsed by the glory of the future (2 Corinthians 4:17). The tears, the doubts, the failures—they are all swallowed up in the joy of eternal life. This is the promise of the New Covenant, sealed by the Spirit, ratified by the Son, and guaranteed by the Father.

Living as a people of the consummation

So, what does it mean to live as a people of the consummation? It means living with hope—not wishful thinking, but confident expectation.

It means aligning our lives with the reality of the kingdom that is coming. It means bearing witness to the age to come by the way we love, forgive, serve, and endure.

Peter exhorts us in 2 Peter 3:11–12: *"Since everything will be destroyed in this way, what kind of people ought you to be? You ought to live holy and godly lives as you look forward to the day of God and speed its coming."* Eschatology is not escapism — it is motivation. It calls us to holiness, urgency, and faithfulness.

Living as a people of the consummation also means resisting despair. The world groans under the weight of sin, violence, corruption, and death. But we are not without hope. We know the end of this amazing story. Christ wins! Evil is vanquished! Righteousness reigns! The New Covenant people are called to live with a settled joy that confounds the chaos of the age.

We are also called to mission. The consummation is not merely about personal salvation — it is about the redemption of a people from every tribe, language, and nation (Revelation 7:9). We live now as ambassadors of reconciliation, proclaiming the gospel of the kingdom until the King returns. Every act of evangelism, every disciple made, every church planted — it is all part of God's consummating work.

And finally, we live with worship. The consummation is the completion of worship. It is the day when every knee will bow and every tongue confess that Jesus Christ is Lord. It is the fulfilment of our deepest longing — to see God face to face and to dwell with Him forever. Even now, we worship in anticipation of that day. Our songs, our prayers, our sacraments — they are echoes of the eternal liturgy.

COVENANT AND CREATION

This seems like a strange place to talk about creation and the covenant - in the final chapter of the book. In my first draft, I had this as chapter 2, but the more I wrote, the more I felt it would be better to reflect on this in the final chapter. I hope you see why I made that choice as you conclude this book.

The covenant framework rooted in creation

The doctrine of covenant does not originate in the covenant with Abraham or even with Moses on Mount Sinai. It finds its roots much earlier — in the very act of creation itself. To understand the full scope and beauty of the biblical covenants, we must reflect on where the Bible begins: *"In the beginning God created the heavens and the earth."* (Genesis 1:1). The story of God's covenantal dealings with humanity is not an afterthought to fix a broken world but the unfolding of a divine design woven into creation from the start.

Creation itself is covenantal. When God made the world, He ordered it with intention, structure, and purpose. The rhythm of creation — six days of work and one day of rest — reflects covenantal structure. God's repeated declaration, *"And God saw that it was good,"* reveals a Creator committed to both beauty and flourishing.

Humanity is created not as an accident or afterthought but as the crown of creation, made "in the image of God" (Genesis 1:27), male and female, with the vocation to *"be fruitful and increase in number; fill the earth and subdue it. Rule over... every living creature."* (Genesis 1:28). This divine mandate is not merely a command; it is actually a covenantal commission. Theologians have referred to this as the *"covenant of creation"* or even the *"Adamic covenant."* Although the term *"covenant"* is not explicitly used in creation account in Genesis 1-2, the elements of a covenant — relationship, responsibilities, stipulations, and blessings — are all present.

Humanity is placed in a covenant relationship with the Creator, given both a gift and a task: to enjoy God's provision and His presence, and to steward His world.

The sabbath and the covenant pattern

The inclusion of the Sabbath in the creation account is highly significant in regard to covenant theology. God rests, not because He is weary, but to establish a holy rhythm—a pattern of rest and worship. The seventh day is blessed and made holy, set apart as a sign of completeness and covenant. Later in the biblical narrative, the Sabbath becomes a central sign of the Mosaic covenant (Exodus 31:16–17), but its roots lie in creation itself.

By setting aside the seventh day, God is signalling the covenantal nature of time. Time is neither random nor chaotic; it is ordered around relationship with the Creator. Humanity is invited to live in sync with God's rhythm—to work, to rest, to worship, and to reflect. The Sabbath is a built-in reminder that creation is not self-sufficient. It exists for God's glory and by God's grace. The covenant of creation is not transactional but relational. God provides everything, and humanity responds with trust and obedience.

This divine pattern reinforces the idea that the covenants which follow—Noahic, Abrahamic, Mosaic, Davidic, and the New Covenant—are not arbitrary interventions but continuations of God's covenantal intention set in motion at creation. The Sabbath is a thread that ties creation to covenant, anchoring God's relationship with humanity in both time and holiness.

Humanity's role as covenant stewards

At the heart of the creation covenant is humanity's identity as image-bearers. The phrase—"*in the image of God*"—is profoundly covenantal. To bear God's image means to represent Him, to reflect His character, and to exercise His delegated authority on the earth. In ancient Near Eastern cultures, kings were often described as images of the gods. In Genesis, that royal status is extended to all humans, male and female. Every person is endowed with dignity, purpose, and responsibility.

The command to *"fill the earth and subdue it"* is not a license for exploitation but a covenantal commission for stewardship. Humanity is entrusted with creation, not to dominate it for selfish gain, but to cultivate it for mutual flourishing. This stewardship is an act of worship. Adam's task in the Garden — to *"work it and take care of it"* (Genesis 2:15) — is priestly language. The Hebrew words used here are the same used for the Levitical priests in the tabernacle. In this light, Eden is the first temple, and Adam and Eve are its priests, mediating God's presence to all of creation. This priestly stewardship reinforces the covenantal dimension of creation. Humanity is not autonomous but accountable. We are not owners but caretakers. Our dominion is always under God's ultimate kingship. To live faithfully under the creation covenant is to live in humble dependence, joyful obedience, and loving stewardship. When this relationship is honoured, blessing abounds. When it is broken, the results are catastrophic.

The fall as covenant breach

Genesis 3 tells us the tragic story of humanity's rebellion. The serpent's temptation is not just about fruit — it is an assault on the covenantal order. By questioning God's word and goodness, Adam and Eve step out of the covenant relationship and assert autonomy. This act of disobedience is not merely a mistake; it is a breach of trust, a rejection of the divine covenant.

The consequences are immediate, and they are far-reaching. The relationship between God and humanity is severely fractured. The harmony between man and woman is also disrupted. The ground itself is cursed. Work now becomes toil. Childbearing becomes pain. Death enters the story. Creation itself groans under the weight of covenantal rupture.

Yet even in judgment, there is grace. God seeks the hiding couple. He covers their shame. He promises a redeemer — the offspring of the woman who will crush the serpent's head (Genesis 3:15). This protoevangelium ("first gospel") is the seed of the New Covenant, planted in the soil of the broken creation covenant. God's mission to redeem creation begins not with wrath but with a promise.

This reveals a profound truth: God is a covenant-keeping God even when humanity is covenant-breaking. His love endures. His purposes prevail. The rest of Scripture is the unfolding of this redemptive mission—the restoration of the covenant relationship broken in Eden.

The Noahic Covenant and cosmic renewal

After the flood, God makes a covenant with Noah and all creation (Genesis 9:8–17). This is the very first time the word *"covenant"* explicitly appears in the Bible text, marking a recommitment to the creation order. God promises never again to destroy the earth by flood, and He places the rainbow in the sky as a covenant sign.

Importantly, this covenant is not just with Noah but with *"every living creature" and "all life on the earth."* (Genesis 9:10, 17). It is a cosmic covenant. The scope is creation-wide. The language used here reaffirms the creational structure: the value of life, the importance of fruitfulness, the call to stewardship. This covenant serves as a stabilising force in a post-flood world. It affirms that despite human sin, God's commitment to creation remains.

The Noahic covenant reveals that the mission of God includes not just the salvation of souls but the restoration of the cosmos. God is not abandoning creation; He is renewing it. The flood is not the end of the story but a dramatic reset. The covenant with Noah sets the stage for the more specific covenants to come, particularly the Abrahamic and Mosaic covenants, which will focus on a particular people. But the foundation remains the same: God is the Creator, and He is committed to His creation.

Creation and the glory of God

One of the recurring themes in Scripture is that creation exists to display the glory of God. Psalm 19:1 declares, *"The heavens declare the glory of God; the skies proclaim the work of his hands."* Romans 1:20 affirms that *"since the creation of the world God's invisible qualities – his eternal power and divine nature – have been clearly seen, being understood from what has been made."*

This is not an abstract theological idea but a covenantal reality. Creation reveals the covenantal character of God – His order, His beauty, His faithfulness. The cycles of day and night, the seasons, the stars in their courses – all point to a Creator who sustains and governs.

When Israel forgets their covenant obligations, the prophets often call them back by reminding them of God's creative power. *"Do you not know? Have you not heard? The Lord is the everlasting God, the Creator of the ends of the earth."* (Isaiah 40:28).

Creation, then, is not neutral ground. It is sacred space. It is the stage on which the covenant relationship between God and humanity is lived out. Our treatment of the earth, our use of resources, our care for fellow creatures – these are not merely ethical issues; they are covenantal responsibilities. To abuse creation is to violate the covenant of creation. To honour creation is to honour the Creator.

Covenant, ecology, and Christian responsibility

In our modern context, the implications of covenant and creation intersect powerfully with ecological concerns. Environmental degradation, deforestation, and species extinction are not merely political or scientific issues. They are theological concerns rooted in covenantal negligence. When humanity forgets its role as steward and assumes the role of master, the consequences are devastating.

A robust theology of the creation covenant challenges the church to engage in creation care not as a trend but as a testimony. It is a witness to the world that we serve a Creator who loves His world and calls us to do the same. Christian responsibility toward the environment is not a distraction from the gospel – it is an expression of it. The good news is not only that Jesus saves sinners but that He is Lord of all creation and is making all things new. Romans 8:19-21 paints a hopeful picture: *"The creation waits in eager expectation for the children of God to be revealed... that the creation itself will be liberated from its bondage to decay and brought into the freedom and glory of the children of God."*

This is covenant language. Creation longs for covenantal restoration. And as the church lives out its calling, it becomes a signpost of that future renewal.

The covenant fulfilled in the new creation

The story of covenant and creation, though beginning in the Garden of Eden, ultimately points forward to the promise of a new creation—a restored cosmos in which the brokenness of sin is fully healed, and the glory of God shines unhindered. This eschatological vision is not peripheral to the covenant narrative; it is its culmination. Just as the original creation was covenantal in design, so too the new creation is covenantal in fulfilment.

The New Covenant inaugurated by Jesus Christ is not merely a spiritual reality confined to individual salvation. It is the beginning of the renewal of all things. in 2 Corinthians 5:17, Paul writes, *"If anyone is in Christ, the new creation has come: The old has gone, the new is here!"* This statement is both deeply personal and profoundly cosmic. Believers are made new, but this renewal is a foretaste of the greater renewal that is coming.

Colossians 1:19–20 expands this vision: *"For God was pleased to have all his fullness dwell in him, and through him to reconcile to himself all things... by making peace through his blood, shed on the cross."* The cross is not just the means of individual atonement; it is the means by which God reconciles the entire cosmos. The blood of Christ has covenantal power to heal the breach not only between God and humanity but also between humanity and creation.

This eschatological hope finds its climax in the closing chapters of Revelation. There, John sees *"a new heaven and a new earth"* (Revelation 21:1). He hears the triumphant declaration: "Look! God's dwelling place is now among the people, and he will dwell with them" (21:3). The covenantal promise, *"I will be their God and they will be my people,"* finds ultimate expression in a renewed creation, free from death, mourning, crying, and pain (21:4).

Jesus as the last Adam

One of the most powerful biblical motifs connecting covenant and creation is the portrayal of Jesus as the *"last Adam."* Paul draws this connection explicitly in 1 Corinthians 15:45: *"The first man Adam became a living being; the last Adam, a life-giving spirit."*

Where the first Adam failed in the covenant of creation — bringing death and curse into the world — Christ, the last Adam, succeeds. He lives in perfect obedience, fulfils the covenant's demands, and ushers in resurrection life.

Romans 5:18–19 lays out the covenantal contrast: *"Just as one trespass resulted in condemnation for all people, so also one righteous act resulted in justification and life for all people."* The obedience of Christ undoes the disobedience of Adam.

This is covenantal substitution. Christ takes on the covenant curse that humanity deserved and bestows the covenant blessing we could never earn.

This identification of Jesus as the last Adam also restores humanity's role as God's image-bearers. In Christ, we are remade into the image of God (Colossians 3:10). We are once again given the Spirit, not only to dwell in us but to empower us to live out our original vocation — to represent God on the earth, to steward His world, and to reflect His glory. The new creation is not just a future reality but a present calling. As new creations in Christ, we begin to live now according to the values, ethics, and mission of the age to come.

The church as the first fruits of new creation

The church, as the people of the New Covenant, is called to be the first fruits of the new creation. James 1:18 speaks of believers as *"a kind of first fruits of all he created."* This agricultural metaphor, rooted in Old Testament covenant practice, signifies that what is begun in the church is a preview of what is to come in the world. The church is a prototype of the renewed humanity and a foretaste of the restored creation. This covenantal identity carries profound implications.

The church is not a religious club or a social organisation — it is the embodied community of the new creation. As such, it is called to model the harmony, justice, beauty, and worship that will characterise the new heavens and new earth. This includes our relationships, our ethics, our treatment of the environment, and our mission in the world.

Our worship is not escapism but anticipation. Our sacraments are not mere rituals but covenant signs that point forward. Baptism signals death to the old creation and resurrection into the new (Romans 6:4). The Lord's Supper proclaims the death of Christ until He comes, anticipating the marriage supper of the Lamb (1 Corinthians 11:26; Revelation 19:9). The church, then, exists not only in history but also in hope. We are pilgrims and ambassadors of a world that is coming.

Creation and redemption are inseparable

One of the tragic tendencies in modern theology has been to separate creation from redemption, treating the former as a background setting and the latter as the main plot. However, in covenantal theology, these two are inseparably linked. The God who creates is the God who redeems, and He redeems in order to renew what He created.

This truth has enormous theological and pastoral significance. It means that our physical bodies matter. Our earthly lives matter. Our work, our rest, our creativity, and our care for creation all matter. The gospel is not a message about escaping the material world but about the transformation of the material world through Christ.

Romans 8 captures this beautifully. The creation "waits in eager expectation for the children of God to be revealed" (8:19). It "was subjected to frustration" but "will be liberated from its bondage to decay and brought into the freedom and glory of the children of God" (8:21). Redemption is not only about souls but about soil. Not only about heaven but about earth. This is the covenant vision: a reconciled people in a renewed world, living in unbroken fellowship with their Creator.

Worship as covenant participation in creation

Worship is one of the most potent expressions of the covenantal relationship between Creator and creation. Throughout Scripture, creation is portrayed as a worshipping entity. The psalms are full of cosmic praise: *"Let the heavens rejoice, let the earth be glad; let the sea resound... Let all creation rejoice before the Lord."* (Psalm 96:11-13). Isaiah proclaims that even the trees of the field will clap their hands (Isaiah 55:12).

This poetic imagery here is more than metaphor. It reflects a theological reality: all creation exists to glorify God. As image-bearers, human beings are uniquely called to lead creation in this worship. When we gather as the covenant people of God to sing, pray, listen to Scripture, and celebrate the sacraments, we are fulfilling our creational and covenantal vocation.

Moreover, worship is not confined to what happens in church buildings. Romans 12:1 calls us to present our bodies *"as a living sacrifice, holy and pleasing to God – this is your true and proper worship."* All of life becomes worship when it is lived in response to God's covenant mercy. Gardening, teaching, parenting, engineering, painting, serving – when done for the glory of God and the good of others, these become covenantal acts of worship that reflect the Creator.

The mission of the church in light of creation

If creation is covenantal and redemption is creational, then the mission of the church must include creation care. The Great Commission (Matthew 28:18-20) and the Cultural Mandate (Genesis 1:28) are not in competition. They are complementary. Evangelism and ecology, discipleship and development, soul care and soil care – all are part of the church's mission under the New Covenant.

This mission is holistic. It involves proclaiming the gospel, planting churches, healing the broken, lifting up the poor, stewarding resources, and advocating for justice. It involves repentance, reconciliation, and restoration.

It is about helping people see that Jesus is not only their Saviour but also the Lord of creation. It is about proclaiming that the kingdom of God has come and is coming—and that this kingdom includes rivers, trees, animals, cities, and skies.

To be covenantally faithful in our mission is to engage the world with open eyes and open hands. We do not withdraw from creation but invest in it. We do not exploit it but nurture it. We do not ignore its groaning but join its longing. We live as those who know that the world was made by God, broken by sin, redeemed by Christ, and destined for glory.

The eucharist and the earth

One of the most overlooked connections between covenant and creation is the Eucharist—the Lord's Supper. In this sacrament, believers partake of bread and wine—elements drawn from the earth, cultivated by human hands, and sanctified by God's word and Spirit. These physical elements become means of grace, symbols of covenant renewal, and anticipations of the heavenly banquet.

In the Eucharist, we are reminded that God works through creation to communicate grace. The table becomes a place where heaven and earth meet. We taste and see that the Lord is good—not in abstraction, but in bread and wine. This sacrament roots us in the reality that God is not distant from the material world but intimately involved with it. Moreover, the Eucharist points forward. It is a rehearsal dinner for the marriage feast of the Lamb. It is a taste of the new creation. It is a covenantal sign that the One who created us and redeemed us will one day restore all things. As such, it invites us to live with gratitude, humility, and hope—not only for our salvation but for the salvation of the world.

The role of beauty in the covenant of creation

Finally, we must recognise the role of beauty in the covenantal relationship between God and creation. Beauty is not a luxury; it is essential. It is part of God's self-revelation.

The intricacy of a flower, the majesty of a mountain, the colours of a sunset, the elegance of mathematical patterns, the harmony of a symphony—all these reflect the character of a God who delights in splendour.

To pursue beauty is to honour the Creator. To create art, design buildings, write poetry, grow gardens, or compose music is to participate in the covenant of creation. These are not secular activities but sacred vocations. The church must be a place that not only preaches truth, and models love but also cultivates beauty. Beauty awakens wonder, draws us to worship, and whispers of the world to come.

As we live out our covenantal calling, we become co-creators with God. Not in the sense of inventing ex nihilo, but in the sense of shaping, renewing, and beautifying what God has made. This is what it means to be human. This is what it means to bear God's image. This is what it means to live under the covenant of creation.

Living as covenant stewards of creation

To live under the covenant of creation is to embrace the role of steward—not as a passive observer of the world, but as an active participant in its flourishing. From the beginning, God entrusted humanity with a sacred mandate: *"Be fruitful and increase in number; fill the earth and subdue it. Rule over... every living creature..."* (Genesis 1:28). This was not a license for exploitation, but a commission to nurture, cultivate, and govern creation in harmony with God's purposes.

This original stewardship over creation remains intact under the New Covenant. The work of redemption does not abolish our responsibility for creation; it redeems and renews it. Through Christ, we are restored not only to right relationship with God but also to our original vocation as image-bearers. We are called to exercise dominion in the way that God does—with wisdom, compassion, and justice. This has practical implications for every sphere of life. In our homes, it means living with gratitude and care for the things we use.

In our communities, it means advocating for policies that protect the environment and promote sustainability. In our churches, it means teaching a theology that includes creation care as a vital expression of discipleship. Stewardship is not optional for the covenant people of God; it is essential to our identity and mission.

Creation groaning and the hope of glory

While the covenant of creation affirms the goodness of the world, it also acknowledges its brokenness. The fall introduced a rupture that extends beyond humanity into the fabric of creation itself. Paul's vivid description in Romans 8:22 — *"We know that the whole creation has been groaning as in the pains of childbirth right up to the present time"* — reminds us that the earth shares in our suffering and our hope.

Creation groans, but not in despair. It groans in expectation. It awaits "the revealing of the sons of God" (Romans 8:19) — the unveiling of God's covenant people in their glorified state. This eschatological vision fuels our present action. We do not give up on creation because it is groaning; we labour in hope, knowing that what is begun now will be completed when Christ returns.

The groaning of creation also invites lament. As covenant people, we must learn to grieve the degradation of the world. We must mourn deforestation, pollution, species extinction, and all forms of environmental injustice — not as political activists but as covenant stewards. Lament is a spiritual discipline that aligns our hearts with God's. It is not the opposite of hope but the birthplace of it. In lament, we name what is broken and cry out for redemption.

A theology of place and land

Biblical covenant theology is inherently tied to land. From the Garden of Eden to the Promised Land, from exile to restoration, from Jesus' ministry in Galilee to the new heavens and new earth, place matters. God does not deal with abstract humanity but with embodied people in particular locations. This incarnational principle is central to covenantal living.

The land given to Israel under the Old Covenant was not merely real estate; it was a gift, a sign of divine favour, and a sphere for covenant obedience. Deuteronomy is filled with instructions about how to live in the land in a way that reflects God's character—caring for the poor, letting the land rest, protecting biodiversity, and ensuring economic justice. These laws reveal a profound theology of place: the land is God's, and we are its tenants (Leviticus 25:23).

Under the New Covenant, the promise of land is expanded, not erased. The church is no longer a people tied to a single geography but a global community that embodies the kingdom of God wherever it is found.

Yet even in this expansion, the theology of place remains vital. Christians are called to be rooted, to care for their neighbourhoods, to honour the land they inhabit, and to cultivate local expressions of the gospel.

Wendell Berry, a Christian farmer and poet, writes, *"There are no unsacred places; there are only sacred places and desecrated places."* Covenant faithfulness means treating every place as holy ground. Whether we live in a small city apartment or a large rural farmhouse, we are called to love the land, bless it, and steward it for future generations. This is how covenant meets creation in the ordinary.

The sacramentality of the created world

The created world is not God, but it bears His fingerprints. Scripture affirms that *"The heavens declare the glory of God; the skies proclaim the work of his hands."* (Psalm 19:1). Nature is not merely raw material; it is revelation. Though not redemptive revelation like Scripture, creation offers a general revelation that reveals the power, beauty, and faithfulness of the Creator.

This understanding leads to a sacramental vision of the world—not in the sense of blurring the line between Creator and creation, but in recognising that physical realities can mediate spiritual truths.

Just as water, bread, and wine convey grace in baptism and holy communion, so too can a sunrise, or a mountain range, or a newborn child awaken us to God's presence. The world is charged with divine meaning for those with eyes to see.

This vision stands against both secularism and sentimentalism. Secularism sees the whole world as being mute and meaningless; sentimentalism romanticises it without any accountability. But covenant theology calls us to see creation as a theatre of God's glory—a place where heaven and earth intersect, where material and spiritual realities converge.

This has the power to reshape our spirituality. Devotion is not confined to the prayer closet; it extends to the kitchen, the garden, the classroom, and the marketplace. Worship is not only what we sing on Sundays but how we work on Mondays. Creation becomes a living text through which God speaks, and every bush may burn with His presence, if we are willing to turn aside and look (Exodus 3:2-3).

Eschatology and the renewal of all things

One of the most radical affirmations of covenant theology is that God's plan is not to abandon creation but to renew it. Christian eschatology does not teach the annihilation of the world but its transformation. This is the promise of *"a new heaven and a new earth"* (Revelation 21:1)—not a replacement but a restoration.

Jesus speaks of this in Matthew 19:28 when He refers to *"the renewal of all things."* Peter echoes it in Acts 3:21, proclaiming that heaven must receive Christ *"until the time comes for God to restore everything, as he promised long ago through his holy prophets."* Paul affirms it in Ephesians 1:10, describing God's purpose *"to bring unity to all things in heaven and on earth under Christ."*

This is the *telos*—the ultimate goal—of the covenant. It is not disembodied bliss but embodied glory. It is not escape from creation but communion within it. It is not an end but a beginning. As the grand old hymn says, *"Jesus shall reign where'er the sun, does its successive journeys run."*

The renewed creation will be the eternal dwelling of God with His people—a covenant relationship unbroken, a creation unmarred, a cosmos rejoicing. This hope must shape our ethics. If God cares enough to redeem the world, we must care enough to protect it. If creation has a future, it has value now. If the earth is our eternal home, then our current lives are not rehearsal but rehearsal dinner—preparing us to live as covenant citizens of the coming kingdom.

Christ, the centre of creation and covenant

At the heart of this entire vision is Jesus Christ. He is the Alpha and the Omega, the beginning and the end (Revelation 22:13). He is the Word through whom all things were made (John 1:3) and the One in whom all things hold together (Colossians 1:17). He is the Mediator of the New Covenant (Hebrews 9:15) and the Lord of creation (Colossians 1:16).

In Christ, covenant and creation are united. He embodies the faithfulness of God to His promises and the fullness of God's purpose for the world. He is the second Adam, the true Israel, the Lamb of God, the risen Lord. His incarnation sanctifies matter; His crucifixion heals creation; His resurrection inaugurates new creation.

To follow Christ is to enter into this covenantal life. It is to say "yes" to a story that began in a garden and will end in a city—a garden city, where the river of life flows and the tree of life yields fruit for the healing of the nations (Revelation 22:1-2). It is to live now in light of what is coming, to act today with tomorrow's hope, to be a signpost of the kingdom in the midst of a groaning world.

This is not easy. It requires faith, patience, and perseverance. It means resisting the culture of consumption and convenience. It means embracing simplicity, community, and humility. It means seeing every act of kindness, every word of truth, every work of justice, and every moment of worship as a seed planted in the soil of the new creation.

The covenant story in cosmic perspective

The story of covenant and creation is not a side note in Scripture—it is the story. It is the grand narrative that gives meaning to our lives, our world, and our future. From Genesis to Revelation, from Adam to Christ, from Eden to the New Jerusalem, the covenantal heartbeat of God pulses with love, purpose, and renewal.

This story invites us to live differently. It calls us to reject despair and embrace hope. It urges us to see the world not as disposable but as destined for glory. It challenges us to care for creation not out of guilt or fear but out of gratitude and joy. It summons us to be a covenant people in a fragmented world, a foretaste of the harmony to come. And ultimately, it directs our gaze to the One who holds it all together—the Creator who became Redeemer, the King who will return, the Bridegroom who will dwell with His bride forever. In Him, the covenant is fulfilled. In Him, creation is restored. In Him, all things become new.

- 20 -
CONCLUSION

As we finish this journey from Sinai to Calvary, we are left not merely with theological insight, but with a call to worship, to faith, and to covenantal living. The tension between the Old and New Covenants is not a contradiction — it is a divine progression.

The Law that was given at Sinai was holy and good; it revealed the character of God and exposed the sinfulness of humanity. But it was never meant to be the final word. It was preparatory. It was provisional. It was a shadow cast by a much greater reality that would come in Christ.

Calvary is the turning point of all history — the moment where the veil was torn, the curse was broken, and the invitation into God's everlasting covenant was extended to all mankind. At the cross, the righteous demands of the Law met the extravagant mercy of grace.

What the Law could not accomplish in the weakness of our flesh, God accomplished by sending His Son in the likeness of sinful humanity to be a sin offering.

Through Jesus Christ, the New Covenant is inaugurated — not by stone tablets or temple rituals, but by His blood and His Spirit, written on the hearts of His people.

The journey from Sinai to Calvary is not just Israel's story. It is ours too. It is the story of a faithful God Who enters into covenant with a faithless, rebellious people. It is a story of promise, failure, mercy, and fulfilment.

It is the story of every heart that has ever longed for deliverance, every soul that has groaned under the weight of sin, and every life that has been redeemed by the blood of the Lamb.

In this story, we see that the Bible is not a tale of two gods or two opposing systems, but one seamless narrative of redemption.

God has never changed. His justice and mercy, His holiness and compassion, His sovereignty and love—these remain perfectly united in the person of Jesus Christ. The Old Covenant points forward to Him. The New Covenant is fulfilled in Him and in Him, we find both the destination and the way.

As people of the New Covenant, we walk not in the shadows of the Law but in the light of the Gospel of Jesus Christ. Yet we do so with reverence, remembering the path that led us here.

The Law still instructs us, the prophets still warn us, and the covenants still shape us—but it is the cross that defines us. It is Christ who sustains us and it is the Spirit who empowers us to live as covenant people in a world desperate for truth and grace.

So may we never forget the mountain of fire and thunder that revealed our need. And may we always cling to the hill of suffering and glory that secured our hope.

From Sinai to Calvary, the covenant story is the gospel story—and it is still being written in the lives of those who follow the Redeemer.

The veil is torn. The tomb is empty. The covenant is fulfilled.

Now, go and live in its freedom.